Cyberbranding

....

Brand Building
in the Digital Economy

FINANCIAL TIMES PRENTICE HALL BOOKS

James W. Cortada
*21st Century Business: Managing and Working
in the New Digital Economy*

Aswath Damodaran
*The Dark Side of Valuation: Valuing Old Tech, New Tech,
and New Economy Companies*

Deirdre Breakenridge
Cyberbranding: Brand Building in the Digital Economy

Dale Neef
E-procurement: From Strategy to Implementation

John R. Nofsinger
*Investment Madness: How Psychology Affects Your Investing...
And What to Do About It*

Cyberbranding

Brand Building
in the Digital Economy

Deirdre Breakenridge

An imprint of **PEARSON EDUCATION**

London • New York • San Francisco • Toronto • Sydney •
Tokyo • Singapore • Hong Kong • Cape Town • Madrid •
Paris • Milan • Munich • Amsterdam

Library of Congress Cataloging-in-Publication Data

Breakenridge, Deirdre.
    Cyberbranding : brand building in the digital economy / Deirdre Breakenridge.
        p. cm.
    Includes bibliographical references and index.
    ISBN 0-13-089710-8
    1. Brand choice. 2. Electronic commerce. I. Title

HF5415.3 .B685 20001
658.8'27--dc21

2001023521

Production Editor: *Wil Mara*
Acquisitions Editor: *Tim Moore*
Editorial Assistant: *Allyson Kloss*
Marketing Manager: *Debby van Dijk*
Buyer: *Maura Zaldivar*
Manufacturing Manager: *Alexis R. Heydt*
Cover Designer: *Anthony Gemmellaro*
Cover Design Direction: *Jerry Votta*
Art Director: *Gail Cocker-Bogusz*
Composition: *Pine Tree Composition*

FINANCIAL TIMES

Prentice Hall

© 2001 Prentice Hall PTR
Prentice-Hall, Inc.
Upper Saddle River, NJ 07458

The publisher offers discounts on this book when ordered in bulk quantities. For more information contact: Corporate Sales Department, Prentice Hall PTR, One Lake Street, Upper Saddle River, NJ 07458. Phone: 800-382-3419; Fax: 201-236-7141; E-mail: corp-sales@prenhall.com

Printed in the United States of America

10 9 8 7 6 5 4 3 2 1

ISBN 0-13-089710-8

Prentice-Hall International (UK) Limited, *London*
Prentice-Hall of Australia Pty. Limited, *Sydney*
Prentice-Hall Canada Inc., *Toronto*
Prentice-Hall Hispanoamericana, S.A., *Mexico*
Prentice-Hall of India Private Limited, *New Delhi*
Prentice-Hall of Japan, Inc., *Tokyo*
Pearson Education Asia Pte. Ltd.
Editora Prentice-Hall do Brasil, Ltda., *Rio de Janeiro*

To Jeff, Megan, Mom and Dad whose love and support made this book possible.

TABLE OF CONTENTS

It has become fashionable in recent months to beat up on the Internet evangelists who told us how brands like eToys.com and Furniture.com were going to make the world forget about Toys "Я" Us and Ethan Allen. The notion that young, aggressive entrepreneurs were going to change the rules of business and steal the bread off the tables of traditional companies was too good a story to ignore. Netscape's Marc Andreessen and Yahoo's Jerry Yang and David Filo were poster children for the new era. Stock options promised to turn even low-level programmers into millionaires.

During my four years as an editor of *Internet World* magazine, our publication was one of several voices to warn that the Wall Street rollercoaster ride would ultimately hit a big descent. We saw fundamental challenges related to customer acquisition costs, low-margin merchandise, poor customer service, and the logistical nightmares of shipping dining room sets and other products across the country. But still the IPOs kept coming and every wild success drove more half-baked business plans into the public markets.

Nearly a year after the April, 2000 NASDAQ correction, almost as much ink and as many screen pixels have been devoted to chronicling the collapses as were spent on feeding the hype. But many of those who've joined the Internet backlash overlook the fact that the network has changed the business world significantly since the Mosaic Web browser emerged from the University of Illinois supercomputer center in 1993.

As Deirdre Breakenridge so aptly chronicles in the pages that follow, every business needs to have an Internet strategy. The Net may no longer be the province of instant millionaires, but it is definitely a channel through which tens of millions—possibly hundreds of millions—of people will be exposed to your company and its brands.

Brand managers who once concerned themselves with finding a jingle to imprint on the American consciousness through 30-second radio and TV spots now have the opportunity to hold the attention of potential consumers much longer and to vastly improve their impressions of a brand. The new challenge is to come up with the tools, contests, or other Internet content that leaves the potential consumer satisfied and coming back for more. The many examples of smart cyberbranding that Breakenridge cites range from Benjamin Moore's paint calculator to Pampers' parenting institute to Nabisco's arcade, and they deserve the close attention of anyone trying to use the Internet to raise brand awareness.

Each illustrates the Net's ability to grab the attention of interested consumers—those leaning into their computer screens with mouse in hand rather than those leaning back on their sofas in front of the television. While some just want to be entertained, others are in search of information to guide them in purchasing decisions or bigger lifetime decisions. The brands they associate with helping them achieve their goals are likely to benefit.

Determining just what you need to do to carry your brand into cyberspace is the hard part, of course. As Breakenridge points out, you still need to know your audience and the best approach for reaching it. Successful Internet brands like Yahoo! and Amazon have demonstrated the power of personalization—knowing enough about their customers to offer them the information and products most likely to fit with their interests. Both companies have also demonstrated the importance of having solid plans for building out your Web activities to ensure that customer demands do not get beyond the levels of service that your technology or your people can provide.

In the end, however, smart cyberbranding is not about building the next Amazon or Yahoo! or eBay. Current market conditions all but guarantee that no pure-play Internet start-up will achieve their phenomenal levels of brand awareness anytime soon. The new phase of the Internet revolution is about how businesses—often derisively referred to as "old economy" companies—take advantage of the new medium to vastly improve their bottom lines. And Breakenridge has done her part to point them in the right direction.

Thomas J. DeLoughry
Westwood, New Jersey
January 2001

What the Marketer Needs to Know

1 The Power of Branding

Objective

For marketers to harness the power of branding. From the nineteenth century through today's technological advances, brands maintain their power by:

- Keeping a historical promise
- Evolving over time
- Influencing our choices
- Having no boundaries
- Surpassing cultural issues
- Growing stronger with technology

It's the twenty-first century, and we all want to know the secrets of brand building. With companies like Yahoo! and Amazon coming to market and branding in record time, what should marketers learn from these field leaders who capture our attention? First and foremost, we recognize and applaud the power of the brand. The question is not, and will never be, "To brand or not to brand." Consider two factors. Marketers are long past questioning the notion that branding works. And the Internet is proving to be a powerful communication channel to find brand success. Combine the two factors and there's synergy.

Consider two factors. Marketers are long past questioning the notion that branding works. And the Internet is proving to be a powerful communication channel to find brand success. Combine the two factors and there's synergy.

Let's start with the field leaders. Hats off to these new brand builders who have accomplished monumental branding strategies in lighting speed.

A QUICK BRANDING STORY—YAHOO!

Yahoo! (www.yahoo.com) continuously tops the charts with its number one rating as the Web's hottest property. It is continually praised for simplicity of design and accessibility. Yahoo! just might be the Web's "quickest and most logical, never failing to give what people need, when they need it" type of site.[1] Yahoo! was quick to brand its name and become an online and offline marketing machine. It is known as "a classic example of brand building, Silicon Valley style."[2] The search engine came to life targeting three distinct groups, capturing the needs of each one separately. Consumers enjoy Yahoo! for fast and easy access to information on any subject. The brand also evokes fun, with a bit of wackiness in its name alone. For the more serious audience, financial analysts and the media, Yahoo! is professional and operated efficiently. Last, for advertisers and media buyers, Yahoo! is the plan that provides the most visibility and online exposure to large audiences. Yahoo! has done a phenomenal job at branding itself through a variety of cobranding efforts, partnerships, and alliances such as Ziff Davis's *Yahoo! Internet Life* magazine, and through sponsorships and contests with a host of well-known companies including Visa (the Yahoo! platinum Visa card that helps to make the shopping season easier in December 1998), MCI (Yahoo! and MCI unveiled a new Internet online service in January 1998), and Ben & Jerry's (Yahoo! teamed up with Ben & Jerry's to connect schools to the Internet in September 1997).[3] And what has Yahoo! been up to lately? It has teamed up with Pepsi for a five-month online/offline marketing campaign to reach consumers. "Combining two of the world's biggest brands . . ." is only just the beginning.[4] Pepsi is giving Yahoo! 1.5 billion bottles for its name to appear under the cap and Yahoo! is lending Pepsi its online expertise and Internet reach to wired teens and young adults. The branding possibilities are tremendous.

ANOTHER SPEEDY BRAND—AMAZON.COM

Amazon.com (www.amazon.com) opened its "virtual doors" in 1995 and from that point forward has developed its brand through the company's mission: to use the Internet to transform book buying into the fastest, easiest, and most enjoyable shopping experience possible.[5] Moving from books and toys to music and videos, Amazon continues to maintain its branding promise simultaneously with the growth of its customer base, product offerings, and product categories. Amazon branding strategies include personalization with every service offered to its customers (with a friendly greeting by name and knowing the user's preferences). Branding also extends to an Amazon family of Web sites including The Internet Movie Database (www.imdb.com), an authoritative source on movies and entertainment dating back to the nineteenth century; Livebid.com, a host of live-event auctions on the Web; and Planetall.com, which offers users a calendar, address book, and reminder service all in one. Amazon also has one of the most well known affiliate programs, with kiosks on search engines and popular Web sites, utilizing the broad reach of the Internet to brand its name and logo (and sell products too). In addition, Amazon has invested in leading retailers including Drugstore.com and Gear.com to provide these sites and their audiences with the same types of services afforded to Amazon audiences: the ability to find vast selection and incredible customer experience all tied to a remarkable brand.[6]

Amazon was proud to announce its first-quarter 2000 earning, up 95% from the same quarter in 1999. Sales increased to $574 million from $294 million. Where to next? With its original vision intact, Amazon continues to build its image as an e-brand that allows customers to find everything they need online.[7] Amazon continues to strive for a powerful global presence, with growth in more product categories, service expansion, and the sense of an Amazon community providing total personalization for the user. The power of branding has found itself in this Internet brand.

Now, for a slight dose of Internet reality. Not many professionals find themselves with a Yahoo! or even the likes of an Amazon. Sure, there are plenty of heavy Internet hitters out there in cyberspace: eBay.com, CNET.com, MSN.com, AOL.com, and a slew of others that deserve recognition. With the rise and fall of dot-coms, the challenges of brick-and-mortar brands moving their business online, and a host of issues that surround the Internet, these field leaders and heavy hitters are the exception to the rule. Now, for the good news—the power of the brand coupled with Internet technology gives the marketer the tools for brand success. It is up to the marketer to understand the power of the brand (by trade we know this) and the issues the brand faces on the Internet (everything from the basic fundamentals of Web site design to the complex issues of global Internet brands).

Technology works for us. We know it is our future. We see how society is rapidly evolving with technological advances—sometimes quicker than we can manage the change and digest the technology. Ten to fifteen years ago we rented and watched videotapes, listened to cassettes, and used the computer as a word processor. Life is so different now. Our youth population is growing up with many more technological options than we thought might ever be possible. Talk about rapid advancement—it's no longer a novelty to listen to CD-ROMs and watch DVD movies. Computers allow us to access the World Wide Web for both information and entertainment in various forms (audio, video, and Web casts). Information is at our fingertips 24 hours a day, 7 days a week. And just as we get used to logging on and surfing the Web, we see technology change again with a shift toward wireless Internet communication on cellular/PCS handsets. However, throughout this evolution of technology (dating all the way back to the days of the first printing presses), one concept has remained constant—the power of the brand and its effect on consumer behavior. And although technological change is thrust upon us, brands survive disruptive change as long as their historical promises stay intact. Looking back to the nineteenth century, the seeds of branding have more than just sprouted. They have grown strong roots over time.

We see how society is rapidly evolving with technological advances—sometimes quicker than we can manage the change and digest the technology.

THE HISTORICAL BRAND PROMISE

After the Civil War, the once–buffalo-covered west all the way to California was teeming with wild cattle. Herds were driven to waiting markets. Cattle drives brought much needed cash to a nation that was suffering from the afteraffects of civil war and also served to feed the new settlers and those caught up in the gold rush to California and the silver rush in Nevada. Common to both the rancher and the cowboy was the practice of cattle branding—a means to identify

key ownership of cattle on the open western frontier. In fact, cattle-men were naming their ranches after their brands, holding these symbols of ownership in the highest esteem. In the frontier spirit of the era, a Bavarian immigrant named Levi Strauss arrived in San Francisco in 1853, at the tail end of the '49er gold rush, and in 1873 he and a Nevada tailor, Jacob Davis, patented the process of putting rivets in jeans to make them stronger.[8] One of the distinctive trade-marks of the company to this day is the leather patch with simulated "brand" meant to tell consumers of then and now that they are buy-ing the real thing.

Also in the late 1800s, John Styth Pemberton, an Atlanta phar-macist, made a concoction of coca leaves, cola nuts, and caffeine. When he mixed them together in an iron tub, who would have thought we would end up with a famous brand that has stood the test of time?[9] Today, Pember-ton's concoc-

Brands date back over a hundred years, and consumers have been supporting brand power every step of the way.

tion, Coca-Cola, is one of the most well known and valued brands. According to the financial world, the value is estimated at $39 bil-lion.[10] Let's face it: there are numerous companies that can manu-facture cola syrup and serve up a similar drink. Scores of suppliers around the globe could develop this syrup and put a cola on the market. However, not one of these new products could ever replace Coca-Cola, as it is known today. The brands that date back to the nineteenth century, like Coca-Cola, Quaker oats, Heinz, and Ivory soap, all maintained their historical brand promises. Advertising has played a major role in their evolution. In fact, as early as 1890, advertising was a popular phenomenon. Companies were placing ads in magazines and newspapers, on streetcars and matchbooks, and even on billboards. History reveals that companies were aware of the power of branding, when they were placing more dollars into the development and branding of products as consumers with considerably more disposable income continued to be influenced by brands. Brands date back over a hundred years, and consumers have been supporting brand power every step of the way.

Why do consumers support brands? Is it the emotional bond they form with the brand or the expectation of its performance? It's both—consumers rely on the bond along with the expectation that the brand fulfills a need. But even more, it's the historical promise (whatever is expected of the brand at the time of its birth) that must remain intact in order for the brand to evolve successfully with the technology that communicates its message. That's why the brands of the past are still recognized today and even though some have altered over the years, their earlier meanings are embedded in product messages. For instance, Coca-Cola started with the slogan "the drink that makes the pause effective" and in 1929 discovered a more concise statement that added to the product's success—"the pause that refreshes." Over time, Coca-Cola coined the phrase "it's the real thing," but we still know the drink is refreshing as well. Take the classic example of Jaguar, a vehicle that was introduced around 1935 by an English company, Lyons Swallow Sidecar Company. Throughout the history of the Jaguar brand were mergers and acquisitions, including the one that created the British Motor Corporation and most recently Jaguar's purchase by Ford Motor Company. It did not matter what happened to corporate ownership of the vehicle: the Jaguar brand still remains an image of "feline grace, elegance and power."[11] And in the case of the Heinz brand and its "57 varieties," would you believe that those 57 varieties never actually existed? Perhaps the strategy was not so much for product accuracy but more for consumer branding and awareness. In essence, the company's founder, H. J. Heinz, just liked the number 57. His historical branding strategy succeeded. To this day, the number 57 still appears on all the Heinz ketchup bottles and the "57" is equated with Heinz products.[12]

BRANDS THAT EVOLVE
TO STAND THE TEST OF TIME

An interesting statement that appeared in an article entitled "Assessing Brand Equity" emphasized how a product can be quickly outdated but a successful brand is timeless.[13] There are quite a few timeless brands that have managed to survive drastic changes, everything from technological advances to world wars. Although a good slogan is only one component in the branding mix, the brand identity quiz shown in Figure 1.1 illustrates slogans for 20 brands

. . . a product can be quickly outdated but a successful brand is timeless.

that have stood the test of time. The quiz is representative of how timeless brands have evolved with power in both name and meaning and to this day are recognized by their slogans.[14]

These brands have several characteristics in common. Indeed, they evolved over the years proving their strength in name, meaning, and symbolic representation. They have all demonstrated the test of time, and each one has maintained, for the most part, a historical promise (with an embedded meaning that started at inception). These timeless brands have survived long after products were

---

TEST YOUR BRAND KNOWLEDGE.

Figure 1.1

1. Good to the last drop
2. We bring good things to life
3. That heavenly coffee that only a millionaire can buy
4. Smooth sippin' Tennessee whiskey
5. When it rains, it pours
6. Say it with flowers
7. The quicker picker-upper
8. Mmmm mmmm good
9. 99 $\frac{44}{100}$ % pure
10. The pause that refreshes
11. Put a tiger in your tank
12. The skin you love to touch
13. Even your best friend won't tell you
14. 57 varieties
15. This Bud's for you
16. Breakfast of champions
17. Don't leave home without it
18. The beer that made Milwaukee famous
19. Snap crackle pop
20. The foot doctor

Note: Answers in Appendix A

outdated. As a result, they are distinguished among competitors and remain well-known choices for consumers.

BRANDS INFLUENCE OUR BEHAVIOR

How is it that branding efforts over the years have influenced our choices? Let's take a look at the many ways that brands are viewed and the different thoughts behind a successful brand:

- Brands create clear ownership of a particular benefit.
- Brands are unique and differentiated.
- Brands maintain a personal connection in the sales process.
- Brands are associated with a clear set of values.
- Brands fulfill a need or expectation.

Addressing the initial question, brands influence our choices by being:

> . . . more than logos. Many elements combine in a brand to generate an emotional bond with a customer. Brands are about personality . . . you're buying the personality, the experience.[15]

Further,

> Designers develop distinctive uses of color, form, materials, and letter forms, as well as attitudes toward function and content that bring a brand to life.[16]

Keeping these brand characteristics in mind, is it any wonder that we make certain associations and have definite feelings when we come in contact with a brand? For example, the Tiffany's gift box—an unmistakable shade of blue with a pristine white bow—signifies class, style, and elegance. Take this box to a party and you will hear more "oohs" and "aahs" than any reaction a J. C. Penney box would elicit. The Tiffany box is only one example of many. What do you think of when you see the Rolex crown, McDonald's golden arches, or 501 jeans? Well, if you are like most, you see the Rolex crown as a symbol of wealth and prestige, McDonald's arches automatically make you think of fast food, and 501 jeans epitomize the classic all-American look.

Here's another little branding challenge. The objective of the test is to read a word and note which company pops into your mind first. Try it.

- Jeans: ?
- Overnight [delivery]: ?
- Clothes: ?
- Software: ?

According to ZDNet.com, the most popular responses are most likely Levi's, Federal Express, The Gap, and Microsoft. The explanation is simple, but the concept of branding is complex. These companies have succeeded by embedding their names into our minds and our lives.[17] It's the *emotional bond,* the *personality* of the brand, and the *experience* we look forward to each time all mixed together that influence our behavior. Brands are in our minds and have captured our hearts. Brands are the only things to grasp, hold on to, and count on when the rest of our world changes rapidly before our eyes.

It's the *emotional bond*, the *personality* of the brand, and the *experience* we look forward to each time all mixed together that influence our behavior.

BRANDS WITH NO BOUNDARIES

The concept of branding is universally known. Only countries have borders; brands do not, as long as they are respectful of global issues. Brands travel across global boundaries and impact different nations in various ways. Global marketers strive to achieve a balance between art and science. The art of branding is its creative meaning that is universally accepted by all. Global brands are capable of enlightening scores of populations, bringing experience and fulfillment of expectations. The science is the careful research and development of the global brand, the precise method of communication, and the calculated timing of its message. When the balance of art and science is achieved, it doesn't matter if Coke is bought in a store in the United States or on the roadside in Mongolia. Either way, the Coke brand evokes a refreshing experience and a "good time" feeling.[18] When it comes to the actual cultural translation,

Only countries have borders; brands do not, as long as they are respectful of global issues.

there's a commonly known story about Coca-Cola and its original branding efforts in China. When researching suitable characters that sounded remotely like Coca-Cola in Chinese, the characters translated into a couple of different meanings including "female horse fastened with wax" and "bite the wax tadpole."[19] Even so, it's the experience of the brand that is universal.

GLOBAL BRANDS AND CULTURAL ISSUES

It's amazing to realize how brands fulfill the needs of various cultures. However, it's an ongoing challenge for marketers to realize that worldwide brands carry the burden of cultural intricacies. As a matter of fact, in Asia-Pacific regions, "a common Chinese idiom describes Asia as an area of great treasures but a place filled with hidden dragons and tigers."[20] The explanation is straightforward, but nonetheless an issue for marketers and companies to face when promoting global products. With linguistic and cultural pitfalls, western civilization needs to understand a region completely and thoroughly before launching a brand in that region. There are far more issues to address in global branding. Research is always imperative in a global effort. Common mistakes include lack of research in the translation of names and spelling. Specifically, not verifying translation in the Asia-Pacific region can be the downfall of a brand. Do you think it's a coincidence that Pepsi-Cola has a meaning in Chinese of "a hundred happy things" and is considered a lucky name?[21]

it's an ongoing challenge for marketers to realize that worldwide brands carry the burden of cultural intricacies.

Here's another example of how cultural differences posed a problem for a global advertising manager in his efforts to promote a brand of children's toothpaste. His initial efforts were not pleasing to his Bangkok office, yet the same measurements were increasing sales in Australia, Canada, Europe, and the United States. No matter which version of the commercial he used (all versions had a parent patting a child's head), there was a sense of uneasiness. The responses from the Bangkok office varied, but mostly were "too American." Finally, after much effort (and wasted time), the cultural mystery was solved when the Bangkok office told the global advertising manager that the commercial with the "pat on the head" from parent to child was an action that was unacceptable for their culture. Touching another person's head is frowned upon in many Asian regions. However, in most parts of the world the message conveyed the parent's appreciation for the child's brushing and using the toothpaste. Because it is imperative that the global brand be perceived to have the same values, the same message needs to be communicated in an acceptable manner for Asian-Pacific regions.[22]

Other issues are faced in the international naming process. Dunlop, a well-known manufacturer of tires, faced a branding obstacle when trying to research a name for a new product. The process took over two years with little success. The European Economic Community has over 5 million registered trademarks, and as a result, international naming is a long-drawn-out procedure. Dunlop actually instituted an international competition among its employees. The competition elicited 10,000 responses, and finally, 30 names were selected. Unfortunately, none of these names were available in more than a few countries. This is an ongoing problem in the international naming process, and Dunlop went back to the drawing board.[23]

Beyond the challenges are the global branding opportunities. The Law of Borders states, "There are no boundaries to global branding. A brand should know no borders."[24] Companies around the world know they have succeeded with global branding strategies when the magic word for most of us is *imported*. There's something special about opening a new bottle of Montrachet imported from France and carrying around a Gucci pocketbook from Italy.

Companies around the world know they have succeeded with global branding strategies when the magic word for most of us is *imported*.

Americans are caught up in the "imported" label, just as Levi's jeans are the rave in Russia. This is apparent when the product crosses a border and we are automatically willing to pay top dollar for the imported brand. There are definite perceptions involved with our choice of global brands. Countries are recognized for what they produce successfully. We would not get as excited about wine from Greenland and clothing from Iceland. If the perception of the country is different, then this alters our expectations and willingness to pay a higher price. As long as consumers' perceptions are fulfilled and expectations met for each culture, branding continues to be accepted and is a powerful force around the globe.

SUMMING UP THE INGREDIENTS
FOR THE GLOBAL BRAND

The Sterling Group conducted a survey in the United States, Japan, Germany, the United Kingdom, and Brazil of 250 nationals in an attempt to reveal the prime ingredients for creating a successful global brand. The results of the survey indicated several top ingredients of a global brand. For instance, *brand essence* occurs when the brand's composition is harmonious with consumers globally and the brand is able to "transcend cultures." *Brand culture* is born from the inside out. Great global brands are products of unique corporate culture. *Brand style* is the unique style with which the consumer can easily identify and form an exclusive bond. *Brand experience* defines the brands that are winners and are not a means to an end but a means to an experience. *Brand difference* is the quality of having an edge over the competition, creating uniqueness and competitive difference. The brands that are communicated the most get the best coverage and are the most well known. These brands have achieved *brand exposure*. When a brand speaks to the heart (as well as to the head) of a consumer, it forms a powerful emotional bond referred to as *brand heart*. The leaders behind the brands who have opinions and are closely connected to the brand product are the *brand champions*.[25]

All of the key ingredients form a powerful mixture and when combined will add brand value to the benefit of consumers and companies who produce the products. From the consumer's perspective, brand value means knowing that a product has a stamp of authenticity, and that repeat use or purchase will provide the same pleasurable experience as

From the consumer's perspective, brand value means knowing that a product has a stamp of authenticity, and that repeat use or purchase will provide the same pleasurable experience as the time before.

the time before. It's a type of reassurance that you know you can count on every time. Is that the reason why we see so many tourists at McDonald's all over the world? Even in a foreign country, consumers gain reassurance from a trusted brand. From a company's standpoint, the bond between the consumer and the brand translates into increased usage over time. Brands influence purchasing behavior and "secure a future stream of profits."[26] Consumers will pay more for something they want and that which has an intrinsic value to them. For a company, this could mean continuous purchase of a particular brand product over time, or consumers' purchasing extensions of that product (for example, Coke's extending its market to Diet Coke drinkers). Disney is another perfect example. Because consumers believe in the quality of Disney's movies, they do not think twice about purchasing Disney clothing and Disney toys, paying higher prices for these brand products.

WALL STREET ENDORSES BRANDING

Even Wall Street believes in the power of the brand. There have been several articles that demonstrate the value from a financial perspective. One such article, "Successful Branding from Main Street to Wall Street," touches upon the pressures to cater to Wall Street. So, how is a CEO expected to keep a company growing and maintain interest from the investment community? What has become an obvious answer is to grow the brand in order to build confidence among investors and audiences alike. There must be a constant communication effort to maintain brand value and have it in the forefront of the audiences' minds. One means to accomplish this task is consistent advertising. But there is still a pressing question that nags at executives with respect to advertising dollars: Will the dollars convert into ROI? One study by James Gregory, CEO of Corporate Branding Partnership, illustrates a direct correlation between ad dollars and a company's ability to turn a profit. By studying *Fortune* 100 companies for a period of seven years, Gregory saw a clear pattern developing between advertising and an increase in stock prices as well as bottom-line returns. Those companies that exhibited "erratic behavior" were the companies that did not show a serious dedication to branding, instead going through periods of advertising and then cutbacks on ad dollars.[27] The moral of the story, according to Gregory, is that in order to build a reputation, companies must engage in long-term brand building. This, in turn, results in better financial performance.[28]

BRANDS AND TECHNOLOGY EVOLVE TOGETHER

The power of branding is a long-time tradition that is here to stay. From the wranglers and the days of cattle branding on the western frontier, to the Internet and the new "free open range," companies have developed their creative messages to appeal to audiences around the globe. We are, in fact, affected by branding every minute of our lives. How has branding come so far? The ability to brand effectively is due to the progression of technology and the way communication channels are advancing at a rapid pace. Our world changed from total reliance on print presses in the past, to broadcast television and radio. Even with these channels, marketers have always faced their share of issues and opportunities.

Along comes the World Wide Web, and with the ubiquitous Internet, guess what? We are now expected to brand at warp speed!

What's a marketer's latest challenge? Along comes the World Wide Web, and with the ubiquitous Internet, guess what? We are now expected to brand at warp speed! Not only are the branding issues of the past still with us today, but also there's a whole new set of rules in cyberspace.

We have established the power of branding. Now we need to harness that power in cyberspace.

Timing has changed, thinking has to be revisited, and methods need to be redeveloped. Is it impossible to take a solid branding foundation that a marketer has developed over the years and work successfully with this new medium? Yes, of course. Is it easy? Well, not exactly. But, if we can set the ground rules, keep an open mind, and always rely on what we know about branding from our past experiences, it's a good start to understanding the depth and complexity of branding on the Internet. We have established the power of branding. Now we need to harness that power in cyberspace.

---

something that forms an emotional bond between the consumer and the product. For the company, the promise and the added value are the differentiating factors. As a matter of fact, when branding is done well, the process makes a product unique and distinguishes it from a competitor's. Zolnierzak states, "Sure, there are many insurance companies but there's only one Rock. You can probably name a handful of brokerages, but there's only one Bull, and when it comes to the many companies that can manufacture stain in a can, it's only Minwax that turns a house into a beautiful home."

Zolnierzak states that brand managers have realized for years that brands need to be developed and nurtured. It's no secret that branding takes time and money. There must be a clear articulation and decision that the brand promise be communicated in every way (via every medium). So with the development and maturation of the Internet, the days of relying on advertising on network television and national print publications to deliver the brand's promise are over.

But we as marketers must realize that the Internet gives us a whole new dynamic. Zolnierzak states that "It isn't just a medium, it's an experience." And for marketers who realize the difference, it's a great opportunity. In the past, a consumer had limited opportunities to interact with a product or service until an actual purchase occurred—and even then the interaction might have been limited. For example, when consumers purchased motor oil for their cars, they *never* experienced the product. You can't smell, taste, or feel the motor oil you're using. You can't watch it work; you can't see the results. Motor oil operated totally on faith. You poured it in and trusted that it would work. This is just one example of how brands relied on communication rather than experience to drive the delivery of the promise. The Internet has fostered a dramatic change. A consumer can now experience and interact online before an actual transaction. Take the Campbell's soup Web site. Pre-Internet, you couldn't enjoy the product until you bought the soup and brought it home. But today, the Campbell's soup Web site invites consumers to participate in contests, search for their favorite recipes, and put together shopping lists including the ingredients to their favorite Campbell's soup dish. Although there is a new level of opportunity available via the Internet, the branding will always remain of utmost importance. The basics of branding have not changed. Marketers must always evaluate and leverage brand power and, most of all, take advantage of a new powerful tool—the Internet.

2

Making the Transition to the Internet

Objective

A quick tour for marketers to consider a few key complexities of making the transition to the Internet, including:

- A transition that supports the brand
- Ongoing battles over Internet commitment
- Growing statistics that reinforce the commitment
- Devoting dollars to the Internet
- Industries taking the plunge
- Internet issues that turn into opportunities
- The smooth transition of the brand

A TRANSITION TO SUPPORT THE BRAND

Timing is a key consideration for every marketer. Amazon had impeccable timing. The site launched when the idea of a virtual bookstore intrigued and thrilled audiences who flocked to the site, first for curiosity, and then for sheer convenience. Amazon was also quick to consider the benefits of selling through personalization (without ever infringing upon the rights of the user to the extent of feeling pestered). Like the very best bookstores, it swiftly learned shoppers' preferences and made relational sale recommendations. As a result, the visitor instantly felt "involved" with the site. Amazon asks every visitor his or her opinion with respect to product reviews, and always has something new and fresh to stimulate its audiences. The rate of change on the Amazon site excels at a pace that would crush the brick-and-mortar establishment. And to address the privacy and credit card issues that concern so many Internet users, Amazon's emphasis on safety parallels Volvo's efforts to make a vehicle that is safe for highway driving. The list of considerations continued, with Amazon immediately taking heed of studies of how many words the normal attention span of readers can bear. With text that is minimal (a body of words never over 150) and visual face-out covers, the site is appealing to the everyday user. In terms of marketing, not a stone left unturned. It's a challenge to get a consumer to break away from an existing brand preference to try a product from a newly created company. Amazon's clever marketing strategies proved to be a key component in driving traffic to the site, retaining an audience and enticing them to make purchases.

> **Amazon was also quick to consider the benefits of selling through personalization (without ever infringing upon the rights of the user to the extent of feeling pestered).**

In 1999, during the holiday season, Amazon used something as simple as a minipostcard (gift certificate) in the form of a direct mail piece to online consumers. The card was so appealing it was enough to make a one-time purchaser into a frequent buyer. This $10.00-off gift certificate was delivered via snail mail to Amazon customers in memorable, sheer holiday red-and-green envelopes. The card, which immediately caught your eye with its unique use of color (very bright blue and yellow), had an easy-to-read saying: "All aboard Amazon.com Toys." An interesting piece, it was "eye candy," on the one hand, and true to its word, on the other, with a fabulous discount (not requiring the online consumer to make any minimum purchase, such as spend $50.00 and get $10.00 off). With this type of bargain, online shoppers were searching for the Amazon toy gift cards. It was considerations such as this that put Amazon on the cybermap. However, the million-dollar question still remains. Despite all of the branding success, the company has yet to make a profit. Nonetheless, Amazon continues to motivate other companies to develop their Internet presences and to brand online.

Then there's Barnes & Noble at the other end of the spectrum. What a great place to read your favorite book, enjoy a cup of coffee, and attend an author's book signing and discussion. Barnes & Noble did not pay careful attention to the needs of its consumers and lost out on a wonderful opportunity to be the first brick-and-mortar with a virtual bookstore. Out of nowhere came Amazon and captured a sizable Internet market. When Barnes & Noble tried to play catchup, the damage was done. Visitors on the Barnes & Noble site who had previously visited Amazon.com felt that many book entries were similar, and the impression, real or imagined, was that the information may have been borrowed. At the least, the content was, for a while, not substantially different enough from Amazon.com, although prices were often lower. The Internet traveling public was savvy to the situation and felt disrespect for the Barnes & Noble brand. Although Barnes & Noble is making Internet headway, in most cases, damage to the brand is irreversible.

Opinion Research Corporation International includes Amazon.com among the top five net names. In addition, when Intelliquest in a survey asked approximately 10,000 Web surfers to name brands in association with a product, for books Amazon was chosen 56% of the time. Not bad at all for the new kid on the block.[1]

Amazon makes the complexities of Internet branding look easy. But the truth is that marketers are struggling over how to handle cyber-brands. New dot-com companies can look forward to a laundry list of considerations with respect to site functionality, content, design, ease of navigation, customer service, or privacy, and the list goes on. But even before any of these issues are taken into consideration, you would think the first obvious question would be whether or not the brand has permission from its audience to be in cyberspace. For example, will consumers stop going to auctions and go to eBay instead? The same consideration holds true for the brick-and-mortar. Take the case of a well-known not-for-profit organization, Lighthouse International (an organization for the vision-impaired): has a visually im-paired audience that may not

. . . the truth is that marketers are struggling over how to handle cyberbrands.

choose the Internet as its medium of choice given this organization permission to be online? The only way to find out whether consumers will go to online auctions and bid for items and whether the vision-impaired will log on to a Web site that would enable them to be a part of an Internet community (one designed for specialized needs) is to conduct market research. Without a research campaign prior to launch and subsequent postlaunch research to guide a serious effort, companies take an incredible risk. It's a myth that even the marketer of a traditional brand can throw the brand online and keep loyal followers happy with just a presence. On the contrary, having an established offline brand means there's more at risk in taking that brand to a new level. After the permission rule is satisfied, considerations filter all the way down to putting the best foot forward to execute the same efficient customer service and providing an online experience that is just as pleasurable as the off-line encounter (if not more so). That's why there was no excuse for what Toys "Я" Us went through in the 1999 holiday season. Brand followers were not forgiving when Toys "Я" Us had significant problems fulfilling orders for catalog items and shipping those items. These are again considerations that cannot be taken for granted.

It's a difficult plunge to take that giant Internet step, and it bears close consideration. Once permission to be in cyberspace is granted, then companies will get there quicker by addressing organizational

challenges first: human resource availability, or finding the right people with the right skill set; cost and budget issues; evaluation of relationships with third-party suppliers; defining roles and responsibilities of employees; defining an online and offline marketing effort; providing customer service for online retail; and—most of all—upper management support every step of the way![2] Some companies, however, try to slowly get their feet wet—as evidenced in a certain brochurelike presence—in implementing their

It's a difficult plunge to take that giant Internet step, and it bears close consideration. Once permission to be in cyberspace is granted, then companies will get there quicker by addressing organizational challenges first.

conversion from traditional marketer to cyberbrander and do not carefully plan the transition between the existing business model and the e-business model. One possible explanation for the slow start is that the Internet does not have enough history under its belt to allow companies to analyze historical benefits. In most cases, the past dictates the future: People are driven by their successes and avoid repeating past mistakes at all costs. Without not enough history behind the Internet, and stock prices that reflect a lot of price and no earnings, some companies are leery of diving into Internet waters headfirst. But that is not to say that traditional marketers haven't come a long way. In May 2000, an article appeared in the *New York Times on the Web* entitled "Many Traditional Marketers Are Becoming Devotees of Cyberspace." The

> ...marketers have lagged behind in the transition to the Internet but are now making up for lost time.

article stresses how traditional marketers have lagged behind in the transition to the Internet but are now making up for lost time. A new study, "Web Site Management and Internet Advertising Trends," published by the Association of National Advertisers, supports the traditional marketers' Internet leap. The study concludes that advertisers are turning to the Internet for its ability to reach consumers, the benefits of two-way communication, and the high potential of Internet branding.

THE ONGOING BATTLE OVER INTERNET COMMITMENT

Top management of brick-and-mortar businesses knows the value of online branding and how the reach of the Internet is beneficial to the brand. To date, companies have been making the

> To date, companies have been making the transition, but their commitment is weaker than it should be.

transition, but their commitment is weaker than it should be. Maybe a motivation to reach a stronger commitment would be to consider the Barnes & Noble scenario, a slow start and then a fight to regain brand allegiance. Whether small or large, a company needs to make a firm commitment as quickly as possible with respect to the Internet. The Internet, like any other communication channel, will be a successful and profitable medium if researched, understood, and used correctly to communicate a brand message. If a firm commitment is

The Internet, like any other communication channel, will be a successful and profitable medium if researched, understood, and used correctly to communicate a brand message.

made, then it should be understood that the proper amount of thought, effort, and resources must be allocated toward Internet branding strategies. The Internet is here to stay, and unfortunately, too many companies are missing out on a tremendous communication tool. From the brick-and-mortar companies that utilize regional portals,

Internet branding is quickly catching on and providing fruitful new opportunities to companies in cyberspace.

i.e., NJ.com, with directory listings to drive traffic, to the giants on the Internet—Yahoo!, MSN, NBC Internet, and Time Warner Online, with the millions of dollars they have spent to establish a well-known presence—Internet branding is quickly catching on and providing fruitful new opportunities to companies in cyberspace.

GROWING STATISTICS REINFORCE THE COMMITMENT

At a San Francisco conference held by the International Quality and Productivity Center in December 1999, the president of the Brand Consultancy presented a workshop entitled "Turning Your Brand into a Cyber Brand." Back in 1999, companies were only just turning their brands into cyberbrands. The discussion focused on how in 1999 there were 92 million adult Internet users (that's approximately 40% of the U.S. population). Further statistics project that Web growth will continue at a torrid pace with 60+ percent of U.S. households online by the year 2003. The number of women Web surfers continues to increase steadily, and senior citizens, proving to be more active and vibrant than ever, are taking advantage of the Internet.[3]

The steady growth of online consumer purchasing in most product categories is a driving force that convinces businesses they should make a firm commitment to Internet branding. Consumers are online doing everything from checking e-mails and bookmarking Web sites, to buying homes and making bank transactions. Even vacations can be planned online with e-tickets and an agenda to boot. And it does not stop here: Consumers are chatting more, getting financial information, and satisfying entertainment needs with audio and video clips.[4] It is interesting to note the most commonly purchased items and requests for information relate to travel, PC hardware, books, apparel and accessories, and PC software. E-commerce

There is a direct correlation between the amount of information that is available online and the amount of time people are spending online.

retail sales have skyrocketed, with over $30 billion in the year 2000.[5] This figure alone gives us every indication that the Internet is attracting consumers who are becoming Web-savvy, spending more time online and ultimately sinking larger dollar amounts into product purchases that at one time would never have been considered an "Internet purchase." We see the change in the last five years of consumer behavior online as people have put more trust into the Internet to satisfy their needs for shopping, banking, stock trading, and entertainment. There is a direct correlation between the amount of information that is available online and the amount of time people are spending online. The global Internet numbers are growing too. According to an article entitled "Now for the Really Worldwide Web..." in *Silicon Alley Report,* because of the adoption of

The Internet will open doors to new markets, and, therefore, must focus on global needs.

the Internet in other countries around the globe, a dot-com must think globally as well.[6] The Internet is not sleeping in other countries. In fact, it is emerging in more places every year. Although the United States is approximately two years ahead of foreign nations, the numbers are steadily increasing. For instance, there were approximately 5.4 million Internet users in Russia in January 2000, a dramatic increase over an estimated 1.2 million at the end of 1998. In addition, the expansion of the Internet into Latin America is driven by the rapid increase of users in this region. The numbers in Latin America are projected to grow from 9 million in 1999 to approximately 38 million by 2003.[7] Japan is also considered among the regions with high Internet penetration, with approximately 15 million Internet users.[8] This is a wake-up call for global brands on the Internet. The Internet will open doors to new markets, and, therefore, must focus on global needs. As a matter of fact, the most frequently visited Web sites, according to Nielsen Net Ratings Japan, are Yahoo!, NEC, MSN, Sony Online, and GeoCities.[9] Currently, U.S. retailers expanding into these foreign markets are addressing multiple currency and multiple language issues on their sites.

DEVOTING DOLLARS TO THE INTERNET

With all of the statistics on consumer behavior on the Internet, a sizable increase of e-commerce, and overall growth in Web usage among varying audiences, a nagging question

...making the transition does not mean diving into the Internet and abandoning mainstream media.

still remains for business owners: How much of the advertising budget should be devoted to online branding? It certainly seems to prove that the Internet is a powerful tool. However, making the transition does not mean diving into the Internet and abandoning mainstream media. That's been done too many times with little success. The advertising market, with Internet advertising to reach approximately $7.36 billion by 2005 (with room to grow), is still dominated by other communication channels that are receiving larger ad dollar amounts. In 1999, the total advertising market was approximately $117 billion in the United States. Of that $117 billion, close to $45 billion was spent on television commercials, about $41 billion went into newspaper ads, and another $26 billion was split between radio and magazine ads. Internet advertising is a much smaller portion of the total advertising market. Although Internet advertising will have a bright future, it should never be considered a "be all and end all" strategy when it comes to branding. Effective branding results from finding a happy medium between online and offline marketing strategies.

Then there's the extreme opposite case, the business that has all of the offline advertising (direct mail, billboards, bus advertising, newspaper ads, etc.) and makes no attempt at cyberbranding. Take a hypothetical example of a Pontiac/GMC car dealer who puts up a Web site and wants to sell cars by driving traffic to his brick-and-mortar dealership. Thousands of dollars will have been spent within the first six months to develop a Web site and the owner of the dealership will not have seen any results or profits. He wonders why his peers down the highway have sold more cars within the previous few months than he has sold in a year. By making the Internet transition and not allocating the proper resources to cyberbranding, with a plan that drives traffic to the Web site, the dealer allows an investment to go down the drain. You have heard this before: The Internet is more than just developing an aesthetic site; it's all about driving traffic to that site and utilizing offline and online efforts in conjunction with the brand. It's imperative to utilize the Internet effectively by integrating online and offline branding. Aside from placing the car dealer's URL on every piece of collateral material and traditional ad, the dealer should have become familiar with what the regional portals (a site that provides specific regional information) had to offer with respect to directory listings and banner advertisements. Or, perhaps, as a first cyber-branding effort, enlisting in the regional search engine would have been helpful, or sponsoring an e-mail program to the subscribers of a regional online publication for increased exposure. With more consumers making major purchases online, being found on the Internet is a priority. In this extreme case, cyberbranding would have made a difference. On a national scope, when Half.com launched its branding campaign, it included advertising online as well as cable, radio, and print (and don't forget the guerilla marketing promotional stunt to have a town named on its behalf). The company targeted print ads to appear in the *New Yorker* and the *New York Times*, not to mention a host of commercials on cable channels including MSNBC and ESPN. Then, for a well-rounded campaign, Half.com aired radio spots on national live talk radio.[10] If you think about it, how many dot-com ads do you hear on the radio in the morning or driving home from work? How many dot-com television commercials appeared during the Super Bowl? The market estimate is that only 1 out of every 12 companies advertising during the Super Bowl will survive post-commercial. There's a great deal to consider when it comes to advertising dollars. With noisy markets, companies need to employ online and offline strategies to reach fragmented audiences and drive traffic to a cyberbrand.

THE INTERNET IS A POWERFUL PIECE OF THE BRANDING CAMPAIGN

The Internet, like any other communication channel, is not a total and complete branding strategy. First, think of your audiences. How do they break down on the Web? Sure, there are the audiences that spend more time on the Internet choosing online media and interaction rather than the traditional media. But there will always be audiences that split Internet time with traditional media. And let's not forget the Internet disbelievers who don't spend any time surfing the

Web—are there any that still exist? In an interview with Eric Straus, president of Straus Media Group of Poughkeepsie, New York, the issue of offline and online branding surfaced (see the Straus Media Group mini-case study at the conclusion of Chapter 2). Straus bought his first radio station from his father in 1989 and since then has acquired nine more stations to assemble the largest media network in the Hudson Valley. When discussing brands and cyberbrands, Straus stated, "Mainstream media will always be a key to branding success. Banner ads will only get you so far. Take radio, for example. It did well in 1999 because of the dot-com business." However, an article on branding appearing in *CEO Conference* magazine in February 2000 mentioned how many of the dot-com start-ups were not making savvy decisions on television advertising and were spending money foolishly. The article, entitled, "Branding on the Internet," goes as far as saying, "Reserving dollars to improve site functionality may be more important in the long run than pouring money into advertising." This statement touches upon issues and certainly raises significant questions. However, both achieving the balance between offline and online advertising and site functionality are key factors to the success of the online effort.

Sure, there are the audiences that spend more time on the Internet choosing online media and interaction rather than the traditional media. But there will always be audiences that split Internet time with traditional media.

INDUSTRIES TAKING THE PLUNGE

As traditional companies continue to make the transition, redeveloping their business models as e-business models, we still see our share of industries proceeding at a pace we'd have to call much less than warp speed. An interview with Sheila Cohen, vice president of marketing, Lawyers Homepage Network, details the progress of various industries in their attempts to move online (See "Industries Moving Online" interview).

Traditional companies are facing their fair share of challenges when journeying into cyberterritory. They have existing cus-

It's a matter of stepping up to a challenge the Internet poses. Larger challenges mean larger rewards. The bigger the obstacle, the larger are the profits if it is tackled successfully.

tomer relationships and business paradigms to suit traditional needs. It's a matter of stepping up to a challenge the Internet poses. Larger challenges mean larger rewards. The bigger the obstacle, the larger are the profits if it is tackled successfully.

INTERNET ISSUES TURN INTO INTERNET OPPORTUNITIES

What are marketers finding to be the most common issues when making the transition to the Internet?

1. Understanding new audiences and meeting their needs
2. Making the transition from communicating as a mass-market company to the individual online consumer (and instant two-way communication)
3. Acknowledging new competition that was not a consideration pre-Internet

Opportunity number 1: New relationships are formed with new audiences as traditional businesses go online. So, for example, in the case of the Arts & Entertainment Network (A&E), its Biography.com Web site invites younger groups to partake in the site with a searchable database of 25,000 interesting biographies. Because of younger audiences, A&E must gear its site to this group in a manner that young audiences will find attractive, interactive, and appealing.

INDUSTRIES MOVING ONLINE

Sheila Cohen is vice president of marketing for Lawyers Homepage Network, a virtual law office for attorneys. Cohen has been marketing and branding products for over 22 years. In a discussion of how various industries are making the online transition, she gave her viewpoint on three industries and what seems to be a rocky road for them.

Supermarket Industry

Although many supermarkets have built their Web sites, few are making the transition to e-business smoothly. Then along comes Priceline.com, spending enormous amounts of money on star power endorsement (William Shatner singing its praises), and tries to "raise the bar." Through Priceline.com, supermarkets and consumers were able to get a good taste of how to buy groceries online. Priceline in all of its efforts attempted to pave the way for grocery stores. In addition, you also have companies like Peapod and Net Grocer that create a network of Web-based shopping using the supermarket as a distribution channel. Who is going to win? Will it be

the Internet supermarket, where an online consumer buys and pays for groceries and then physically goes to the supermarket to pick up their prepaid items, or a full service market where groceries will be delivered to you at work or at home? It all depends on which way the market swings. This is another industry slow out of the gate—and the race continues.

Retail Industry

About a year ago, it was obvious that many retail chains were sadly behind the technology revolution, including household names like Barnes & Noble and Macy's that have spent years and billions branding offline. However, they did not seem to fully understand e-commerce and the needs of a Web-based shopper. And, in terms of fulfillment, they must have forgotten that delivering a promise is a key to customer satisfaction and retention. The retail industry has been slow to embrace brand equity and transfer it online. Frankly, a web shopper's expectation is the same as what he or she would expect from a brick-and-mortar location. Consumers want the same selection and variety that they would see in a physical store setting. But when Macy's Web site did not live up to its catalog selection a couple of years ago, consumers were disappointed with slim online pickings. So, what happens? Consumers go to shop at e-toys or Amazon.com if they can't find that "cute something special" from the Macy's online catalog. Macy's then has to scramble to get the customer back.

The Legal Industry

The legal industry is long known for its paperwork court filings and long briefs. It's ironic that an industry bogged down with paper is so slow to make the transition to the Internet. Lawyers, for the most part, are not tech savvy, making the transition even more sluggish. But, finally we are seeing lawyers who are in fact catching on—a good example is Lawyers Home Page Network (www.lawyershomepagenetwork.com), and its consumer site CaseMatch (www.casematch.com), founded by David Rizzo, an attorney himself. On this Web site we see lawyers utilizing the power of the Internet and conducting many functions of their daily business online. The LHN site allows member lawyers to take advantage of this virtual law office with everything from research tools to case management to marketing their firm and finding new clients. It took some time, but the legal industry is definitely catching on!

Opportunity number 2: Web sites provide one-on-one interaction and two-way communication. Companies that have traditionally engaged in mass marketing are used to reaching groups of people and must alter their methods. Mass marketers will quickly find that a Web site is all about the individual consumer and satisfying individ-ual needs. This is a new bond that has to be developed through interaction and strategies to keep a visitor coming back to a site for more information and activity. The Internet provides this opportunity (as well as this challenge) of being able to personalize and sensitize communication. Better yet, the Internet also allows immediate two-way communication. So, if you continue to "mass-market" to individual consumers, they will let you know exactly how they feel or they will not be back to your site. The brand will benefit from the ability to have two-way communication and implement feedback for further customer satisfaction. Otherwise, with so many choices on the Net, a consumer is just a click away from the next best thing!

Opportunity number 3: On the Internet, the whole scope of competition changes. So, for example, if A&E's major offline competitor is the Discovery Channel, that does not mean that in cyberspace Discovery Online poses the same kind of threat. As a matter of fact, A&E has more to worry about with Amazon when it comes to biographies. This forces A&E to think differently and evaluate competition in a whole new light. The Internet evokes creative thinking that is "out of the box," because audiences and competitors don't necessarily follow those traditional business plans we are all so used to.[11]

The Internet evokes creative thinking that is "out of the box."

THE SMOOTH TRANSITION OF THE BRAND

The nature and scope of the Internet is so vast that a traditional company no longer can simply satisfy a traditional business model and expect the brand to flourish. There are new considerations for the online company. That means that not only are audiences changing, but their expectations are increasing as well. Companies must develop sites that are delightful and engaging or face the threat of losing customers to the closest competitor. And when it comes to competition, that has all changed too. Just when you think you have figured out exactly who the brick-and-mortar competitors are, in come the new dot-com start-ups and a bunch of online giants that keep merging to add more products and services to their sites.

The nature and scope of the Internet is so vast that a traditional company no longer can simply satisfy a traditional business model and expect the brand to flourish.

To recap, here's an abridged list of considerations to keep in mind when it comes to transition and commitment in cyberspace:

- How much do you know about the Internet and whether or not your audience will accept your brand's presence online? Permission, permission, permission! Ask and you shall receive.

- Is the online audience the same as the offline audience? What other groups should be included in your research? The wide reach of the Internet allows new audiences to become involved with online brands. Don't overlook these secondary groups, as the Internet has incredible growth statistics.

- How can we integrate all of our offline efforts to drive traffic to the online site and vice versa? By devoting time and advertising dollars to a well-thought-out marketing plan. The plan should integrate all the branding efforts (using consistent brand communication) and be written simultaneously to fit into the e-business plan.

- Do the competitors extend beyond brick-and-mortar competitors? Yes, you will see competitors triple in numbers based upon the scope and variety the Internet has to offer.

- What are the competitors doing with their Web sites? Make sure you know how competitors are impressing online visitors. Warning—Don't just borrow content; your audience will know it and lose respect for the brand.

- How do we develop a site that is gripping and engaging, far more than just a brochure online? Interactivity and immediate and rewarding two-way communication is more than the brick-and-mortar will ever be able to offer prior to the purchase of the brand.

- What types of interaction will add a new level to the brand's promise? Audio, video, Webcasts, and the aspect of communities converging online with chat sessions, to name a few.

- How do you meet and exceed audiences' expectations of the brand online? By providing a site that allows visitors to interact with the brand online and by allowing users to find appropriate, interesting, and updated content that enhances the value of the brand.

RADIO GOING ONLINE: REGIONALHELPWANTED.COM

Eric Straus is president of Straus Media Group in Poughkeepsie, New York. For the past 10 years, he has grown his business 20-fold. Straus Media Group is the largest media network in the Hudson Valley—a $5 billion market. Straus has radio stations in Poughkeepsie, Ellenville, Kingston, Catskill, and Hudson, as well as offices in various cities. His radio stations include program formats from adult contemporary to nostalgia to news talk radio.

Straus has been conducting the operations of his radio network in a "traditional" manner. His main objective is always to run the best programming possible while trying to cut costs. By hiring top-notch sales experts to increase sales, he is able to sell long-term business on his radio stations. Straus's success is built upon improving his advertisers' businesses, and Straus works to find the long-term marketing answers for long-term customers.

Even with all of the Internet hype, Straus never put much thought into the World Wide Web. Recently, as he listened to his advertisers, he found that they were always frustrated with not being able to find good help—their dollars were constantly eaten up by newspaper classified advertising, with little or no luck with new hires. In turn, Straus saw an opportunity to solve his clients' problems while at the same time gearing radio toward the Internet. With an idea in mind he made a deal with a computer guy (as he puts it), a deal that has the computer expert building Web sites and the two of them splitting the revenues. So, where does radio fit in? Straus joins together radio groups who are competitive in the same markets to sponsor help-wanted dot-com sites across the country. These regional help-wanted sites provide a valuable and resourceful service for individuals in regional areas seeking employment as well as for area business owners who need to post available employment opportunities. Straus's regional help-wanted dot-com service is a completely separate venture from his traditional radio network. It is representative of how the Internet allows a vast array of opportunity for different industries. Straus was able to go beyond the conventional transition (putting his station and programming online) and foster a business that breaks a traditional mold.

Challenges

- How does Straus convince general managers (GMs) to work together with competitors in their markets?

- How do the regional help-wanted sites reach 70% of the adults in the market when 5 out of 10 read the newspaper?

- How does a regional help-wanted site compete with daily newspapers?

Outcome

Before RegionalHelpWanted.com, no competitive radio groups in the same market attempted to work together. And although the common response from GMs was that they preferred to work alone, it's not enough to beat out the big boys. This is a business where those big boys, the daily newspapers with circulations over 50,000, are making at least $5 million a year in newspaper help-wanted classifieds. Straus convinces GMs that in order to compete with the big boys, radio groups must work together in order to reach enough people.

Straus tested his concept online with his first site, HudsonValleyHelpWanted.com. With much success from this site, he took his idea on the road to a conference in Colorado that was hosted by the Radio Advertising Bureau (RAB). Straus' presentation at the conference evoked interest among GMs across the county. As of March 2000, Regional Help Wanted was in four markets, with four markets expected mid-March, and another four markets by April 1, 2000. With this steady rate of growth, it was expected that Regional Help Wanted would be in 150 markets within 18 months. Is it any wonder that Smith Barney analysts predict that 70% of classified advertising will move online? It's a whole new revenue stream. Now it's working for radio as well.

3 The Impact of the Internet on the Brand

Objective

For marketers to understand how the Internet has tremendous impact on a brand. Marketers need to "think" Internet and develop cyberstrategies by considering the following:

- The components of the cyberbrand
- New levels to which cyberbranding takes the brand
- More ways to "think" Internet in support of the brand
- Internal and external dimensions of the brand
- Cyberbranding theories
- The cyberbrander's checklist

THE COMPONENTS OF THE CYBERBRAND

Take a name, a logo, a company, a promise, and a full set of values and expectations and mix them all together. What do you get? The traditional meaning of a brand. If you take the same mixture of elements and put them on the Internet, does this make a cyberbrand? Just moving the brand online does not make up the all of the components of the cyberbrand. The Internet allows the brand to move into a new realm and affords consumers the opportunity to experience the brand on an interactive level. It's the "cyber" part that provides hands-on experience and immediate involvement with the brand prior to the purchase of a product or

> **It's the "cyber" part that provides hands-on experience and immediate involvement with the brand prior to the purchase of a product or service.**

service. Every interaction with the brand has the potential for an immediate reward. The Internet allows consumers to access information, get involved in surveys and polls, and collect digital coupons or enter into free sweepstakes and contests, and is customer service–ready with e-mail responses, answers to consumer FAQs, and round-the-clock, 24/7 service. These are the differentiating factors that define the "cyber" aspect of the brand that are found in no other form, on any other medium.

NEW LEVELS TO WHICH CYBERBRANDING TAKES A BRAND

Every brand has the potential to flourish on the Internet. Taking the brand to a new level is the ability to "think" Internet. This ability increases the bond between the consumer and the cyberbrand. Before Benjamin Moore, a popular brand of paint, went online, the company's name and logo were a symbol of quality and trust a homeowner (or business owner) could depend upon. The Benjamin Moore brand name still carries the same meaning, but the Internet adds a new dimension to the brand. Benjamin Moore's consumer and business audiences (homeowners, architects, designers, and professional contractors, to name a few) go to its Web site for more than the ability to view a full online paint catalog for home, office, or building use. Why? Because of relationship marketing. In cyberspace,

Taking the brand to a new level is the ability to "think" Internet. This ability increases the bond between the consumer and the cyberbrand.

Benjamin Moore offers one-on-one experience with the visitor. Automatically, the expectations are different. The visitor on the site anticipates being able to use the Benjamin Moore paint calculator to figure out the dimension of the structure to be painted, and exactly how much primer and topcoat is necessary to finish a room from floor to ceiling. These added extras on the site go one step beyond the traditional mixture of brand elements.

Another area loaded with information is the "About Color" section in the Homeowner's portion of the site with articles relating to color and lighting. The article entitled "When Color Is Critical, Switch On the Light" educates a homeowner with respect to the difference between how we see color on the color card chip and the color that dries on the walls of our home. The article offers tips on how to avoid disappointment.[1] With articles that change on a frequent basis, Benjamin Moore's Web site audience expects to return to the site and see updated information and new tips and technique articles. As a matter of fact, at one point on the Benjamin Moore site there was an interesting piece on the appropriate colors to use for each room of your home. Did you know that red in the kitchen provokes overeating? Benjamin Moore is appealing to audiences in a new way, visually, emotionally, and interactively, with hands-on helpful resources to keep them coming back for more—driving traffic to the online brand.[2] This is only the beginning for the cyber-brand. Another way that Benjamin Moore might continue to "think" Internet is in offering online contests (contests are among the top reasons consumers frequent Web sites). For example, The "new homeowners before and after Benjamin Moore paint" contest would offer new homeowners the opportunity to submit before and after pictures of their homes for display and judging online (one picture before the paint job and the other picture post paint job). Drawing consumers into a contest that lets them take pride in their homes, tied into the emotional bond with a brand of paint they trust, drives traffic to the Benjamin Moore site, and gets consumers to buy paint products (just to be a part of the contest).

Another strong example of a brand making the commitment to the Internet and adding a new dimension to its meaning is P&G's Pampers online. We all know Pampers as a reliable brand of dia-pers, one that has been around for decades. However, Pampers in cyberspace goes one step further to benefit new parents and aid them with the concerns and issues regarding parenthood. The Pampers Web site welcomes parents to the "Pampers Parenting In-stitute" (PPI). On this site, parents (and even day care and preschool professionals) can access information on children's safety issues and childhood diseases and learn the latest information on physical and emotional developmental stages from the professional experts. The extension of the Pampers brand on the Internet evokes a feeling of commitment to families in many ways. And with a host of information updated on a frequent basis, loyal brand customers will visit the Pampers site repeatedly for tips on child rearing from the experts. What's another way for the Pampers brand to "think" Internet and harness the power of Pampers online? Pampers might open a section of its Web site devoted to parents who want to share those "adorable" children stories. Most proud parents jump at the chance to tell their favorite "cute son or daughter account" (you can only tell friends or relatives so many times before they tune you out). If Americans can go on national television (on Oprah Winfrey and Leeza) and share their problems, then what's wrong with sharing cute kid stories on the Internet? The benefit to the Pampers brand is that millions of parents have a story to tell—an-other case of increased traffic to the site—and that parents will identify with a brand that supports their need to be fully absorbed in their children.

The last example of branding to a new level is Mattel's Barbie.com which allows interaction with the brand from the moment the pink site downloads. There are approximately seven areas that permit loyal Barbie fans to be directly involved with the product before any purchase of a Barbie doll. The "Hot & Not" Poll section asks kids about their favorite activities—e.g., video games—and also shows them results of polls from the day before. Posting results from earlier polls is an excellent technique to get an audience to return to the site to see how their peers feel about these same topics. Another popular section is the "My Design Barbie," which allows users to create their own personalized Barbie. Hands-on interaction allows a youthful audience (an age group that loves to dress up and wear makeup) to choose Barbie's eye color, hair color, lip color, hairstyle, and cool fashion outfit with accessories and even to select a personality for Barbie (which corresponds to the special occasion of your choice). Of course, once you design your Barbie doll, the next logical step is to purchase that special doll or send it to a friend. Pre-Internet, Barbie was in a box, on a shelf, and she came in a predetermined outfit, with predetermined hair and eye color. Mattel's Barbie site is all about hands-on interaction. The viewers on this site know and love the Barbie brand and have the opportunity to have fun with Barbie online, before any purchase. The interaction online creates a stronger bond between the consumer and the brand. Again, these are only a few ways that Mattel can take Barbie to a new level on the Internet. One more way for Mattel to "think" Internet involves little girls who enjoy telling stories about their favorite Barbie doll. The Barbie site could have a section that allows girls to create a favorite Barbie scene. Maybe it's a scene with Barbie and Kelly in their pool, or Barbie horseback riding, or even at a fashion show. Online creation and coloring of the scene, and then an area to tell a story for submission into a contest, would have little girls across the country online hoping that their story is highlighted as the "Barbie story of the month." This is one more example of how the Internet takes the brand to a new level and increases involvement with the user resulting in continued brand loyalty.

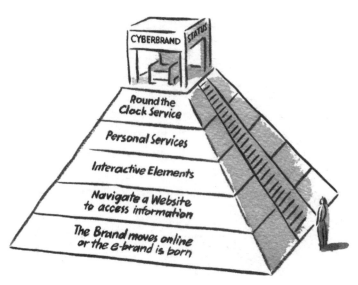

MORE WAYS TO "THINK" INTERNET IN SUPPORT OF THE BRAND

The proof is out there. We see every day how brands need to move beyond a name and logo, *especially* in cyberspace. Branding on the Internet is more than characteristics and attributes. It's all about hands-on experience and interaction with brands, something that was not always available pre-Internet. The best way to

> ...brands need to move beyond a name and logo, *especially* in cyberspace. Branding on the Internet is more than characteristics and attributes. It's all about hands-on experience and interaction with brands, something that was not always available pre-Internet.

prepare for the online brand or e-brand (dot-com start-up) is to start thinking Internet. Try your hand at Internet thinking in the next few examples.

Example 1: The Situation

A national day care center, caring for infants up to age 5, is known across the country for its nurturing environment, a place where the atmosphere of the home is extended into the classroom-learning situation. The center is an extension of the child's home. However, leaving a child in the hands of a day care provider is one of the most difficult decisions made by a parent. There is an enormous amount of trust placed upon the center. In this instance, the brand has to satisfy an emotional need for the parents, who are concerned about the safety of their children. Is there any way that the cyberbrand can calm their fears and allow them to feel more comfortable with the child care situation?

Questions:

- What can this brand do to have a powerful cyberpresence, leverage brand opportunity online, and create a stronger bond with parents who are hesitant to leave their children in day care?
- What would happen if the company simply put its brochure online?
- What type of interaction will appeal to parents who want to experience a day in the life of their children?
- How can the brand online be developed so parents can visit a site that fulfills their expectations?

Solution:

The Web site as an extension of the center's brand must allow parents to experience a day in the life of their child, and interact with the center and their children as many times as they like, in the following ways:

- Interaction with day care directors and teachers via e-mail, message boards, and parent–teacher conferences online. Immediate response is the key to soothing an anxious parent, and the Internet can accommodate parents' needs.
- Chats or Q&A sessions with medical practitioners and psychologists to bring the latest medical information to parents. A brand that has experts available for the support and well-being of the family unit is a brand that cares and deserves loyalty.
- Webcasts of center special events and activities for parents who are tied up at work and cannot make it to a dance recital or holiday show. It's one more way to experience those special times that parents would otherwise miss because of busy work schedules.
- Communication with other parents (via a message board or chat session) to discuss the joys and frustrations of

parenthood and the exciting stages of a child's development. We already know how much parents love to share stories.

- Allowing parents to get involved in home activities with their children by providing online curriculum to further the classroom learning experience. Parents want and need to be a part of their children's growing and learning process. When the brand offers a way to allow the parents and children to work together at home, it benefits the parents just as much as the children.

Clearly, the foregoing examples illustrate how the day care center has moved from expectations of the traditional brand to expectations of an online brand. A brochure and a behavioral report card have much less impact than a cyberbrand on the day care families. The cyberbrand brings much more experience and fulfillment into their lives. Building the brand is financially rewarding, whether traditionally or as an online extension. However, when it comes to the Internet, the online experience, interaction, immediate rewards, responsiveness, and service complete the picture. Parents will feel closer to their children by experiencing a hands-on day care experience.

Example 2: The Situation

A well-known line of clothing marketed to young females, aged 12 to 17, has a brand name that evokes the feeling of what's "hip," "cool," and "extreme" among its youthful audience. Moving the brand online will open new doors to creating an unforgettable experience for this group. However, the cyberbrand faces the challenge of evoking a community feeling among an age group who are just discovering who they want to be, the nature of their likes and dislikes, and what is accepted and rejected by their peers.

Questions:

- How does the company maintain its stylish image and remain a guiding force for this audience when it makes the commitment to the Internet?

- Is there more to moving the brand online than having an online catalog of clothing and a shopping cart?
- How does the company drive traffic to the Web site and get young females to take part in an online brand that is all about being a part of a community that shares ideas and experiences in a friendly way?
- How will teen expectations be fulfilled?

Solution:

The company has to move the brand online and create a teen community by utilizing the following cyberbranding strategies:

- Allow young women to express themselves with one-on-one interaction. Young women must feel a part of this community with easy access to message boards for communication with one another. It's always hip to know what your peers are thinking. And on the Internet, there is no threat to stating an opinion (unlike a classroom setting). Young women do not have to feel intimidated to participate in the community discussions.
- Provide surveys and polls on the site to get visitors answering questions about themselves and get them looking forward to how their peers feel about similar issues. Again, this aspect of sharing is a healthy way for teens to vent or "blow off steam" and be heard and acknowledged.
- Conduct chat session forums for teens to talk to their favorite TV star idols or members of their favorite musical group. Any way to follow a favorite star or music artist will capture the attention and the hearts of millions.
- Provide community contests to let viewers compete with and/or judge their peers. With this audience, the sky is the limit when it comes to contests. From writing essays to forming musical bands to community service, contests are traffic drivers.

A new teen community is now the extension of the brand. Not only will these young girls feel good about wearing the brand as the "coolest" line of clothes, but they will also experience interaction on a Web site that allows them to feel important, and a part of a "hot" Internet community that satisfies an emotional need to be liked and well received by their peers.

Example 3: The Situation

A car dealer has a line of vehicles of a well-known family brand—one that promotes quality vehicles as well as customer service satisfaction. But when the company moves the brand online, it must maintain this set of characteristics and attributes as well as add a new dimension of interaction.

Questions:

- How does the car dealer provide an online experience that goes beyond quality vehicles and automobile customer satisfaction?
- Is there an opportunity for this car dealer to provide any other types of information that might be related to families interested in making an automobile purchase?
- Will the brand be able to live up to the same set of characteristics and attributes online?

Solution:

The car dealer must offer consumers information and an experience that goes beyond a visit to the brick-and-mortar dealership, with a Web site that has the following:

- Editorial content including articles on car safety and road hazards. Letting visitors know what experts are saying on these topics just might save a life and projects the image of a brand that cares.
- Information on the popular destinations. Listing the top 10 places in their geographic area that families can drive to in their new vehicles (amusement parks, museums, family-friendly restaurants, etc.) is a way to become more involved with this audience and what the families do in their vehicles.
- An opportunity to become a member of an online auto club that gives discounts on services and coupons toward purchases at area businesses (cyberpartnerships add

value to the brand and drive traffic to the Web site). Regional merchants will benefit from the ability to promote one another's Web sites to drive traffic back and forth between sites.

- A link devoted to customer service and one-on-one interaction with an online dealership representative. And the ability to have two-way communication with a car salesperson or a service representative is ideal.

The car dealer now appeals to its car buyers not only with the quality of its vehicles but also with the 24 hours a day, 7 days a week service promise that the Internet provides. The car dealer's site also affords the customer those extra Internet benefits, including tips on travel and great deals from participating in an online automobile club. Even though the brick-and-mortar dealership can provide service, pamphlets on safety, and maybe even an offline auto club, the consumer won't find it in the privacy of his or her own home or sitting at a desk at work (where consumers tend to spend most of their time and get the most done).

INTERNAL AND EXTERNAL DIMENSIONS OF THE BRAND

It's extremely important to think Internet before making the commitment to cyberspace. However, in order to think Internet, companies must fully understand both the internal and external dimensions of a brand. And in the

It's extremely important to think Internet before making the commitment to cyberspace. However, in order to think Internet, companies must fully understand both the internal and external dimensions of a brand.

case of moving the brand online, or even the birth of a dot-com, the same considerations must be made. In an interview, Alan Bergstrom, president of the Brand Consultancy, clarifies the importance of understanding the internal and external dimensions and how this translates into brand opportunity (see "Branding—Internal and External Dimensions" an interview with Alan Bergstrom).

Learning and discussing traditional brands, brand extensions online, and e-brands evokes an interesting question. Is there a difference between how the traditional brands are moving online with brand strategy and how e-brands are developing their cyberstrategies? According to Alice Uniman, president of Phoenix Brand Strategies, there is an enormous difference (see "The Brand Perspective," an interview with Alice Uniman).

CYBERBRANDING THEORIES

According to *Advertising Age,* understanding the cyberbrand has to do with the three "i" theory. The first "i" is *information,* which does not necessarily mean simply company brochure information, but information that an audience expects from a brand in cyberspace (which depends on the brand's characteristics and attributes). The second "i" is *interactivity,* that hands-on experience that adds a new dimension to any brand pre-Internet. The third "i" is *instinct,* to avoid emulating another company's Web site branding and marketing efforts simply because it looks like a good idea.[3]

More theory behind cyberbrands brings us to the new four "p's." In addition to Marketing 101, with *its* four "p's" (price, product, promotion, and placement), welcome the *new* four "p's" with an online branding twist. The first "p" is *permission.* This notion was touched upon in the Bergstrom interview, in which he, too, agreed that having permission from an audience to be online increases acceptance of the brand as opposed to consumer criticism. The second "p" is *penetration.* There is the belief that online traffic will eventually transfer to smaller, niche sites and marketers need to be smart about

> In addition to Marketing 101, with *its* four "p's" (price, product, promotion, and placement), welcome the *new* four "p's" with an online branding twist.

where they form cyberpartnerships and promote their brands in terms of allocating cyber advertising dollars. The third "p" is *personalization.* Knowing your customers and understanding their personal needs will allow for a more enjoyable personalized online experience. The last "p" is *profitability,* realizing that the strength of the brand online will leverage an opportunity that will lead to stronger recognition and brand awareness.[4] That's why some venture capital companies insist that dot-coms are evaluated by brand consulting firms pre-IPO, because the power of the brand reaps profit.[5]

BRANDING—INTERNAL AND EXTERNAL DIMENSIONS

Alan Bergstrom, president and founder of the Brand Consultancy in Atlanta, Georgia, began his marketing career as a military intelligence officer and at one point served in the Reagan administration as a daily intelligence briefer. He later ventured into the consulting field, helping American businesses to handle emerging trends and identify brand strategies to position themselves for the future. After years of brand consulting for firms in the Atlanta area, in 1996 Bergstrom formed the Brand Consultancy, a company that focuses specifically on brand strategy, leveraging the brand to attract and retain loyal employees and loyal customers (in addition to creating more demand for a company's products and services and often obtaining a premium price if positioned properly).

According to Bergstrom, brands have both internal and external dimensions. The internal dimensions involve the employees of the company, the culture of a company, and the styles and personality it embodies. He states, "This not the easiest sell to many companies." Brands have to appeal to their employees, and employees must be proud of the brand. It's the same approach you take externally when attracting customers, where you try to create a real powerful emotional bond or affinity that customers attach themselves to. When that bond is created, employees, like customers, become great "brand ambassadors." The power of the brand makes a person want to work for a particular organization. It makes sense if you think about all of the dot-com start-ups and how these companies are attracting the best talent—it's a result of the opportunity, the excitement, and the potential of the brand. The key is to build a strong brand to attract the brightest employees. For Brand Consultancy's clients, branding is a "holistic" approach—it's much more than a name and a logo. And no longer is branding "just about advertising." Every part of the organization must be involved in delivering the brand promise that is made in advertising and in other communications. The brand must be able to deliver what it promises, and that requires people throughout the organization creating the proper "brand touch-point" impressions every time the customer encounters the brand, whether it's in the advertising, the customer service, the product or service itself, the distribution channel, or the Internet. As a matter of fact, "We choose brands because of their attributes and characteristics, the impressions we form about them, and the value we receive from them," states Bergstrom. If a company fails on any brand encounter, it misses the chance to maximize an opportunity, or worse yet, it may destroy a positive impression that already existed or create confusion about what the brand stands for and appear to deliver against its promise. Successful brands "walk the walk."

THE BRAND PERSPECTIVE

What is a brand? Alice Uniman, President of Phoenix™ Brand Strategies, offers this definition—a brand is a "promisemark." A brand promises its customers the consistent satisfaction of a specific set of expectations. Consumers buy brands, not products or services. After all, consumers can't buy products off the factory line. They can only recognize your product by its proper name, not its common name.

Why are brands important to their "owners"? A successful brand engenders long-term customer loyalty that, over time, allows the brand to accrue equity and true asset value. In turn, such brand power permits the brand to command higher profit margins, higher stock prices, a higher level of insulation from competitive attack, and a far greater ability to weather and effectively respond to technological change and shifts across elements of the marketing mix.

So, is there a difference between a brick-and-mortar brand moving to e-commerce and an e-brand? According to Uniman, who has been in the brand-building business for 20 years, there is a significant difference. In a lengthy discussion, Uniman raised some interesting issues about the difference between these two general brand types.

Uniman stated that it's easy to see the difference when you consider the following scenario. Start with the obvious fact that an e-brand is dependent on the WWW for its mere existence—and the brick-and-mortar gang is not. At least, not yet.

For the GEs, P&Gs or GMs of the world, then, the Internet affords a powerful brand-building tool to strengthen their total marketing clout. Often, the brick-and-mortars leverage the Net's capability to serve as a channel for relationship marketing efforts and not necessarily as a retail channel to directly sell product. (Although many, many of them already do move product sales through the WWW.)

From a customer relationship-building perspective, the Internet is another avenue for customers to get information. After all, the Internet is that personal salesperson that you can visit at three o'clock in the morning when you are in your pajamas. Classic relationship marketing activities have been conducted for a long while across a number of venues—customer satisfaction surveys, consumer clubs, reward programs, to name a few. Now, the Internet presents another immensely effective way for companies to facilitate their relationship marketing efforts.

So, the next logical question is, Do brick-and-mortar companies have a cyberbrand? Not so far. But they do have a powerful channel to expand and enhance the identity of their offline brands. The core, brand-building fundamentals employed by such companies are unlikely to change markedly. That's probably why the brick-and-mortars' Internet activities receive little publicity and why most of them rarely play a role in the "e-hype."

Long-lived, strong brands have maintained and nurtured their valuable equity through many changes—product design and manufacturing technology evolution, the proliferation of retail channels, a virtual explosion in number and types of media vehicles through the years, and seismic shifts in consumer attitudes and lifestyles. So managing change, to such successful marketers, is a state of being. Even if the GMs or P&Gs are not at the center of all the cyberarticles, they are not necessarily "asleep at the wheel." The savvy brick-and-mortars are involved in the Internet, hold a long-term view about its potential, and have the business resources to stick with it.

Uniman focused the discussion on the e-born brands. Unlike offline brands, their existence *is* the Internet. Such brands are a bit more restricted in the number of elements in the marketing mix they can utilize to build their business. As well, these brands are, in a funny way, more fragile than offline brands. They can't be protected from competition by a patent or a unique, a secret formula, or some proprietary piece of technology.

The importance of superb branding skills becomes, therefore, that much more critical if an e-brand is to have a long shelf life. Some of them are clearly going to have to learn that lesson the hard way. As well, it is essential for an e-brand to deeply appreciate the importance of brand identity components, because when the Web site is altered, so is the very design of the brand and both the perceived and actual consumer use experience. Today, a strong offline brand can probably survive a substandard Web site. An e-brand cannot.

With the intense flurry of new dot-coms, with the rich supply of venture capital, and with the IPO of the day, it makes a lot of folks wonder (even some on Wall Street and the investors who make out like bandits) how many e-brands will survive at least beyond the next 12 months—and even whether some of the quite young and already quite wealthy founders even care. Given the phenomenally high stock valuations—the "P" in the P/E ratio—and phenomenally low earnings levels, expect a giant shakeout.

So, why do so many believe that only the e-brands will crack the e-commerce code? As far as Uniman is concerned, it's unlikely to be all the dot-com "newbies," but rather offline brand leaders who will author the cyberrules.

THE CYBERBRANDER'S CHECKLIST

From this point forward, you should be gearing your thoughts toward the Internet. All of your thinking should be "Internet" thinking and you should feel empowered by the potential of the cyberbrand. And every

All of your thinking should be "Internet" thinking and you should feel empowered by the potential of the cyberbrand.

time you hear the word *cyberbrand*, you will automatically be thinking that your online brand has met these requirements:

- Permission to be online
- One-on-one interaction
- Personal experience
- Immediate rewards
- Service and responsiveness
- Relationship marketing
- Content beyond a static brochure

THE AUTOMOTIVE INDUSTRY GOING ONLINE: SAAB CARS USA

Saab customers can be described as predominantly professional, affluent, independent-minded, and well educated. They are "premium" car buyers, not luxury car buyers. When defining brand attributes and characteristics, which appeal to these customers, the Saab brand has both functional and emotional dimensions:

Functional

- Unique design
- Superior comfort and spaciousness
- Designed-in safety and security
- Smart engineering
- Technical simplicity

Emotional

- Individual and personal
- Unique and unconventional
- Secure and safe
- Intelligent technology

To leverage this brand, every stitch of communication had to fully reflect the brand strategy. Saab Cars USA worked with an advertising agency to develop the campaign entitled "Find Your Own Road." As a part of this campaign, Saab Cars USA wanted to extend its brand online. As a traditional brick-and-mortar car manufacturer, it needed to differentiate itself from other traditional car manufacturers and at the same time maintain consistency with the Saab offline brand advertising, a campaign that utilized a series of color drawing animations and messages reflecting the brand attributes outlined above.

The underlying premise of the brand message is centered on independence and not being a "crowd chaser." The Saab brand stands for being your own person, defying convention, and seeking a spirit of uninhibited fun—the type of individual who drives a Saab.

Challenges

- How does Saab Cars USA utilize its Internet site as a place where a Saab customer can be his or her own person and create an individual experience?
- How does Saab Cars USA grasp the power of technology for a satisfying customer service experience?
- How does Saab Cars USA establish the brand online so

that it maintains an individual, personal, unique, unconventional, safe, and secure image?

- How does Saab Cars USA remain consistent with its offline advertising campaign?

Outcome

Saab Cars USA developed a Web site that enabled individuals to express individuality and uniqueness of character. The site allowed users to create links to other Web sites that were of personal interest, including active sporting destinations like tennis, mountain biking, and kayaking; and music and cultural destinations, such as modern jazz, the arts, or dance.

With respect to technology, Saab Cars USA was first in the automobile industry to allow customers or potential customers to order a car on the Internet through a local dealership. A consumer could select a vehicle with desired options and choose a delivery area. The site would then identify a dealership and have the vehicle order and delivery instructions compete via the Internet. For Saab Cars USA, the Internet represented a safe and secure environment for the purchase of an automobile, reinforcing those attributes or "pillars" of the Saab brand. The company was also successful with its online test drive service. A consumer could place a test drive order over the Internet and have the car delivered by a local dealer to his or her door (home or office) the next day for that test drive. The Internet afforded Saab Cars USA the opportunity to communicate one-on-one with the consumer to leverage that personal and individual experience that the brand represents. Saab Cars USA was successful at communicating the offline traditional brand strategy on the Internet. As a result of the brands being communicated so well, an audience, whether it knew the brand strategy or not, could easily figure out what Saab was all about. Saab's brand message was delivered consistently in words, visuals, and actions in every medium; that made the brand promise real.

SOURCE: The Brand Consultancy, Atlanta, Georgia.

CHAPTER

(4) The Emergence of the Cyberbrand

Objective

The twenty-first century has brought the cyberbrand to life. Accompanying its presence is loyalty from consumers who believe in the Internet. Marketers need to grasp the importance of the cyberbrand and treat it with the same respect and consideration that has always been given to traditional brands. Marketers branding online will gain insight into this importance by taking the following into account:

- That consumer trust and cyberbranding go hand in hand
- The differentiating factors of the cyberbrand
- The benefits of having a well-known traditional brand
- That consumers care about brands online
- Tricks from the "new kids on the block"
- The convergence of the traditional brand and the cyberbrand

CONSUMER TRUST AND CYBERBRANDING
GO HAND IN HAND

The cyberbrand has emerged. It's not "just arriving," or "starting to emerge." It's here, it's now, and it's packing a punch so powerful that consumers are logging on daily to see what cyberbrands have to offer. The importance of the cyberbrand grows in proportionate measure to how much time, energy, and trust consumers place in the Internet. Whether it's researching information on the Web, shopping online, or using the Web as a source of entertainment, consumers are becoming

> **The cyberbrand has emerged. It's not "just arriving," or "starting to emerge." It's here, it's now, and it's packing a punch so powerful that consumers are logging on daily to see what cyberbrands have to offer.**

increasingly tech savvy and extremely comfortable with all of the Net's offerings. In a recent survey by *Screaming Media,* the results revealed that for millions of Americans, the Internet is a trusted and indispensable information source relied upon just as frequently as traditional media channels including television and newspapers.[1] Other significant findings included that survey participants chose the Internet over television as a source of the most interesting information, 67% to 18%. In addition, 65% chose the Internet as the easiest source of information, and 63% were in agreement that the Internet has the most in-depth information. With respect to consumer trust, the survey also states that participants place the same amount of trust in the online version as they do in offline news and information.[2]

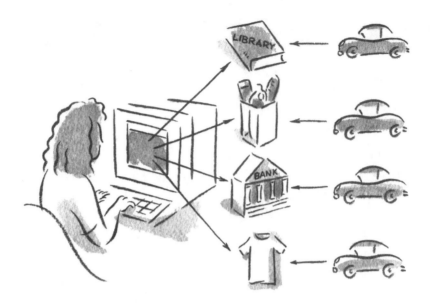

Yes, the cyberbrand has emerged and continues to gain momentum and strength as more people place their trust in the Internet as the number 1 source of information. More evidence of consumer trust is seen in the growing Internet numbers: online purchases, banking, trading, and the rising numbers of advertising dollars from companies that know cyberbrands have emerged with immeasurable benefits. Perhaps 100 years from now, marketers will view the cyberbrands of today more like the traditional brands of the past. Yahoo! will be like Coca-Cola and Ivory soap. Maybe, in the future, there will be "solar" branding or "orbital" branding. The point is that marketers will always be branding to influence consumer behavior and will utilize the technology of the times to capture the hearts (and the pockets) of consumers globally. So, when a statement

Perhaps 100 years from now, marketers will view the cyberbrands of today more like the traditional brands of the past.

pops up in conversation or in an article that refers to branding as "old-fashioned," marketing professionals automatically know the inherent value of branding, and it's certainly not old-fashioned. On the contrary, it's the force, coupled with technology, which has allowed companies over the years to forge into the future and move brands to new interactive levels.

THE DIFFERENTIATING FACTORS OF THE CYBERBRAND

The mixture of the brand and the technology that communicates its message is a powerful combination. And with each combination there's a *differentiating factor*. Back in the days of just print and broadcast media, these channels also had positive brand factors including the print media's instant credibility as a reliable source of information and the broadcast media's opening up consumers' ears and eyes to a new world of audio and visual entertainment. With each factor was the opportunity for the brand to be more persuasive to evoke consumer action. The Internet and the cyberbrand entice consumer action with several differentiating factors. The Internet is the only place where a consumer can interact with a brand for hours prior to an actual purchase (and now, that purchase is online as well). Because the Internet is technologically advanced, inter-

The Internet is the only place where a consumer can interact with a brand for hours prior to an actual purchase (and now, that purchase is online as well.)

action with the brand can be in the form of audio, video, or 3D animation. One-on-one communication is available at all times—it's the user and the brand together, with a hands-on experience that strengthens a bond between the two. The two-way communication appears in various forms including chat sessions and message boards to communicate with other users and the ability for consumers to request information or make a service inquiry that is given an immediate response. In addition, as a result of the Internet's reaching a point of trust with consumers (one of today's major issues), they are more apt to use credit cards, give out banking information, and make transactions that would have been unheard of decades ago. With more trust in the Internet, consumers take advantage of the convenience and ease of performing daily tasks that otherwise take up much of their time. These differentiating factors are the aspects of the cyberbrand that "pack the punch" and evoke action.

Take a look at Disney, for instance, a brand that has maintained its strength by changing with the times and the new technology. Walt Disney in his memoirs stated, "Disney is a family thing, a set of constant expectations in the public mind. I'm not Disney anymore. I used to be Disney, but now Disney is something we've built up in the public mind over the years. It stands for something, and you don't have to explain what it is to the public. They know what Disney is and what it represents. They know they're going to get a certain quality, a certain kind of entertainment."[3]

When Mr. Walt Disney started his company, the brand was attached to his name. Through years of organizational focus, brand planning and strategizing, and consistent brand communication, the Disney name and logo transcended Mr. Walt Disney's life to become among the top 10 brands in the world.[4] Today, Disney leverages its powerful brand online with an Internet presence that catches the spirit, fun, and family entertainment the brand has always conveyed. From the moment the Disney site downloads, a visitor's attention is captured with so many interactive options. From the action-packed games to the lovable music of Disney (captured by downloadable sound clips) and all of the wonderful animation that allows children to travel on a cyber Disney adventure, the site translates into brand value. So, for children who know and love the Disney brand, no more waiting for their parents to take them to the movies or waiting for Mom and Dad to go to the Disney store. It's easy for children to experience a Disney adventure by visiting Disney's online arts and crafts center, checking out the paint and play section of the Web site, or listening to the Disney soundtracks. For the big kids (adults fall under this category as well), information is provided in the "Fun for Families" area on a 24/7 basis for movies, Disney vacations, and a host of activities. Did Mr. Walt Disney ever expect his name to mean so many things to so many different people around the world? Both offline and online, the brand stands for quality entertainment and an experience that fulfills expectations of the Disney brand promise. The online brand allows Disney to flourish in ways that were not possible pre-Internet—instant Disney fun, ease of use, and convenience, all without making a single purchase (yet enticing consumers to be a more connected part of the products). By being offered extra one-on-one interaction, convenience, and immediate rewards, loyal Disney fans remain faithful Disney customers.[5]

THE BENEFITS OF HAVING A WELL-KNOWN TRADITIONAL BRAND

Disney is just one of the many examples illustrating the importance of a powerful traditional brand and how having an online brand carries tremendous importance. Disney online reaches millions of consumers, further enforcing the spirit of this world-renowned brand with stimulating visual interaction. Most marketers realize that a brand gains momentum, as every promise is fulfilled, for every customer. And each time a consumer is satisfied, loyalty to the brand goes without question.

> Most marketers realize that a brand gains momentum, as every promise is fulfilled, for every customer. And each time a consumer is satisfied, loyalty to the brand goes without question.

Translation: Consumers will pay premium prices when expectations are satisfied. After all, that's why a large percentage of the youth population walks around in Guess, Tommy Hilfiger, and DKNY. The reverse is also true—Wrangler is no longer a sign of the times. How many teenagers are bragging about their Wranglers? With our vast knowledge of brand power and the struggle to keep messages alive and fresh in the minds of audiences, is there any doubt that a cyberbrand would carry the same weight as an offline brand? If we know that brands are so important, then shouldn't cyberbrands be given the same careful consideration? Yes, and yes again! The rush to the Internet does not go without warrant, because in some cases first to market wins, but not without careful planning and consistent branding strategy—if there's an offline brand, then the online counterpart must be familiar to consumers, yet capture a new interactive experience for them, like what we have seen with the Disney brand. Or, with respect to the dot-com start-up, there are careful steps to assure the brand's life and strategies to thrust the e-brand past its launch and into the minds of consumers who recognize the brand immediately, like Yahoo!, Amazon, or eBay. There are too many instances when companies should have proceeded with caution but did not and thus caused irreversible damage to the brand. Toys "Я" Us is the traditional example. The brand was moved online with high expectations from consumers that Toys "Я" Us would fulfill their holiday shopping needs. A poorly planned holiday season marred the brand and sent consumers running to e-toys. It's unfortunate, and happens all too often. We know why brands are important. There's no excuse for not protecting every aspect of the customer experience and fulfillment of the brand promise. For the e-brand, mistakes are happening just as often. Boo.com was the online fashion retailer that went out of business within its first six months of existence. The new start-up had famous names to back its efforts, including Bernard Arnault, the Benetton family, Goldman, Sachs & Co., and J. P. Morgan. Boo.com launched with promises to create a fashion experience that would allow global service and advanced technology to consumers who would view merchandise in three dimensions. The end of Boo.com came quickly when consumers could not access the site or take advantage of the technology that was promised to them. As a result of these technical problems, the site took double the time to develop. By the time the technology issues were straightened out, it was too late. Consumer excitement and anticipation turned into an unpleasant experience that led to the e-brand's downfall.[6]

There's an obvious advantage to having a well-known brand offline: consumers who know the brand take the time to explore and experience it online. If consumers are willing to travel to a brick-and-mortar location, then the Internet is pure convenience. The whole point of cyberspace is to provide convenience and that extra something special we cannot experience offline. So, if a company makes the commitment to take the brand online, every aspect of branding should be well thought out and protected. Being unprepared for a large shopping season or not properly managing the technology that is promised will shatter the expectations of an audience that goes online for an exciting cyberexperience. Any incident that has the potential to damage the brand should be an immediate call to action—reexamination of brand-building strategies and a reevaluation of the importance of a cyberbrand.

> **There's an obvious advantage to having a well-known brand offline: consumers who know the brand take the time to explore and experience it online. If consumers are willing to travel to a brick-and-mortar location, then the Internet is pure convenience.**

> **Any incident that has the potential to damage the brand should be an immediate call to action—reexamination of brand-building strategies and a reevaluation of the importance of a cyberbrand.**

In an article that appeared in *Computerworld* in 1998 entitled "Building Brands on the Web," the author discusses the advantage of an existing radio brand, National Public Radio (NPR), and how its Web site is related to the offline brand, with a little something extra for its loyal listeners on the Net. They're not only listening to the radio. For NPR's "Car Talk" program (www.cartalk.com), fans can visit a Web site to access their favorite broadcast programs that are archived on the site and various forms of entertainment including contests and trivia. The site includes what's consistent with the NPR brand promise with an added twist—again, it's that one-on-one interaction that allows more entertainment for program followers, more than they can get from the radio dial alone. Communication of the online brand, just like its offline counterpart, can make or break the brand promise. If sports fans went to ESPN.com and could not access the latest information on sports news and events, would those fans lose trust in ESPN.com and think twice the next time around? Yes, indeed. That's why ESPN makes a promise to its loyal audience and keeps that promise with a Web site that fulfills expectations of the offline brand. ESPN.com is online with the same related sports information that is on its television programming, yet moves in a new direction, into the online interactive realm. The brand allows one-on-one interaction for the user with video highlights and the ability to listen to audio highlights, to participate in two-way communication in sports chat rooms, and to gain hands-on brand experience in anything from football and basketball to Nascar racing and hockey. ESPN.com offers a host of information that is frequently updated, and accessibility at a moment's request with immediate rewards for sports fans of every age. The Web site is also geared toward a younger audience (more so than the offline brand). Children can enjoy hockey games and trivia and access information on their favorite teams and players. In addition, ESPN.com accommodates its paying members, who join the ESPN.com community, with Fantasy Football games and a wealth of opportunities with respect to sports entertainment. Again, the online brand can make or break the brand. ESPN realized the importance of the cyberbrand and in this case makes the brand a pleasurable experience for users every time. It's the opportunity of a lifetime to get that much closer to a loyal customer, and careful consideration with this brand was definitely exercised.

CONSUMERS CARE ABOUT BRANDS ONLINE

Is there any proof that consumers care about brands online, or is it strictly convenience? An article appearing in the *Electronic Advertising and Marketplace Report,* published by Simba Information, Inc., reveals that brands do play a role in online purchases. The article discusses research conducted by a consulting firm that reveals how online purchasers of computer products are placing far more emphasis on the brand name. Whether consumers were buying PCs, hardware, or software, or even storage parts, much more value was placed on the manufacturer's brand name. Case in point—online or offline, again, branding does matter.[7] As a result, companies are realizing more today the value of building their brands online. Offline, we see how the brand is a promise, built upon the company's history and its current position in the market. The brand encompasses facts about the company's heritage and its future aspirations. In addition, the offline brand is important because it comes with a set of values that build toward a promise to employees, customers, and partners.

It's the online brand that is considered to be every "touch point" or electronic experience a customer can have with a company. And with every experience, a lasting impression is formed, one that builds upon

It's the online brand that is considered to be every "touch point" or electronic experience a customer can have with a company.

the brand or detracts from its overall appeal. As companies worldwide see the connection between online brands and consumer preference, more emphasis is placed on the Internet. The importance of the cyberbrand grows as each online visitor interacts with the brand in a different and unique way. Companies are strategizing differently as a result of the Internet. They are redefining the way they interact with consumers, making the brand an experience long before the purchase of the actual product or service. The brand online does more than communicate an idea. Think back to the days when mom-and-pop stores were flourishing in your hometown. These small, friendly stores had the best approach to customer service, with the owners always remembering your name and how you liked your cold cuts sliced. Not only did they remember your food preferences, but also they knew the names of the members of your family, and always had something pleasant to say when you were at the checkout counter. You never had to search for the item that you wanted, because you knew exactly where it was or they would find it for you, and most of all they lived by the notion that the customer was always right—a way of thinking that is somewhat archaic in today's market. Since the mom-and-pop stores of the past, time has gone by with little hope of recapturing that small-town friendliness.

...along comes the Internet and "personal" is the name of the game.

However, along comes the Internet and "personal" is the name of the game. It may not be as sincere as mom and pop, but it certainly works.

Many of the cyberbrands understand this concept and carry the personal message on their sites; Amazon and CDNow were among the first to start the trend. How does this affect consumer perception and judgment? In all honestly, quite a bit. It is

It is just as easy to frequent a Web site that makes a consumer feel welcome as one that does not.

just as easy to frequent a Web site that makes a consumer feel welcome as one that does not. It's a simple principle. Consumers will always choose what will offer more personalization and experience and ultimately what will make them happy. So, then, it should not be a surprise that when a site knows the consumer's name, remembers what he or she likes, and makes his or her shopping experience more pleasant, ultimately, that consumer will be back to purchase more items in the future.

TRICKS FROM THE NEW KIDS ON THE BLOCK

There are a handful of new companies that are capitalizing on their brand-building efforts and quickly realizing the importance of branding. With U.S. households becoming more familiar with names like Yahoo!, America Online (AOL), and Palm Computing, it is evident that these companies believe in the power of the brand. How did these new kids on the block become so brand-smart that GE and P&G might take notice? And why is it that more than half of U.S. households recognize the names AOL and Yahoo! immediately? Furthermore, Palm Computing took only 18 months to sell its first 1 million units, significantly less time than it took Sony Walkman to sell the same number of units. These companies are investing in brand-building strategies, creating recognizable brands not only quickly but also at less expense. They are employing strategies far beyond advertising, which is considered only "one element in a bag of creative brand-building tricks."[8] Here's trick number one: forget the old saying "Why purchase the cow if you can get the milk for free." Give away the milk and the cow. Free samples are an immediate attention grabber. Take AOL, for instance: it's king of the giveaway strategy, at one time distributing diskettes to American households and then upgrading to CD-ROMs. A one-month free trial is the best way to get the consumer to try the service. There's no better explanation than a hands-on experience. Even if the consumer does not sign up for the AOL service, the brand is still visible in a household, doubling as a coaster or a Frisbee for the kids (it's been done). Another example of the giveaway strategy is 3Com's Palm Computing offer that provided members of a 3Com conference a Palm Pilot for half price. There were 600 attendees at the 3Com conference that walked away with a half-price deal. Just by getting the word out and by creating a stir, executives at subsequent 3Com events opted to buy Palm Pilot products for the full price.

Another useful tip is to utilize the reach of the ubiquitous Web. Online advertising reached the predicted $4 billion in 2000, according to Forrester Research. Beyond standard banner advertising, take notice of Amazon.com and its ability to franchise in cyberspace. Amazon capitalizes on the opportunity to appear on sites everywhere on the World Wide Web. Amazon partners receive a percentage from the company (somewhere between 5 and 15%) of any revenue that is generated on their site. In 1998, the associate franchising program (or the affiliate program) encompassed over 40,000 sites on the Internet. There are other companies striving to duplicate the likes of the Amazon model.[9] Last, a secret that rarely gets out of the bag—public relations like never before. The power of branding is complemented by the influence and credibility of a third-party endorsement. Consumers are more likely to believe the words of an objective third party than a company saying, "Try our product, it's the best." Some of the latest brand builders have been employing public relations strategies to make even more "noise" about their products and services. It worked for Yahoo! with a marketing campaign focusing on its youthful and instantaneously famous founders, David Filo and Jerry Yang, who got involved in speaking engagements that generated substantial press for the young entrepreneurs. Powerful public relations strategies include guerrilla-marketing stunts such as Java's launching an intense guerrilla effort against its opponent, Microsoft, by tying in JavaBeans™ with the explosion of the coffee house fad. Or what about the young man who changed his legal name to "The Dot-Com Guy?" Other efforts include lobbying around industry issues to gain exposure, further enforcing the attributes and characteristics of the brand, whether it's independence or defiance, or anything else.

CONVERGENCE OF THE TRADITIONAL BRAND AND THE CYBERBRAND

It's true that some of the newer brand builders, as mentioned, have built their brand recognition quicker. Does a newer brand that is acknowledged sooner have the staying power in the market like an older brand? We see how Coke and Disney have taken decades of investment and continuous brand-building strategies to create the giant brands of the world. Where do the newer brands fit in? Do these brands

There is opportunity on the Internet for both traditional brands and new e-brands to prosper. Therefore, forward-thinking companies will rely on the importance of branding and the power of the brand to forge ahead successfully.

have the patience and the understanding of the importance of branding to continue brand-building efforts? There is opportunity on the Internet for both traditional brands and new e-brands to prosper. Therefore, forward-thinking companies will rely on the importance of branding and the power of the brand to forge ahead successfully.

These companies will take their brands to reach new market heights and communicate through channels, such as the Internet, that have the ability to promote everlasting life. It's the power of the brand together with technology that produces what we will call the "optimum brand." There are two types of optimum brands that marketers will strive for in the twenty-first century. The first optimum brand is the one that recognizes its traditional roots and can change with technology to develop a strong cybercounter-

It's the power of the brand together with technology that produces what we will call the "optimum brand."

part that enhances overall brand value (Disney, Microsoft, NBC, to name a few). Here, we have the successful convergence of the traditional brand and its online brand counterpart. The second type of optimum brand relates to the new dot-com start-up that quickly incorporates several traditional, offline branding strategies along with cyberstrategies to have an existence that extends beyond the Internet (like Yahoo! appearing under a billion Pepsi caps or teaming up with Ben & Jerry's, and E-Trade, which has signed a deal with Target stores to open an investor zone for customers). Either way there is a convergence: traditional brands need the cyberaspect to forge ahead to meet consumer needs of the future, and e-brands require a bit of a traditional foundation and "roots" to survive and flourish in the twenty-first century. Hence, we have the emergence of the cyberbrand.

Anne Holland is the CEO and founder of MarketingSherpa.com and has extensive experience as a Web strategy consultant to online content business. She has been marketing via the Internet since 1995. Holland discussed her experiences with companies moving online and the importance of exercising careful thought on the Internet.

With offline companies, according to Holland, the first error is to purchase a "bad" URL or domain name. Usually the information technology (IT) officer in a company makes the decision with respect to the company's online name. "A much better procedure would be to have a committee meeting with executives of the company who logically pick out as many domain names as possible," states Holland. She believes that these names can range from all of the variations of a company's name (and those of its brands and planned brands) to common spelling errors made by consumers. For Holland's company, MarketingSherpa.com, she made a point of purchasing a URL to catch a common spelling error in the word *sherpa*, making sure to obtain the domain name with the word spelled incorrectly (with an "i" for *shirpa*). *Reader's Digest* had the right idea. It bought roughly 300 domain names—every possible name or variation of the brand name that a reader might refer to. For branding, this makes a great deal of sense. However, there are cases in which companies are not quick enough to grab their URL. In the case of Phillips' *PR News,* the company wanted to purchase PRNews.com. But when *PR News* tried to secure this name, it had already been taken. (Note: The same thing happened to the *New York Times,* which is now stuck with NYTimes.com.) The next step was for the company to decide on a new online brand name. It may not have been the "greatest solution," according to Holland. It chose PRandMarketing.com, capturing only the "PR" portion of the offline brand name while not replacing it with a sufficiently "snappy" or ear-catching name to really do any easy branding.

Holland offered a few suggestions with respect to a new name. Ideally, a company should try to keep its brand name for its URL. But when that doesn't work out, try to keep the following in mind:

- The name must be easy to spell.

- It must be able to pass the telephone test (most dot-com names are passed by word of mouth).
- Stay away from using dot-net. Not many people search by dot-net.
- Remember that dot-org is reserved for not-for-profit companies.

Holland elaborated on another aspect of moving online that deserves careful consideration: the cyber portion of a brand should have a separate staff from the offline brand. For example, *Washington Post Online* staff are located in a Virginia building several miles away in location and attitude from the *Post's* offline headquarters in downtown Washington, D.C. The *Post* could also have housed the cyber portion of the company downtown, but made the strategic decision to devote a separate staff and location to the online brand. Having separate companies is one way to make a firm commitment to the Internet. As Holland puts it, it is the difference between a company that is in "attack mode" and one in "defense mode." When companies are in attack mode, they have a full-time cyber department and a full-time cyber staff. Their financial decisions are also made to different criteria than the parent offline brand. An attack company takes financial risks, accepts outside investments, and operates with different bottom-line goals than its parent company might be able to. On the contrary, defense-mode companies have what is known as an "offline way of thinking." They are only testing the waters and do not want to take too big a risk when it comes to the Internet. For these companies, the solution is to make the Internet a part of someone's job rather than having the attack-mode attitude of "Let's give it our all."

Holland gave a clear example of how many companies are slowly changing their mindsets. At a Direct Marketing Association (DMA) Net marketing show in February 1999, almost every company participating in the show had initiated an online presence, but had done so in a fairly tentative defense mode. Most attendees said their jobs were split between Web marketing and "regular" marketing. Speakers stressed the importance of separate Internet players, separate budgets for Internet departments, and the necessity for separate job functions (online versus offline), urging, "Get 100% dedicated to the Web quickly, because it's not a part-time job!" A year later at the DMA Net marketing show in March 2000, clear progress had been made. After the overwhelming success of the Christmas 1999 shopping season online, most show attendees reported that their companies were now shifting as rapidly as possible to attack mode.

Companies need this type of critical thinking when it comes to the World Wide Web, which leads to Holland's final thoughts about online brands: there is no complacency when it comes to the Internet. Offline brands moving online and e-brands born in cyberspace must put careful thought into their branding strategies. There is always the fact that "no matter what your great idea is, there are at least 10 more people who you've never heard of working to take the same idea to market." Competition is fierce, and no one can sit back and be complacent. Look how competition is changing. E-brands are moving offline and suddenly challenging brick and mortar. Take Alloy.com. Moving offline, the company is creating print products for teens. *Yahoo! Internet Life* magazine is another good example of an e-brand forging ahead to capitalize on offline ventures. Expect to see brick-and-mortar stores launching from online-only brands in the coming year.

Holland stressed that not being complacent is by no means a way of suggesting companies should rush in their Internet efforts. Rushing to the Internet without a well-thought-out plan can damage a brand. Offline companies, without the pressure to rush to grab venture capital funds that tie e-brands into a frenzy, can afford to sit back a bit and really do this thing right. Holland offered a piece of advice to offline companies with respect to a new online venture: slow down, take a breath, regroup, and get into the attack mode. Hire the most experienced and talented team you possibly can. (Yes, they will be expensive, and yes, you will have to give them equity and a suit-free place to work.) Give this team a budget larger than you ever imagined, plus the power and freedom to move forward at hyperspeed without having their hands tied by offline company committee meetings, business cannibalization fears, rules about which of your competitors they can't partner with, or internal power struggles. Then be prepared to flexibly change your online business model as many times as it takes to make your Internet brand work for you.

5 Using Technology Properly to Cyberbrand

Objective

To provide marketers with immediate and simple tips to use technology properly. Beginning with the development of a Web site right down to how to avoid the misconceptions of cyberbranding, marketers need to consider the following:

- Cyberbranding trial and error of the 1990s
- Cyberbranding misconception number 1: With the Internet, there's a worldwide audience
- Cyberbranding misconception number 2: Having a 24/7 Web site allows a company to pay less attention to consumer needs
- Cyberbranding misconception number 3: Launching a site means Web surfers will find it
- Cyberbranding misconception number 4: The Web creates an equal opportunity for the little guy to compete with the giants of the industry
- Cyberbranding misconception number 5: Powerful graphics are the key to a "killer" Web site
- Simple cyberlessons learned

CYBERBRANDING TRIAL AND ERROR OF THE 1990s

The 1990s were a decade of Internet trial and error. Web sites were launched, and quite honestly, many lacked the proper amount of prelaunch market research into the online needs of primary and secondary audiences. In addition, site functionality was much less than perfect, the technology promised to online consumers was unavailable when users

The 1990s reflected a lack of cyberbrand emergence. The power of branding was apparent and the force of technology was also present, but there was little success in bringing the entities together.

tried to access it, content was stale, and the average presence was brochurelike. The 1990s reflected a lack of cyberbrand emergence. The power of branding was apparent and the force of technology was also present, but there was little success in bringing the entities together. Only the field leaders, such as Yahoo!, MSN, Amazon, and eBay, succeeded with optimum brands; they found convergence early on and built models for other companies to emulate. Now we see much more convergence and more optimum brands arising; these brands are seizing the power of technology and utilizing the power of the brand to create the omnipotent force. However, from the trial and error of the 1990s to the twenty-first century with its calculated and conscious Internet efforts, there is always room for improvement.

There's a common phrase that creates a stir among professionals and confusion as well, used to describe the false impressions of the Internet and Web site development: the misconceptions of cyberbranding. In order for a brand to reach "optimum" status, it must use technology properly. And what is the value of technology if the brand is isolated on the Internet with no means of being found?

In order for a brand to reach "optimum" status, it must use technology properly. And what is the value of technology if the brand is isolated on the Internet with no means of being found?

Let's get to know the meaning of cyberbranding. Simply stated, cyberbranding is an opportunity to create awareness of a brand online, develop name and logo recognition, communicate a brand message, drive traffic to a Web site, establish an identity with primary and secondary audiences, build a customer base online, increase sales over the Internet, and create a reputation so that as much as a mention of the brand elicits a feeling of a pleasurable experience. You can easily find the top 50 Web properties on Nielsen's Net Ratings. These are brands that have captured the essence of the cyberbrand and have been cyberbranding properly. There are also smaller-scale efforts that deserve recognition exhibiting simple steps taken by companies that have discovered the power of technology and the necessary measures to allow their Web sites to be found and to be functional on the Internet:

- Ascovalve.com, a division of Emerson Electric, features English, Spanish and Portuguese Web site versions for its worldwide clients.
- A consumer goes to CancerQ.com to "Ask the Dr." a personal question with regard to a relative's disease and receives an answer within a two-hour time frame.
- Consumers use a keyword search on a search engine like AOL, Yahoo!, MSN, Lycos, or GoTo.com, and a listing of site descriptions appears.
- A consumer goes to Northjersey.com for specific information and is not bombarded with unnecessary content that does not pertain to his or her geographic region.
- At Tommy.com, consumers do not have to wait for long downloads of graphics to view summer fashion trends and Tommy Hilfiger product information.

These tactics illustrate sites and marketers that have been doing their cyberbranding homework. They have avoided the simple obstacles that start with research and Web site development and continue on with the techniques used to drive traffic to a Web site. They have avoided the misconceptions of cyberbranding.

MISCONCEPTION NUMBER 1: WITH THE INTERNET, THERE'S A WORLDWIDE AUDIENCE.

One of the first questions is, Does the brand need a worldwide audience? Too many companies are not carefully targeting the appropriate audiences in their geographic locations, or the specific groups that need to hear a message. Market research prior to the launch of the site is a critical tool to discover the needs of primary and secondary audiences. Market research might be in the form of existing-customer information or focus panels, one-on-one interviews, and questionnaires distributed to customers.

For AscoValve.com, a division of Emerson Electric, it was necessary to construct a site that was available in three different languages. AscoValve, an off line brand, originally launched **Market research prior to the launch of the site is a critical tool to discover the needs of primary and secondary audiences.** its Web site in English and then, after extensive research, realized that large portions of its customer base were in Spanish- and Portuguese-speaking countries. As a result of the research, AscoValve quickly redesigned its site to have full text and product catalogs in Spanish and Portuguese. Larger companies on the Internet must face issues with respect to being fully equipped to **Larger companies on the Internet must face issues with respect to being fully equipped to handle the needs of a global audience.** handle the needs of a global audience. For instance, a company that has been branding offline globally cannot establish a Web site that is only in one language. In 1999, statistics revealed that of the 180 million Web users, only 107 million read English. There is also the issue of global access and interactive design. The media employed for a target audience or even secondary audiences can be the difference between success and failure on the Net. For example, the personality of a company in the United States is altogether different from what the same company projects for its brand in other countries. Take the rules of color. The color yellow in some Asian countries connotes anger, while in other countries it suggests a positive, favorable image and will increase product purchases when incorporated into the design and packaging of products. Other color examples include forest green, which in Germany is a recommended hue. Royal blue is a color that immediately gains the attention of the British. Colors translate into different meanings for different cultures, so it is extremely important to be aware of this phenomenon when designing a site for the global marketplace.

Because the Internet has the ability to deliver messages so broadly, and so quickly, marketers must take the time to research audiences and prepare for how global visitors will perceive a site. It is not always in a company's best interest to strive for a global site. To avoid the misconception of believing the Internet affords a brand a worldwide audience, the best strategy is to market research to understand the brand's reach, audiences' preferences, and what they will expect from your brand. And if it is a worldwide audience that you seek, be sure to communicate the brand in a fashion that is acceptable to all of the cultures that will have access to its global commerce landscape.

MISCONCEPTION NUMBER 2: HAVING A 24/7 WEB SITE ALLOWS A COMPANY TO PAY LESS ATTENTION TO CONSUMER NEEDS.

This statement could not be farther from the truth. The nature of the Web as a medium is instant communication and gratification. The Internet translates into immediate two-way communication between a company and its audience. Customer service is as important in the digital world as in the real world. Neglecting clients online will drive them away, and it's a guarantee, that with all of the choices on the World Wide Web, they will not be back to a site that neglects their interests. Customer service is built into a brand. What is expected offline is doubly important in cyberspace because of the nature of the

What is expected offline is doubly important in cyberspace because of the nature of the medium and the instantaneous results it's been known to produce.

medium and the instantaneous results it's been known to produce. At CancerQ.com, if a visitor enters the section of the Web site to "Ask the Dr." a question relating to cancer, the visitor receives an answer within two hours from a licensed physician or oncology specialist. On any medical Web site, areas designated for answering questions with regard to a user's medication, specific medical matters, or general health issues need to provide answers in an acceptable time frame. For the consumer on the Internet, this means immediately. No longer can a company get away with one of those instant reply messages that simply acknowledge a request and then answer the question 24 hours later. A consumer, even one who is loyal to a particular company, will not stand for a less-than-adequate communication turnaround time, especially when it pertains to medical advice or health-related issues. Discovery-health.com has an unacceptable time frame when it comes to answering medical inquiries. Consumers who register on the site are disheartened when they ask a question and receive a message that states, "Your question has been received. Please check back in a few weeks to see if your question has been answered. We're sorry, but we cannot personally answer every question...."[1] That is the equivalent of calling up a pharmacist or a doctor and being told that your question cannot be answered for a week and to check back when he or she is not as busy. A patient, in this day and age, would not continue relations with that pharmacist or doctor. After experiencing such a less-than-adequate response, it's highly unlikely the patient would have the same bond or feeling of loyalty.

Regardless of the type of Web site, consumers on the Internet expect to visit a site and receive immediate rewards and answers to their questions. In addition, every item featured on a site, in an online catalog (think of the consumer walking through the aisles of a brick-and-mortar, viewing shelves stocked with products), should be available to the consumer including product description and information and a reasonable price tag attached. Consumers expect products to be order-ready (in small, medium, and large quantities), packaged securely, and even gift wrapped, if necessary. Most of all, products need to be shipped in a timely fashion and, of course, returnable if they do not live up to consumer expectations. Barnes & Noble actually

> **Regardless of the type of Web site, consumers on the Internet expect to visit a site and receive immediate rewards and answers to their questions.**

accepted incorrect Internet orders for return at a brick-and-mortar location. That's an example of customer service working to benefit the brand and the overall customer experience. The Internet process, ideally, should be a hassle-free experience that strengthens the bond between consumers and the brand. This is not asking the impossible. Although many companies starting out in the 1990s did not get it right the first time around, Web sites are now being launched fully tested and prepared to handle the needs of demanding online consumers. To go one step further (as Internet audiences expect), make the experience even more enjoyable for the visitor by concentrating beforehand on the customer's preferences; for example, provide special features on the site, such as personalizing a user's visit by making suggestions on items that may be of interest, or continuously furnishing consumers with new-product notifications after they leave the site. When customer expectations are exceeded, the consumer and the company have formed a stronger relationship, with service beyond what the consumer has ever experienced offline. The Internet makes customer service a 24/7 priority, and remember, what is expected offline is expected in less time on the Internet—it's the nature of this powerful channel.

When customer expectations are exceeded, the consumer and the company have formed a stronger relationship, with service beyond what the consumer has ever experienced offline.

MISCONCEPTION NUMBER 3: LAUNCHING A SITE MEANS WEB SURFERS WILL FIND IT.

An all-time favorite misconception and one that is most popular on the Internet is that if a site is launched, Web surfers will automatically find it. When a company builds a physical structure, there is a slight advantage. People walking by the store peek in the window, become interested by the visual presentation of the window display and enter the store to browse around or to purchase a product. However, it does not work this way in cyberspace. Sure, someone can stumble upon your Web site. But most Internet users these days are savvy and surf the Web with ease, traveling to specific sites with specific intentions. According to recent surveys conducted by Zatso (formerly ReacTv) and the Pew Research Center, the days of aimless surfing are long past.[2] Consumers have a goal—they know exactly what they want to accomplish online. The Internet is ubiquitous, and it is unlikely that an audience will find a site if

Consumers have a goal—they know exactly what they want to accomplish online.

the company does not take the steps to direct them to the site's URL. The use of metatags, developed in the HTML coding of a site, will allow a site's content and key words to be picked up by major search engines. There are two types of metatags. The first allows the Web site to use key words that will automatically be recognized by the search engine. A gardening site might use key words including *gardening, garden, herbs,* and *flowers* to be picked up by search engines. The second metatag is a descriptive tag that allows a site to enter a one-sentence description coded into the HTML text. The description appears in the search engine listing and provides the search engine user with a concrete site explanation.[3] However, contrary to popular belief, simple listings in search engines are not enough. On the large search engines, a user usually moves on after viewing 10 to 15 entries (if that many) that are pulled up by the search engine.

It is imperative that companies employ online and offline marketing. For offline marketing, a company's URL address should be prominently displayed on any collateral pieces right down to the giveaway items like pens, mugs, business card holders, mouse pads, or T-shirts, which are an opportunity to display a Web site address to drive traffic to the site. In the twenty-first century, CD-ROM interactive programs used as direct mail pieces are taking the place of static brochures, with links to a company's Web site, and CD-ROM business cards are a novelty to high tech firms trying to impress new technology on their clients.

When marketing online, a factor to keep in mind is to pay careful attention to the technique that best suits a brand and its message. On the Internet, this is the difference between broadcasting and narrowcasting. When it comes to a specific group that you are targeting, either by profession, age, or even education, a narrowcast message is necessary. Narrowcasting is the strategy that targets a message for a specific group and allows a brand to be found by its audience. Narrowcasting is much more practical on the Internet. So, instead of registering in a Yahoo! search engine for that widespread broadcast message, companies might want to consider choosing a regional portal; for example, a lawyer in New Jersey may choose NJ.com or Inthegardenstate.com and list his or her practice in a lawyer's directory. It is a principle similar to offline marketing. Mass-market media, e.g., network television and national radio, are messages broadcast to the masses. Utilizing local cable stations and local television programming is much more practical for a brick-and-mortar that caters to customers within a 10-mile radius.

When marketing online, a factor to keep in mind is to pay careful attention to the technique that best suits a brand and its message. On the Internet, this is the difference between broadcasting and narrowcasting.

Messages and communication channels need to be extremely targeted to gain maximum exposure among a specific audience. The Internet provides marketers with the tools to communicate a targeted message and to build foot traffic. Using metatags, directory listings in search engines, and link exchanges, with sites that have similar demographics, to drive traffic all promote one central effort. It's the ability to be found on the Internet and to generate as many hits (whether they are original hits from a search engine or a referral hit from a partnering site) as possible on a Web site to build traffic and measure a return on investment (ROI).

Messages and communication channels need to be extremely targeted to gain maximum exposure among a specific audience. The Internet provides marketers with the tools to communicate a targeted message and to build foot traffic.

MISCONCEPTION NUMBER 4: THE WEB CREATES AN EQUAL OPPORTUNITY FOR THE LITTLE GUY TO COMPETE WITH THE GIANTS OF THE INDUSTRY.

Although things are a little brighter for the smaller guys on the Net, these companies still do not have the same opportunities. Larger companies have significant advantages:

1. They have the funds to hire better designers of their Web sites.

2. They have the resources for timely updates to their Web sites.

3. They have the money to advertise their sites both online and offline.

The top Web properties are giants in the industry. Among the most well known, of course, are MSN, IBM, and General Motors, which spend millions of dollars to promote their sites (and this is only a drop in the bucket for these companies). In addition, the television network–owned Web sites, such as NBC and CBS, have an obvious marketing advantage. Their Web sites are promoted on stations that already have millions of viewers—advertising is an easy means for these networks. The same goes for radio stations on the Internet. The New York all-news station 1010 WINS is constantly plugging its Web site URL as a place to find further updates

On the brighter side, however, smaller companies with local patrons do not have to compete with the big guys anymore.

on news and weather. It's difficult for smaller companies to compete against the larger entities that have the resources to cyberbrand, unless it's a new dot-com with venture capital backing the promotional efforts.

On the brighter side, however, smaller companies with local patrons do not have to compete with the big guys anymore. These companies are taking advantage of local and regional portals that are much more reasonable with respect to advertising rates and are extremely targeted to specific user demographics. For example, because the Internet is used to create social interaction, the smaller companies are participating in multiple list dwellings; for example, a college campus may go online to form a unique community. On the University of Florida's Web site (www.ufl.edu), an area designated for the Gainesville community has directories for advertisers to list their stores with links to their sites. Merchants in the vicinity of the campus participate in this portal by advertising their products and services. Other businesses get involved in sponsoring online events for the campus residents. The campus audience takes advantage of the many features on the site, including daily news and events on campus and activities within a two-mile radius of the community. For the online campus, information and events range from those of clubs and fraternities to sporting and recreation. At the same time, the college audience unknowingly receives the branded messages of local businesses that participate as advertisers and sponsors. These multiple list dwellings are definitely a step in the right direction for small companies that do not have the dollars to compete with larger advertisers that post their messages on Yahoo! search engines or on news and informational sites.

Regional sites are becoming increasingly popular with residents who want to be a part of an online community.

Another excellent example of a regional portal that caters to the needs of a specific community is Northjersey.com. Regional sites are becoming increasingly popular with residents who want to be a part of an online community. These sites bring residents news and information, entertainment, education, sports, health, travel, etc. Northjersey.com is fully equipped with directories, providing access to local information and online shopping malls that are relative to the North Jersey community. Northjersey.com allows its advertisers to purchase anything from simple directory listings (with minimal monthly fees) all the way to e-commerce packages and the ability to build a site within the Northjersey.com Web site. In reality, on the Internet, the little guys do not have to sit back and be envious of the big guys and their deep pockets. Targeted communication provides the little guys with a distinct advantage, the ability to be closer to a specific audience. Taking the time to find the most appropriate Internet channels will allow a company to put its best foot forward and be found on the Internet.

Targeted communication provides the little guys with a distinct advantage, the ability to be closer to a specific audience.

MISCONCEPTION NUMBER 5: POWERFUL GRAPHICS ARE THE KEY TO A "KILLER" WEB SITE.

For aesthetic purposes, yes, graphics are important. However, too much, or overkill, can work to a Web site's disadvantage. An abundance of graphics can distract the user from the intended message on the site and make it difficult to concentrate on or pay attention to information or relevant content. What's the use of finding the site if the original purpose for being there is cluttered by graphic overload or graphics with slow downloads? A balance of graphics and purposeful content is the key to retaining your audience. As the Web is utilized more and more for entertainment, sites with games are popping up all over. Uproar.com, Candystand.com, and Nabiscoworld.com have tremendous interactive media appeal for audiences. However, take the dot.com start-up that

A balance of graphics and purposeful content is the key to retaining your audience.

wants to compete in the marketplace with these popular sites: it's faced with issues regarding graphics versus slow download time. It's extremely difficult to make the decision to sacrifice one for the other. Should it be high-quality 3D graphics that take forever to download, or shoddy graphics that download in 30 seconds? In most cases, quality graphics in 3D animation have slow download times, with file sizes ranging from 600K to 800K, depending on the game. This could mean up to three-plus minutes that a visitor must wait to play a game. A perfect example of a site with "killer" graphics but slow download is Nabiscoworld.com's Frog Toss game. With an extremely slow download, the site could easily lose its players.

There's not a great deal that can be done when it comes to high-quality, high-resolution graphics, only a Band-Aid solution for this situation. While the audience awaits the anticipated game, they can get involved in a pregame trivia contest to get them interested and interacting with the site. Sure, this might work on a game site when viewers know what they are waiting for, but in all actuality, a Web site that has a slow download time in general will lose the attention of its audience, and there's little hope of capturing their attention once you have lost their interest.

On Tommy.com, the Tommy Hilfiger Web site, the graphics download quickly, and visitors are captured immediately with a highly audiovisual Web site. Tommy.com has online male and female fashion previews (pictures and music appear in less than a minute), musical artists including Britney Spears who endorse Tommy Hilfiger and a large assortment of Hilfiger products that are extremely captivating for a savvy audience searching for the latest fashion trends. Tommy.com is a good example of a clean, well-designed graphic presentation. The visual movement and stimulation and music and talk on the site

. . . watch out for slow downloads. What you think might be a "killer" graphic, may just "kill" the potential of your site.

capture the user's attention and keep Tommy Hilfiger consumers coming back for more previews and products. On the other hand, Coke.com has long downloads, and much as Coke is a world-famous brand, waiting for site graphics to download (after three minutes) is just too long a wait. Coke might want to consider the Band-Aid solution with some type of "Coke trivia challenge" while the site graphics download. In any case, watch out for slow downloads. What you think might be a "killer" graphic, may just "kill" the potential of your site.

THE SIMPLE CYBERLESSONS LEARNED

There are simple cyberlessons for marketers to remember if they want their brands to reach optimum status. To use technology properly and enhance the brand's ability to be found,

- Identify your audience as a part of the pre-Web site research (and keep in mind that this audience may expand beyond the scope of an offline audience).
- Make the Web site appropriate for the target audience. Trying to be global means taking into consideration various languages and cultural differences.
- Know that customer service is the experience that leaves a lasting impression. With the Web, it is automatically assumed that service is instantaneous and comparable to—if not better than—offline service.
- Be aware that it takes only one bad experience to make a visitor leave a site to never return again—the Web offers so

many choices that consumers are learning firsthand how to comparison-shop and know exactly where to go to find what they need.

- Remember that launching a site in Cyberspace and having a presence is not enough—online brands need to attract and retain audiences. Metatags in HTML text and simple search engine listings are helpful but are not the sole strategies to drive traffic to a Web site.

- Maintain your company's online and offline marketing alike in a well-rounded campaign (TV network and radio stations online have an obvious advantage). Branding offline and online will allow maximum exposure for the brand. The Internet is only one communication channel of many to be utilized.

- Keep in mind that being among the little guys on the Net with smaller resources means there are bigger opportunities that many professionals do not realize when it comes to advertising and sponsors on the Net. There's no need to compete with the big guys unless you are ready to join the ranks of the "deep pockets."

- Employ aesthetics that are visually pleasing enough to draw attention to your site but not overpowering or distracting. The best mix is the proper amount of targeted content with a complementary and quick display of graphics that appeal to the Web site audience.

VISUAL BASICS AND THE MAKINGS OF A WELL-EXECUTED DESIGN

Interview

William C. Miranda heads the design department at PFS Marketwyse. He works closely with the marketing department to cyberbrand various projects.

William has also contributed his illustrations to many of the "to go" series of books. An avid fan of new Web design and technology, he spends his leisure time searching *the Net for sites that stand out from the rest. You can find his links to great sites at www.pfsmarketwyse. com/greatsites.html.*

Overall user-friendliness, accessibility of information and quick download times are extremely important to your audience. But there is one concept that the cybermarketer must absolutely grasp. The quality of graphics and layout of the site are key in portraying the intended image for the brand. Your target audience has an amazing ability to discern a half-hearted attempt at graphics from an effort that is produced on a corporate level. There is no comparison between the effect on a consumer of a well-executed design and that of a poor one. Your audience immediately registers a good visual site into its brains. The level of taste in the work stands out, and visitors pull the site out of the digital pile and render it to memory. In contrast, poor design and layout has a negative effect in that it overshadows the cyberbranding effort, and turns an otherwise good marketing campaign into a visual flop.

If the budget allows (and it always should, in my humble opinion), a good portion should be devoted to quality graphics and production. Hire a proficient design studio or ad agency to handle this phase of the project. I have seen, one too many times, clients requesting savings in design and layout. This always ends with a less-than-desirable logo, layout, and production that only hinders the cyberbranding attempt. A creative agency's Web designers understand that good design is planned out and executed in a manner that ensures your site will look and feel professional. They know that it truly is in the details. They implement certain methods of creating Web graphics that ensure quality and also speed download.

Creative thinking always aids in getting a Web site online that is attention-grabbing. Work the possibilities of themes and other visual tools into the branding effort. This can be used as a springboard for creative graphics. Use interesting images and colors that get noticed and also work for the brand. And by all means, take advantage of animation if it fits into the site plan. The design of the navigational elements is also important. If the Web site is mainly an information site, then graphical elements for buttons and links must be used in such a way that the imagery does not get in the way of the interface. Sites that are created for more trend-setting products or services can use navigation based on imagery.

In its simplest form, all imagery must work together to create a Web site that stands out from the rest, especially if there are many competitors in the market. Keep quality production work high on your list and your target market will take notice.

6 Web Site Design to Enhance the Cyberbrand

Objective

To look outward (beyond the company and past the brand) and realize that the Internet has one central focus—online audiences and their expectations. This chapter will give insight into how specific Web site design considerations enhance the cyberbrand and strengthen the outward focus by examining the following:

■ Understanding that a Web site is not about a company

■ Five Web-site factors

■ Cyber do's

A WEB SITE IS NOT ABOUT A COMPANY

From the moment a Web site launches, it becomes the sole form that encompasses a brand, 24 hours a day, 7 days a week. It's the look of the brand, the feel of the brand, and the essence and experience of the brand together in one unique presence. A Web site is an opportunity—the chance to communicate and impact an audience's behavior instantly. A Web site shares information and promotes interaction.1 Indeed, it is every touchpoint of a company and a brand. That's more than any other channel has to offer in the twenty-first century. As such, a Web site should be outwardly focused. Every issue and consideration stems from the needs of an audience. It's not about the company. It's not about the company's history. It's not about the company's press releases or its brochure. It's about the audience—their needs and preferences.2 For branding professionals, nothing has changed. It's always been about the audience, their likes and dislikes, and what they deem credible. A Web site is an opportunity to dazzle a user with creative site design, visual appeal, ease of function, and accessibility. All of these considerations center on the user, the central focus of the Internet.

> **From the moment a Web site launches, it becomes the sole form that encompasses a brand, 24 hours a day, 7 days a week.**

> **A Web site is an opportunity to dazzle a user with creative site design, visual appeal, ease of function, and accessibility. All of these considerations center on the user, the central focus of the Internet.**

There are five factors that need to be considered when developing a Web site to properly communicate a cyberbrand's message:

- *Number 1: Ease of use.* Web sites should be simple and concise with consistent design for easy navigation and location of information. Apple.com has a clean interface and easy-to-access information. It has a one-click checkout process in accordance with the "ease-of-use principle."

- *Number 2: Provide up-to-date information.* Relevant content should be updated daily (if possible), and weekly at best. iWon.com, a prize-winning Web site, is updated daily for its users, who come back frequently to win cash awards and view surveys and sweepstakes results (the more they visit, the better their odds of winning).

- *Number 3: The importance of a fast download.* Quick downloads are necessary for visitors with slow connections and short attention spans. Yahoo! is the leader of quick downloads and a Web site model most frequently emulated.

- *Number 4: Consistent design and imagery for audience appeal.* Nickjr.com rates well among a youthful audience that visits the site for its design and imagery and an experience that is symbolic of the Nickelodeon brand.

- *Number 5: Provide the right content.* Content must be pertinent to the user and timely with the trends and must revolve around current events and present interests. A plethora of women's sites have launched to face the content issue head-on. Women.com and iVillage appear to be in the lead, but are up against praise and criticism as they race to be "queen of the hill."

NUMBER 1: EASE-OF-USE PRINCIPLE

With an explosion of e-commerce sites, a consumer no longer has to leave the house to get a shopping list filled. From clothing to prescription items, the World Wide Web is accommodating to all. At drugstore.com, a user can find items easily. Visitors can shop by brand, or, if they choose, access specialty areas on the site (located on the navigation bar) including the medicine cabinet, personal care, and nutrition and wellness, to name a few. Drugstore.com is known for stocking those especially hard-to-find items that shoppers may have difficulty purchasing at their neighborhood drugstore. These types of sites have popped up in large numbers, and consumers are buying into the e-commerce process—that is, of course, if waiting to purchase online is faster than actually waiting to buy "on line" (at a brick-and-mortar location). Because e-commerce

> ... consumers are buying into the e-commerce process—that is, of course, if waiting to purchase online is faster than actually waiting to buy "on line" (at a brick-and-mortar location).

sites can be thousands of pages encompassing thousands of products, navigation should be simple, concise, and consistent on all the pages of the site. With thousands of pages and products to choose from, sites should have navigational tools built within the form of searchable databases. There are various ways that are acceptable for audiences to search on a site. Sony.com has an easy search function that allows the user to type in a key word to access a specific product and takes the user di-

> ... searchable keyword databases and pull-down menus of major categories are a necessity (the optimal location is at the top of a site or in the left-hand corner of the main pages) for the user to navigate easily and find products and information quickly.

rectly to a specific page. On the other hand, radioshack.com has a more complicated search with a less apparent search function. An indistinct search tab at the bottom of the home page allows the user to type in a product category, such as portable CD player, and the

search produces a series of catalog pages for the shopper to access within the site. That's too much clicking to find one product. In any case, searchable key word databases and pull-down menus of major categories are a necessity (the optimal location is at the top of a site or in the left-hand corner of the main pages) for the user to navigate easily and find products and information quickly.

It's a frustrating feeling to be lost on a Web site and not know how to get back to a familiar area (an icon back to the home page should be clearly labeled on every page). Whether it's being lost behind the wheel of a car or lost in the layers of a Web site, it's the same uneasy feeling. In a car, having a reliable map is a step in the right direction; the same principle applies on the Net. Some of the best sites have a reliable site map and display that obvious

Some of the best sites have a reliable site map and display that obvious link back to the home page.

link back to the home page. And even if there are links to go outside a company's URL, the site could be designed either within framesets, or with the opening of a new Web browser window that can be closed for backtracking to the original URL. Most of all, information should be placed in a fashion that is logical to the user and makes it effortless to locate.

If visitors have to search for anything on the Net, chances are they will not stick around for long. After all, especially on e-commerce sites, the main goal is to get users to find the product they want and to make a purchase. Apple.com is an excellent example of easy-to-find products with a one-click shopping process. The procedure is one click of the mouse after the user registers information on the site. As a one-click user, shoppers create a "Buy

If visitors have to search for anything on the Net, chances are they will not stick around for long.

with one-Click" button that appears on most of the product pages on the Apple site. The user is able to turn the one-click feature on and turn off with ease. In addition, the Apple site has a clean interface, with graphics that are well done and download quickly for product display. The easy top tab bar is present at all times for trouble-free navigation. Overall, as a result of the clean interface and consistent design and navigation, information is accessible for consumers and professionals who visit the Apple site.[3]

As a rule of thumb, companies need to evaluate shopping cart procedures. If it takes more than two to three clicks to get to the checkout (not including the mouse clicks to add new items to the cart), then the company might as well give the merchandise away—maybe then a visitor would stick around. The Hewlett-Packard site is an example of too many clicks for information and downloads. A large percentage of HP users go to hp.com to download dri-

Any long, drawn-out process contradicts the beauty and nature of the Web—easy information at a fingertip's reach.

vers; however, it takes four to five mouse clicks before even starting the download process. This certainly takes away from the "ease of use" principle. Any long, drawn-out process contradicts the beauty and nature of the Web—easy information at a fingertip's reach.

NUMBER 2: PROVIDE UP-TO-DATE INFORMATION

Up-to-date information is a key to Web site "stickiness." Information that changes frequently is the reason to return to a Web site. And although this is an obvious consideration, even the most experienced marketing professionals overlook it with regard to Web site design. Timely updates in the form of news, daily specials, sale announcements, new coupon offers, calendar entries that post events and activities, tips and techniques on varying subjects of

Up-to-date information is a key to Web site "stickiness." Information that changes frequently is the reason to return to a Web site.

interest, and surveys and contest results are all excellent strategies to attract the attention of visitors and mold them into repeat visitors. Of course, consumers automatically expect that news headlines on media and portal sites will be updated daily, such as the *New York Times on the Web* and MSN.com, respectively. But it's a strategy that extends to all sites that want to draw an audience and keep their attention on a daily or even weekly basis. What does that

. . . if information is not current and "fresh," then users will quickly lose interest and have little reason to return.

mean for the average gift store, floral supply shop, or retail outlet online? It means that if information is not current and "fresh," then users will quickly lose interest and have little reason to return. iWon.com has a strategy that is worth discussing. The more you visit the site, use the search engine, and take part in daily surveys, the better your odds of winning a $10,000 daily sweepstakes, or even a $1 million monthly sweepstakes. iWon.com posts the winners of the $10,000 sweepstakes daily, with pictures and personal quoted comments on their newfound earnings. The site even goes as far as having audio clips of each daily winner discussing his or her sweepstakes success on iWon.com. Not only are registered users of iWon returning to the site, but, as winners inform their families and friends to check out their pictures and audio clips, it's an opportunity to have new visitors become instantly involved in this site's successful "sticky" tactics. Because Web audiences do not have unlimited attention spans, sites must contain that element of "stickiness" in the form of relevant up-to-date information. Up-to-date information keeps a site alive. If there's even a hint of "stale" on the Internet, an opportunity with a user is lost!

Up-to-date information keeps a site alive. If there's even a hint of "stale" on the Internet, an opportunity with a user is lost!

NUMBER 3: FASTER THAN A SPEEDING BULLET . . . THE IMPORTANCE OF A FAST DOWNLOAD

If you are designing your Web site and have access to an ISDN, DSL, or cable line, then you are still considered among the elite on the Web. As far as bandwidth goes, it is still a major factor. ISDN, DSL, and cable have not significantly penetrated consumer markets. On top of slow connections, people have short attention spans that compound the slow download situation. About one minute—and no more—is the average consumer attention span.

On top of slow connections, people have short attention spans that compound the slow download situation. About one minute—and no more—is the average consumer attention span.

There are a couple of tips to help. Using duplicate imagery and preloading graphics cuts down on download time. There are also sites that give pregames or trivia tests as graphics are downloading to get the user involved immediately. Yahoo.com is the pinnacle of the "speeding bullet" on the Internet—quick downloads and easy access to information. As a result, the site is among the top Web properties. No one wants to wait when it comes to the Internet. That's why we use the Internet to begin with. The Yahoo! site is designed to have easy downloads. There's little graphics, only the Yahoo! logo and then a few banner ads for advertisers on the site. There are so many sites on the Internet that could take a lesson from Yahoo! An article entitled "To Yahoo, with Love" discusses how Yoshi Sodeoka, art director at Word.com, published a letter on the site stating that he would "swallow his pride as an accomplished Web designer and return Word's site to a simpler template."[4] Sodeoka found inherent value in Yahoo!'s "simple ingenuity" and felt the need to go back to basics.[5]

NUMBER 4: USING ATTRACTIVE DESIGN CONSISTENT WITH COMPANY IMAGE AND AUDIENCE APPEAL

The design of a Web site should reflect the company and its product(s). Colors, layout, fonts, and graphics all play a part in the design for maximum effectiveness. The careful thought of these elements combined must appeal to the target audience. Successful design has more to do with these elements than it does interactivity and content. It's market research that enables branding professionals to understand primary audiences and figure out what

Colors, layout, fonts, and graphics all play a part in the design for maximum effectiveness.

sort of look and feel will make them respond to a Web site favorably. In-depth research allows companies to understand audiences before they come to a site. Research pinpoints a target audience with respect to gender, age, education, and personal preferences of each group. Pre-Internet research identifies what types of sites an audience will respond to with respect to demographic and psychographic information.

Brick-and-mortar brands online have an advantage. Because these companies have been branding offline successfully, demographic research exists and can be used in Web site development. The transition online must maintain designs and imagery consistent with any offline messages. Nickjr.com is a good example of a children's site that has consistent designs and imagery of the brand that appeal to young audiences. On Nickjr.com, pictures, activities, and site animation reflect those lovable Nickelodeon characters recognizable to children from the television programming. Online, children experience similar adventure stories and hands-on activities, which enhances the impact of the Nickelodeon brand. Through the games and activities and information on Nickelodeon daily programming, children who are familiar with the Nickelodeon brand become closer to it as they continue to watch programs on television and welcome the activities on their computer screens.

NUMBER 5: PROVIDING THE RIGHT CONTENT

Whether the Web site is up or is about to be launched, providing the right content is the key to attracting large audiences and keeping their interest. Relevant content is an ongoing consideration for the life of a site. Every site has a reason for being, whether it is to brand a message, to inform, or to sell a product or service. Messages have to be related to the nature of the site and significant to those who are visiting. That's why as sites grow and expand, it is imperative to choose content and partners selectively. With a recent surge of women's sites, it's a constant race to be the leader, with content as a major issue in the race to the finish line. Women.com and iVillage have both been praised and criticized for their content. The managing producer of Nickelodeon online, Jennifer Eno, discussed her thoughts on iVillage in *Silicon Alley Reporter*'s review of women's sites. According to Eno, iVillage has "too many content links [that] dilute any message to the users."[6] In the same review, Ted Werth, COO of Digital Club Network, discussed Women.com's content "ups and downs." Werth stated, "Most of the content comes from a roster of established magazines, which, on the one hand, gives the perception of higher quality. On the other hand, it says 're-purposed' and not particularly unique."[7]

Every stitch of communication should be useful, interesting, and valuable to users—not superfluous or to the point of clutter.

Relevant content is an ongoing consideration for the life of a site.

There is always that line that should not be crossed where information becomes overkill. Overkill can actually send visitors off in so many directions

Every stitch of communication should be useful, interesting, and valuable to users—not superfluous or to the point of clutter.

that they forget why they went to the site in the first place. Or, worse yet, if consumers are dissuaded from finding the information they need, they may leave a site and not make that product purchase. Not many people go to Amazon.com and forget why they are there. If

Not many people go to Amazon.com and forget why they are there.

you need a book, toys, or music, it's ready without distraction. Content should never "get in the way" and should always work to enhance the meaning of the brand. Good content translates into Web site stickiness and supports the cyberbrand.

CYBER DO'S

- Navigation should be simple, concise, and consistent on all pages.
- Customers should not have to search for information— make it easily accessible, with pull-down menus by product name or category and searchable databases.
- Keep information up-to-date to avoid the look and feel of a "stale" Web site that no one will visit a second time.
- Fast downloads will get an audience involved in a Web site quicker—remember, the average attention span is roughly one minute.
- Design should be consistent and reflect the message the company wants to portray as well as what the audience needs to hear.
- Understand customers before they come to a site—it's much easier to anticipate their needs.
- Too much content can be distracting—customers should not forget why they came to a site in the first place.

EXCEEDING CUSTOMER EXPECTATIONS: BUDGET GROUP

Krista Musur is the manager of Internet marketing for the Budget Group. With a background in advertising and marketing, she manages the online division of Budget with responsibilities that include cyber relationships with Budget.com's online partners. Musur is also an instrumental player in the redesign of the Budget site. According to Musur, Budget's connection to the Internet began in 1996, when the company partnered with Travelocity. However, the road to e-commerce was only just beginning for Budget as its growth on the Net resulted in a need to develop a leading-edge software application that would enable Budget to have incredible flexibility with its systems and allow for a very streamlined booking process. "The original online booking was not as easy for the customers as it could be," states Musur. "The new interface application that Budget developed rearranges information so that several decisions can be combined in just a couple of steps; otherwise, it's a less intuitive process for the user," she says. The nature of the Web is all about ease of use. The competition for Budget is the same in the offline world—prices are competitive in the open market. On the Internet, however, Budget faces a different challenge, that of technology. The winning rent-a-car site is the one that provides the most pertinent information, best value, and simplest booking process.

The following is a mini-case study depicting Budget's transition to the Internet and the challenges and successes faced by the brand in cyberspace.

Background

The Budget name is always remembered among customers as one that translates into value. Whether offline or moving online, the brand message must be consistent. Budget made the transition to online booking and e-commerce communicating this message and opening new doors for the online brand with customers who:

- Crossed all ranges of expertise
- Expected ease of use and excellent tools
- Wanted immediate results
- Were global in origin
- Would tell you exactly what you wanted to know if you asked

Budget first developed its Web site as an online brochure. Its road to e-commerce unfolded in several phases:

- 1996—partnership with Travelocity
- 1997 – introduced online booking via Travelocity
- 1998 – developed direct e-commerce mission and launched
- 1999 – launched Bidbudget, the first online bidding system in the car rental industry
- 2000 – Budget.com redesigned to perfect the booking engine and site navigation and allow a much more personalized experience by prepopulating the booking engine with user preferences

Challenges

- How does Budget use technology to streamline the booking process and meet consumers' expectations online?
- How does Budget deal with global issues as it moves the Budget brand online?
- How is marketing integrated to tie in offline and online branding?
- How important is navigation and ease of use to Budget customers?
- How will Budget make its site "sticky" and still avoid too much distracting content?

Strategies and Results

Budget saw the opportunity on the Internet with travel commerce growing steadily. Online travel sales, according to Jupiter Communications, are projected to reach $16.6 billion in 2003. Budget made a full commitment to the Internet with a complete staff devoted to online marketing. Right from the start, there was a strong commitment from senior management, who understand and value the Internet as an important distribution channel.

Moving to the Internet, Budget faced the following issues:

Technology

Budget was confronted with the challenge of technology when it began with an online booking system that took too many steps to complete the process. Booking could be difficult, and customers were often frustrated over the process. A new booking engine was launched in 2000; plans to improve the process further are under way. Budget is striving to simplify its process and exceed the expectations of its online customers. With the latest redesign, individuals will not have to request rates for individual vehicles. Instead, they can enter their destination city and the dates of travel in order to access all the available vehicles for that location as well as their corresponding rates.

Global Issues

Budget faces a challenge on the Internet because the company has both corporate and licensee locations. As a result, global branding on the Internet becomes more of a challenge. Vehicle selection and local as well as national promotions can vary depending upon the location. In addition, services including Fastbreak (Budget's express service) and Perfect Drive (Budget's loyalty program) may vary around the world. One solution for Budget is to avoid U.S.-centric graphical treatments on the site. In addition, Budget enables customers around the world to book cars both in the U.S. and internationally. The site also includes a global location finder so customers can quickly find the Budget location closest to their destination.

Integrating Marketing

Budget launched a successful customer loyalty program that tied directly into its Web site. The program, Perfect Drive, allows customers to earn points toward free car rentals, Bolle eyewear, Calloway golf clubs, airline miles, etc. Perfect Drive found its greatest success on the Internet—with the introduction of Budget's double points program. Now customers earn double Perfect Drive points when they book their car through Budget.com. In addition, when customers become Fastbreak members, they are automatically enrolled in Perfect Drive and can quickly begin earning points. This type of integrated marketing continues to drive traffic to the Web site.

The launch of Bidbudget and the procurement of the domain name Budget.com were also extremely successful in driving traffic to the site. BidBudget was hailed as a market-leading product and led to a very successful partnership between Budget and Priceline.com.

Navigation and Ease of Use

Clear and simple, navigation and ease of use on a car rental Web site are the differentiating factor that sets a site apart from the pack. Web visitors are savvy shoppers and are doing their comparison shopping more and more every day. The redesign of the site, as mentioned previously, will significantly streamline the navigation. By doing so, it will make shopping and booking quick and easy for customers. They will be able to find all of the answers to their questions quickly and easily, and important features such as Booking, Hot Deals, and Perfect Drive will be prominently displayed.

Content

Budget strives to make content relative and pertinent to its audience. The question has come up several times with regard to expanding content to include other areas of interest for users, e.g., weather forecasts and events in various cities around the world. However, these are serious considerations. Content can make or break a site. And too much of it can be distracting and make Budget customers forget why they came to the site in the first place. Budget may not have weather forecasts, but it does offer its users some "sticky" areas:

- *Contests*: Usually occur in conjunction with a partner. One contest included a weekend getaway (partnering with ebags.com and AOL). The winner received a free weekend with free air travel, luggage, and rental of an SUV. The industry average banner ad clickthrough rate is 2%. However, for this contest, banner ad clickthrough rates were significantly higher.

- *Budget.com Personality Test*: Users are walked through a series of questions designed to determine the best vehicle to match their personality. Are you a Taurus or a Jaguar? And, how many times will you change your answer to become the car that you think best reflects your personality?

Tips to Remember

- Always remember and incorporate, to the extent possible, what the customer wants.

- Let technology support your Web development efforts—streamlining processes will lead to maximum efficiency and customer satisfaction.

- The Web is all about navigation and ease of use. The winners on the Web will be concentrating on making the customer experience as easy as possible.

- People expect more from an online brand. Customers love to communicate directly with a company, and responses are immediate—they'll tell you exactly what they want and how they feel, whether you asked them or not.

- Integrating marketing efforts (online with offline) is an excellent strategy to drive traffic to a Web site and create Web synergy.

- Strong commitment from senior management is key. Devoting resources to an online department is imperative to the brand. Having senior management with a good understanding and appreciation of the Web makes the process a whole lot smoother. This type of support will lead to a successful Internet venture.

BILLBOARD.COM

John Lerner is vice president and director of operations for VNU eMedia, which is part of VNU USA. Lerner has been running the Web division for the parent company for the past five years and is one of the original founders of the electronic media group. Lerner shared, in a full case study, *Billboard*'s transition to the Internet, the challenges facing the brand, and its successes on the Net.

Background

The *Billboard* brand name has been the premier source of music and entertainment news, information, and services for over 105 years. *Billboard* is more than just a trade publication; rather, it's a unique chronicle of the music, video, and home entertainment industries. The company's mission is:

To provide maximum new information in the timeliest possible fashion to help our readers do better business. Moreover, since our audience includes a wealth of experts we aim to offer them surprising and insightful advance knowledge they couldn't possibly locate anywhere else.

(Billboard editor's statement, 1999)

Billboard has an international audience with readers in over 110 countries. *Billboard* brings the "bible" of music and entertainment to the industry with top-notch news and reporting of cutting-edge reviews, as well as the most respected charts for retailers, record company executives, and artists.

Interesting *Billboard* Facts

Of the 150,000 readers of *Billboard:*

- 13% spend more than 40 nights per year in a hotel (average 21 nights for all readers).

- 54% have purchased audio equipment in the last year or plan to purchase audio equipment in the coming year.

- 23% take 10 or more airline trips per year.

Audience: *Billboard* Readership Demographics		
Age	%	Sex
18–24	6	Male 69%
25–34	32	Female 30%
35–44	27	N/A 1%
45–54	26	
55+	9	

Source: 1999 Readership Survey, Harvey Research, ABC statement.

Industry	% Responding	Total Readers
Record companies, manufacturers of hardware, studios	29	43,500
Retailers, distributors, mass merchandisers of records, hardware, software, and accessories	25	37,500
Schools, colleges, students, faculty, library, music fans, and audiophiles	15	22,500
Radio personnel including program and music directors	8	12,000
Recording artists, performers, attorneys, agents, and managers	8	12,000
Music publishers, songwriters, and related fields	4	6,000
Journalists, PR organizations, agencies, etc.	3	4,500
Buyers of talent	3	4,500
Others allied to the field	3	4,500
Miscellaneous	2	3,000

Source: 1999 Leadership Survey, Harvey Research, ABC statements.

■ 52% have purchased computer equipment in the last year or plan to purchase computer equipment in the coming year.

■ 46% use a cellular phone with an average monthly bill of $183.00.

■ 29% have bought or leased a luxury car in the last year or intend to buy or lease a luxury car in the coming year.

Source: 1998 Readership Survey compiled by Harvey Research.

Billboard **Branding (Pre-Internet)**

■ *Billboard magazine.* Weekly global coverage reaches over 150,000 readers in 110 countries.

The music and entertainment industries' authoritative voice.

■ *Billboard conferences.* Hosted by *Billboard*'s expert editors, these major conferences bring industry leaders together to exchange opinions and to network.

■ *Billboard directories. Billboard* Music Group offers directories providing essential information on every facet of the industry—the "definitive" who's who for the entire music and entertainment world.

■ *Billboard Entertainment Marketing.* Drawing on an international name and logo,

(continued...)

Billboard Entertainment Marketing develops powerful licensing opportunities including world-class partnerships with Fox's top-rated *Billboard* Music Awards show and ABC's American Country Countdown.

- *Extensions of the brand.* Targeted publications include *Amusement Business,* which is the premier publication for the live entertainment and amusement industries; *Musician,* which addresses the needs of today's active musicians and *Music & Media,* the leading pan-European trade for weekly radio and music industries.

Moving the *Billboard* Brand Online

Billboard possesses a powerful brand name. With a century of brand equity, the company was able to move the brand online to face new challenges and meet new successes. It was the brand name that was a major part of the process, making the Web a "no brainer." *Billboard* was able to leverage the brand on the Internet, not only as a business-to-business product but also as a business-to-consumer product. The Web afforded *Billboard* the opportunity to extend its reach to the consumer market with ease.

Challenges in the Transition to an Online Brand

- Utilize the World Wide Web as a viable communication channel to provide content that is consistent with offline brand communication.

- Evolve with technology to sell customers.

- Incorporate the Internet into an integrated online and offline marketing campaign.

- Achieve a return on investment (ROI) for *Billboard*'s Internet venture.

- Face the fear of copyright holders (similar to MP3 issues). Music is based on intellectual property, and you cannot be a publisher and not respect intellectual property.

- Handle unknown barriers that "pop up" unexpectedly along the way with technology.

Strategies and Outcome

Billboard actually started online as a dial-up site developed to download software, where users could dial up into a proprietary software system. The Web at this point was a means of distribution that was cost-effective and had a tremendous reach. Then, with the evolution of the WWW, companies were quickly learning that Web site technology was a way to sell customers. Suddenly, the Internet afforded *Billboard* a much larger branding opportunity. However, it was always the underlying notion that whether offline or online, the brand carried a tremendous power in and of itself. The Web, to *Billboard*, proved to be a viable communication channel. Now, *Billboard* was experiencing audience growth and reach like never before, with female audiences increasing tremendously. On the Internet, *Billboard* does not target a particular market; rather, on the ubiquitous Web, it focuses on a diversified pop culture—the people who follow music will follow *Billboard*. The *Billboard* Web site (www.billboard.com) takes brand content online with interactive experiences beyond charts and articles. The Web allows *Billboard* to have areas of multimedia for audiences to enjoy. Never before have the *Billboard* charts had sound clips accompanying them. The Web site also brings *Billboard* videos to its audience. At times *Billboard* faced slight glitches with technology, such as having a radio show that had to change from "streaming" to video "on-demand." Sure, it can be frustrat-

ing, but it's always better to catch these glitches early on, before it's noticeable enough among audiences and quite possibly could damage the online brand.

The power of content from industry experts and the multimedia experience on the site leverage the power of the brand in cyberspace. Was the transition ever a concern for the *Billboard* print publication? Would there be cannibalization of the offline brand? This is always a concern, but for *Billboard*, more so with tertiary audiences. With clever marketing strategies to drive traffic between print Billboard and online Billboard.com, the issue is minimized. For example, the *Billboard* URL is added to the folio of all the magazine's pages. And in addition to *Billboard* Internet audiences' enjoying the site, the *Billboard* weekly publication is still considered the "bible," with everything based on the magazine. At the same time, *Billboard* is considered the top music information source on the Web. The site is trafficked with over 8 million monthly page views and more than 1.6 million monthly visits. It did not take long for *Billboard* online to become established as the industry's best source of Internet information and the "hot" destination for loyal *Billboard*

(continued...)

followers worldwide. As a result, audiences expect the Web site to be current and up-to-date—an attribute of the *Billboard* brand. This attribute is reinforced on the Web with a site that is updated twice daily to maintain the brand image. *Billboard* online gives visitors access to historical archives (10 years of past *Billboard* articles and 40 years of past *Billboard* charts), concert reviews, album previews, online conference registration, and a tour of the search database. In addition to constantly updating information, *Billboard* regularly augments design, although initially it exhibited a skillful approach in building a Web site that was user-friendly and allowed visitors to navigate easily. The Web site content, of course, is fresh and always pertinent to the industry (consistent communication with the offline *Billboard* brand).

Also as a result of *Billboard's* transition online, there are various opportunities for professionals in the music industry to create a Web page and profile an artist on the *Billboard* site. An icon on the homepage, with album cover graphics, is prominently displayed to reach millions of consumers. These feature pages allow artists to display album reviews, images, and artist information, to include links to record label sites and retail information, to insert sound and video clips, and tour listings and appearance information. In addition, the *Billboard* Bulletin, the daily calendar that concentrates on the essentials of industry news, is also found online (by fax as well) to provide the "scoop" that every well-informed industry executives need. Via the Internet, global business learns about executive moves, the latest labels, artist signings, and retail activity.

Billboard, through the power of its brand, has made the transition to the Internet smoothly and successfully. The brand continues to thrive and fulfill audience expectations in the music industry by maintaining its position as the premier source of music and entertainment news, information, and services. *Billboard* fully utilizes the Internet with its tremendous power to communicate the brand—expanding services to loyal followers as well as gaining new audience reach. *Billboard* is able to satisfy its objectives both online and offline:

Billboard analyzes and interprets the present while both anticipating and helping shape the future. We are lonely in our high ideals, determined in our high standards, and dedicated to the excellence of a form of news gathering that has its

*own news making momentum.
There is only one worthy adjec-
tive for what we [Billboard] do
and it's our name: We cover our
international beat the Billboard
way.*
Source: *Billboard* marketing materials, 1999.

Tips to Remember

- When it comes to information, the Web is a great equalizer. It brings you back to basics—back to the product and the promise of the brand. It equalizes everyone and puts us all on the same playing field.

- Great branded content is key—it starts and ends with the expertise of a devoted staff.

- The brand itself will stay the test of time and should be communicated consistently and across many channels. The Internet, although viable, is only one medium of many to consider.

- The Internet allows immediate feedback from users. Use it to your advantage. Online polls are a great source to guide marketing strategies.

- The Internet affords the opportunity to reach a larger audience with more interaction for users to experience.

- Driving traffic between online and offline media is a key to minimizing cannibalization of an offline brand.

- Grow with technology and use the Web to focus on in-depth areas that could not be experienced offline.

2

Impacting Audiences with the Cybervision

7

Start with the Organization and the Cyberbrand Vision

Objective:

For marketers to understand and implement the traditional or "smart business" strategies that aid in development, cultivation, and communication of the cyberbrand vision and promote the success of the Internet brand by recognizing the following:

- Vision beyond the entrepreneurial idea
- Avoiding the "rushed" vision
- Developing the vision through offline versus online comparison
- The importance of the coalition to guide the vision
- Cybervisions that survive

VISION BEYOND THE ENTREPRENEURIAL IDEA

Every entrepreneur has an idea, but in today's new economy, ideas are a dime a gigabyte. A cyberbrand vision needs to be developed, cultivated, and often reworked to suit the needs of the brand online. Hence, every entrepreneur has the potential to create a cyberbrand vision that expectantly possesses everlasting life. This occurs if and only if the vision meets the challenge of the Internet issues head-on. With the rise and fall of every cyberbrand vision there's speculation:

Was the vision realistic, with attainable goals? Did the executive team have enough experience to implement the vision?

. . . when it comes to the Internet, the reality is that 10 other entrepreneurs are cultivating a similar "brilliant, never before seen" idea on the Web, . . .

Was the business model flexible enough to support the vision? There are many questions and not enough history behind the Internet to back up all the answers. Getting the vision right before launching the Web site goes without saying. Yet, with the notion that when it comes to the Internet, the reality is that 10 other entrepreneurs are cultivating a similar "brilliant, never before seen" idea on the Web, it's difficult for the dot-com to have a vision mapped out from start to finish prelaunch. Because the Internet provokes the feeling of "first to market wins," the cybervision suffers. Time frames are terribly compressed, and launches that would normally take 18 to 24 months (the business hatching phase) take only 3 to 6 months.[1]

How is it possible to have the vision fully intact prior to launch of a Web site? This is certainly a question that deserves a considerable amount of attention with brand building in the new economy. The trials and tribulations of online companies in the retail industry, such as Boo.com, and companies in the publishing industry, including APBnews.com and Salon.com, are examples of cyberbrand visions that come to fruition but do not reach their full potential. Companies are faced with financial and technological problems early on that result in employee layoffs and little success to secure future funding. Even so, the nature of the World Wide Web allows companies to get away with launching cyberbrand visions that are not well thought out, with visions that cannot possibly meet the challenges of the Internet. Concerning APBnews.com, the crime Web site, " . . . has run out of money and fired all its staff."[2] For APBnews, there was a tremendous challenge on the Internet to differentiate and create a unique selling proposition (USP), because of the nature of online competition. Although APBnews.com touted itself as the only crime and justice site on the Web, online audiences still found it easier to frequent portal news sites to receive their daily news and information. Again, APBnews' cyberbrand vision had tremendous possibilities yet fell short of its true potential by not anticipating the complexities of audiences and its competition.

> **Companies are faced with financial and technological problems early on that result in employee layoffs and little success to secure future funding.**

AVOIDING THE "RUSHED" VISION

Maybe it's a "cash galore internet economy"[3] that focuses on passion and timing but neglects the vision in its entirety. When it comes to venture capital and angel funding (equity funding whereby the investor obtains stock in a company), strategies differ. Start-up companies on the Internet that receive angel funding usually tend to have semideveloped visions (but that is considered acceptable), and venture capital requires companies to fully develop their visions postlaunch into implementation phases (but that's a catch-22 in a compressed time frame). And much as the new Internet companies would like to slow down and not rush from concept to launch phase, it just isn't happening for many of them. This really has nothing to do with passion and fervor; these are characteristics common to the start-ups. From the onset, the entrepreneur persuades all who come in contact with the cyberbrand vision that it possesses passion, depth, and perpetual life. The trouble exists in the development of the vision, beginning with the power of the team to execute the vision and, from that point on, continuing with the necessary

. . . much as the new Internet companies would like to slow down and not rush from concept to launch phase, it just isn't happening for many of them.

communication to enhance and extend its life. Evidence of the IPO frenzy and "first to market wins" reveals itself with the release of 1999 statistics. In 1999, there were 698 companies that went public, as compared with 350 in 1998.[4] It would be interesting to analyze how many of those IPO companies had fully developed visions and how many were able to follow through with execution of the vision postlaunch.

There are marketing professionals who have the opposite viewpoint and believe that streamlining the launch process is efficient, getting the new company off to a good start. But there's a great deal of evidence out there in cyberspace that paints a completely different picture. In an article in *Silicon Alley Reporter* entitled "Punky IPOs," we can see that when the Webcaster.com site was over six months old, it had $100,000 in assets and no revenue to date.[5] To top it all off, even though the article referred to Webcaster.com as "contentless," it went on to say that it filed for a $33 million IPO in November 1999. It seems that the only marketable presence related to the company is Punky Brewster, its 23-year-old cofounder. The purpose of the site is to make its audience (visitors aged 13 to 35) experience what the article referred to as the "inside world of entertainment." Reading on, it's apparent that this site promised (prelaunch) to get its viewers backstage passes to the entertainment world. However, this hasn't happened yet. Case in point: The cofounders of the site had a "perfect" vision, full of passion with eagerness to succeed, and somehow from concept to launch only a partial vision was executed.

Another example illustrating the execution of the partial vision appears in an article entitled "Spinning Out of Control" that discusses Theglobe.com and its downward spiral from a record-setting IPO in 1998.[6] With descriptive phrases like "the flailing community" and "downward spiral," it begs the question, What happened to the vision? How did the site deviate from its well-thought-out plan to lack of execution of that plan? Apparently the cofounders (a pair of 20-year-old school buddies from Cornell University) rose quickly to Internet stardom with an IPO that climbed dramatically from $9 a share to $97 its first day on the market. Theglobe.com swiftly came down to $28 a share and, from that point on, continued to plummet. The article further states that the cofounders (also co-CEOs) have stepped down to let a more experienced professional in the company assume the role of president. Is this a case of Internet hype, or execution of a half vision? Most likely it is a little of both. There are a rash of Internet companies that rise quickly and then fall just as fast.

On the opposite end of the spectrum are the companies with visions powerful enough to support rapid growth and flexible enough to encounter rough terrain. Take a look at the ultimate vision, that of Cisco Systems: the desire to have all computers around the globe communicating with one another. This is the vision that got the Internet off the ground, the vision that started a cyber precedent (or at least should have). Again, the vision came to life with an idea shared between two individuals, Leonard Bosack and Sandra Lerner. The two were IT people at Stanford University who worked together to connect computers in departments of the university. Finally, when they left Stanford, they shaped the Cisco brand by starting a business that connected not only educational institutions, but governments, organizations, and all computers—no matter how little or inexpensive.[7] The Cisco vision miraculously transformed from a dream into reality. Making the vision a reality is a sign that the brand is fully realized: the strength of the vision is tied directly to the brand. It's referred to as

Making the vision a reality is a sign that the brand is fully realized: the strength of the vision is tied directly to the brand.

the "brand vision," and it's the force behind the focus and stability of a company. Few companies have experienced or ever will experience the same type of impact as the Cisco brand vision has had on the Internet economy. For this reason alone, it is definitely worth evaluating the strategies that cultivate a vision and lead to a successful execution and brand strength.

DEVELOPING THE VISION THROUGH OFFLINE VERSUS ONLINE COMPARISON

John P. Kotter authored a book entitled *Leading Change*, which is well known among MBA graduate students. Although the book focuses heavily on organizational change, there are several valuable strategies that lend a hand to developing and communicating a cyberbrand vision. According to Kotter, "Vision refers to a picture of the future with an implicit or explicit commentary on why people should strive to create that future." In Kotter's book, one of the main components of his eight-stage process deals with developing the vision. Although *Leading Change* does not address cyberbranding, there is a connection between Kotter's brick-and-mortar thoughts and the way companies should proceed with their cyberbrand visions.

Let's differentiate the offline and online visions for a moment to illustrate their similarities and differences. Kotter believes that the vision (referred to as the offline vision) will take root in the corporate culture if it has the following attributes:

- Clarifies a direction
- Motivates people to take action
- Has a long-term interest

According to Kotter, the *characteristics of an effective vision* as detailed in his book are as follows:

- *Imaginable:* conveys a picture of what the future will look like
- *Desirable:* appeals to the long-term interests of employees, customers, stockholders, and others who have a stake in the enterprise
- *Feasible:* comprises realistic, attainable goals

- *Focused:* is clear enough to provide guidance in decision making
- *Flexible:* is general enough to allow individual initiative and alternative responses in light of changing conditions
- *Communicable:* is easy to communicate; can be successfully explained within five minutes[8]

Then, there is the cyberbrand vision, which is similar to the brick-and-mortar vision because it clarifies a direction, motivates people to take action and has every intention of being a long-term interest (as stated in the first three bulleted items above). However, moving past these points, the traditional attributes of the vision are altered to meet the demands of the Internet. In the past, on the Internet we have seen the following digressions from the offline vision attributes:

- *Imaginable:* The portrayal of the future changes so quickly as technology continues to advance rapidly. Companies must always be 10 steps ahead of the competition and ready to modify strategies (and business models) to meet the changing interests and needs of audiences.
- *Desirable:* Long-term is always the intention but some of the 20+ CEOs have abandoned their start-ups and bailed out a little on the early side to let more experienced professionals run the show.
- *Realistic:* The Internet often fosters unrealistic goals and promises; it's that say it now then worry about it later type of attitude. State-of-the-art technology is promised to online audiences and difficulties lie in developing systems to handle these promises.

The Internet often fosters unrealistic goals and promises; it's that say it now then worry about it later type of attitude.

- *Focused:* There is not always a clear path in cyberspace – a great deal of trial and error in the 1990s is evidence of this fact. If the vision does not keep its focus there is the tendency to "go off on a tangent" and lose the meaning of the message. Web sites should not attempt to be everything to everyone.
- *Flexibility:* A great deal of flexibility is necessary to manage rapid advancements as well as the built in two-way communication feature that enables users to guide Web

efforts and directly impact the successes and failures of an Internet company.

- *Communicable:* If it's ideal to communicate an offline vision in five minutes or less, then with the Internet moving at warp speed, fast and effective communication of the cybervision, is a priority.

Comparison of the offline vision and the cybervision and pinpointing recognizable differences provides a company

> **. . . with the Internet moving at warp speed, fast and effective communication of the cybervision, is a priority.**

with a greater chance to meet the challenge of the Internet and be prepared to face the obstacles that restrict the life of the cyberbrand.

CALL IN THE COALITION TO GUIDE THE VISION

Experts say that Internet companies are stealing the best talent. It's referred to as the *talent drought;* there just are not enough "techies" to go around. Venture capital firms are looking for three things:

- The potential of a unique idea
- The value of a solid plan for launch strategy and implementation
- A management team that will bring the vision to life

The last item mentioned is a type of "coalition." This is the trusted and empowered group that will communicate the vision and move the company well beyond its launch phase. This team is critical to the success of the vision. In Kotter's book, traditionally, the coalition is utilized in any change effort.[9] This group has "strong position power," and generally has the expertise, credibility, and leadership skills necessary to get the job done.[10] It is this team that is extremely crucial to the execution of the vision. New dot-coms build coalitions all the time. So, for example, in the world of dot-com start-ups, Kotter's coalition could be analogous to the entrepreneur and the executive team that is pulled together prior to the launch of the cyberbrand. It is this team that prepares for the launch, communicates the cyberbrand vision to all that come in contact with it, and implements the vision's course of action completely and thoroughly.

The coalition in the click-and-mortar world becomes the key players in an Internet division of a company. This group is assigned the role of launching the online brand. In order for the vision to take root in the corporate culture, Kotter stresses that internal communication must be embraced first by employees of the company. For the cyberbrand vision to be embraced, *all* employees of the company, not just an Internet division that manages the technology, must understand and accept the brand in its new realm. This is imperative to the traditional company. An article in *Chief Executive* magazine entitled "Through the Looking Glass" spells out that brick-and-mortars have to shift their culture. In the article, theStreet.com's CEO Thomas Clarke states, "With upstarts like us, there's no culture shift that has to happen. There's no dragging someone from a legacy environment into the new world."[11] Therefore, every member of the company must be aware of and understand the meaning of the cyberbrand vision and the strength and vitality of the brand online. Whether it's "traditional" or just "smart business," there is the belief in the corporate world that in order to project a message (the vision) outward to audiences, it must be communicated effectively and continuously internally, using as many channels as possible. If, and only if, the corporate culture understands and

> ... every member of the company must be aware of and understand the meaning of the cyberbrand vision and the strength and vitality of the brand online.

supports the efforts of the cyberbrand vision, in turn, this will result in what is known as "proud communication" on behalf of employees. When employees believe in the promise of the cyberbrand vision and all of its implications, there's that buzz in the hallways and the feeling of excitement in the air, whether it's in the break rooms or the company cafeteria. The organizations that communicate properly to their employees first, via a strong coalition, are in all actuality allowing these individuals to embrace the cyberbrand vision and empowering them to be faithful cyberbrand communicators and loyal followers.

CYBERBRAND VISIONS THAT EXIST POSTLAUNCH

Moving past the so-called dangers and difficulties of moving the brand online are the companies that have not only ventured into cyberspace, but also have high-tech visions that are making news and making great strides. An article entitled "Old-Line Firms with High Tech Vision," written by Allison Kopichi of Bloomberg Personal Finance, illustrates how the traditional offline brands are successfully executing cyber strategies. Who are these traditional cyber winners who quickly realized how to combine tradition and technology to form an optimum brand? According to the article, Kmart is one, taking the "blue-light special" online with free Web access for its customers. And for United Parcel Service (UPS), it does not matter who sells the goods online—UPS will reap the benefits. The company has invested in the package delivery market by providing Internet purchasers with an easy process to track online orders.[12] What about American Express? Unlike some brick-and-mortars, this company is not worried about cannibalization. American Express did not hesitate to offer online financial services for its customers. Last, Federated Department Stores, which includes Bloomingdale's and Macy's, has quickly caught on with the purchase of Fingerhut. Buying the Internet retailer not only fostered the Federated cyberbrand vision, but also increased sales fourfold in 1999.[13]

Another article, appearing in *CEO's Web Review*, scopes out the benefits of Home Depot's Web site. The Web review points out that the site does not even sell products, but serves to maintain a dynamic presence with its customers. It goes on to say that Home Depot is one of those "smart" brick-and-mortars that developed an online following even before the e-commerce is launched. Home Depot's strategy entices visitors to get involved with do-it-yourself projects, with help online every step of the way.[14] This is a case of using brand recognition and consistent customer service (in cyberspace too, right from the start) to establish a powerful presence.

What do these click-and-mortars have in common? Here are a few hypotheses about their cyberbrand visions. The visions were most likely invented and then reinvented "on the fly," illustrating the flexible vision.[15] Many of these click-and-mortars are finally aligning IT with the business vision that defines how the Internet will complement traditional operations.[16] And even though at one time these companies did not include IT as a part of their sales departments, the two are slowly coming together; the marriage means successful e-commerce.[17] Last, if you get a strong management team that generates enough enthusiasm from every single person who comes in contact with the vision, the dream comes to life quicker than was ever thought possible (because it's Internet time). Put this all together with the fact that these companies have existing brand recognition and trust. What is the benefit? The "click-and-mortar" advantage—a cyberbrand vision that survives after the concept stage and continues to make strides postlaunch.

THE CHALLENGES OF A CYBERVISION: CYNET, INC.

Christopher Levy is marketing and public relations manager for CYNET, Inc., a Houston-based technology firm focused on developing customer-driven business-to-business communications solutions. Levy, with a background in brand marketing (having worked with popular auto brands including Saab, Porsche, BMW, and Saturn during his tenure at Momentum Automotive Group) discussed candidly how CYNET's cybervision came to life from inception to IPO.

Background

Founded in 1995, CYNET began as a fax broadcasting company. When the current management team assumed leadership in 1998, they saw the potential of the available technology and launched the Internet and wireless divisions in 1999 (www.cynetinc.com). At this point, CYNET expanded its traditional offerings to include what is referred to as *unified messaging* (an industry buzzword that describes the ability to send and receive mainly fax, e-mail, and voice messages from a single source). Going one step further with its cybervision, CYNET combined the power of Internet technology and applications with that of wireless solutions, to be positioned in the industry as a

convergent messaging solutions company. CYNET was able to offer to its business-to-business audience full Internet and e-commerce solutions as well as proprietary software (ADC 2000) that is fully customizable for clients, including portals, procurement centers, e-trade, and online shopping malls.

The CYNET vision evolved to meet the needs and demands of an Internet audience:

CYNET's Vision

To be the industry leader in convergent communications by integrating traditional and emerging e-mail, fax, data, voice, and video messaging with Internet applications and wireless tools, to enable simultaneous global communication.

CYNET's Mission

To maximize the efficiency of its clients' business communications and exceed their expectations by creating customized solutions through the integration of convergent messaging, Internet applications, and wireless tools.

CYNET's Audience

CYNET's primary target is "C" level executives (CEO, CFO, COO, CTO, and CIO). Its secondary target audience is managers and directors with technology buying power or influence on marketing, sales, IT, etc.

For CYNET wireless products, the primary audience is the mobile workforce, and the secondary audience consists of sales managers, road warriors, service organizations, and governments.

Challenges with the Cybervision

- Proper planning and execution of the vision pre- and post-IPO
- Differentiating the company from industry giants

Outcome

- *Planning and Execution of the Vision:* The vision came to life with an experienced executive team as noted in CYNET's promotional material.

Vincent W. Beale, Sr., Chairman and CEO: As chief executive officer, Vincent Beale has the charge of ensuring the strength and longevity of the company. His career has spanned over 30 years including positions with distinguished companies including Shearson Lehman Hutton, Paine Webber, and Merrill Lynch.

Bernard B. Beale, Executive VP and COO: As chief operating officer, Bernard Beale uses his talent of working with people to build CYNET's name worldwide. His 20-year career began at AT&T in the accounting department, working with finance and budgets, and then later moved into several investment banking positions with companies such as Equitable and Meridian Bank.

Michael A. Galloway, VP of Technology: Galloway came to CYNET from General Motors International Operations in Berkshire, U.K. His numerous responsibilities included operations management, process engineering, and IT program management. Prior to his position at General Motors, Mr. Galloway held positions with Dresser-Kellogg Energy Services and Merck & Co.

David R. Hearon, Jr., Senior VP of Institutional Development: Hearon has enjoyed a successful career of more than 36 years with the Bell System, Western Electric, AT&T, and Lucent Technology. Involved in numerous telecommunications projects, Mr. Hearon was instrumental in the development of many of the modern telephone systems used in today's complex communications networks.

CYNET's executive team began forming strong alliances at inception to foster the cybervision. Its first major alliance was with ENRON Energy, a *Fortune* 100 company. With an experienced executive team (each member with 20-plus years in the industry) and the power of technology, CYNET was able to capture the attention of investors quickly. These key players "kept the ball rolling" and made sure the company was headed in the right direction, unlike other technology companies that lose focus of their visions quickly. The combination of a "young" (with respect to age of its employees), energetic company and the qualified executive team led to a successful IPO.

CYNET's executive team was also responsible for the extensive planning that went into the company's cybervision. To aid in the development of communication strategies for CYNET's products and services, as well as CYNET, Inc., as an entity, the company constantly reviewed extensive market research from reliable sources such as Forrester and Hoovers. CYNET's strategic planning involved ongoing discussions and meetings with representatives from every department in the company (marketing, product development, engineering, interactive, graphics, and the executive staff). By involving all departments and communicating the vision internally, CYNET was then able to communicate complex information, in a clear and simple format, to its customers. The company's communication priorities require not only informing its clients, but also delivering a consistent message of quality and technology intelligence to properly position the CYNET brand.

■ Differentiating the Company

Heavy competition from industry giants makes it difficult to stand out in a highly saturated industry. In order for CYNET to differentiate itself from the competition, it focused on the elements that are highly demanded from customers, but difficult for large industry leaders to provide. These services include customization of products, effective pricing, and value-added extras that encourage customer loyalty.

In its efforts to implement the cybervision and differentiate the company, CYNET has remained flexible with its business model. In Internet time, "Years are equivalent to a day and CYNET must be ready to adapt at all times," states Levy. CYNET is a company that recognizes the challenges of the Internet, and behind the planning and execution of its cybervision there is the understanding that "change is the only true constant."

8 Empowered Online Audiences

Objective:

The twenty-first century is the age of the empowered audience. Choices are vast, and decisions on the Web are researched and calculated. It's time to focus on the online audiences that know their way around the Internet and are looking for Web sites to further empower them. Brand recognition is realized by understanding the following:

- The makings of an empowered audience
- Offering additional information to build relationships
- Personalization to build relationships
- Customization of products and services to build relationships
- Building relationships through incentive programs

THE MAKINGS OF AN EMPOWERED AUDIENCE

The twenty-first century marks the emergence of the cyberbrand and an age of empowerment. Chapter 7 illustrated how companies empower employees to embrace and become a part of the cyberbrand vision. The result is high energy and high output. At the same time, technological advances empower online audiences to control their daily messages and information. "A lot has been said about how the Internet is turning many industries on their heads while putting consumers in charge of relationships once dictated by businesses," state the authors of the article "Attack of the 50 Foot Empowered Consumer." Greg Sherwin and Emily Avila discuss how most businesses do not realize the changing dynamics of Internet customer relationships. Customers are in the driver's seat.[1] They control the messages about the products and services that interest them. There is a tremendous opportunity to give online audiences more of the control they readily welcome—to further empower them. It's not what the business has to say anymore: less talking and more listening is in order to keep consumers satisfied.

> . . . most businesses do not realize the changing dynamics of Internet customer relationships. Customers are in the driver's seat.

> There is a tremendous opportunity to give online audiences more of the control they readily welcome—to further empower them.

It's not the easiest task to abandon old-school mass marketing ideals to embrace the "empowered customer" concept. It may not be the simplest transformation, but it is certainly necessary when dealing with savvy online visitors, who have more information at their disposal, seek specific Internet destinations, and realize their countless Internet options. Building a strong relationship means focusing on the customer: it's the customer's way or no way. Consumers are taking charge of the technology that intrigues them and know how to satisfy their daily needs on the Internet. At the same time, they remain loyal to the cyberbrands that adopt a new paradigm, one that complements their newly formed empowerment. Now it becomes a race to the finish line. In the new economy, it's a competition to see how quickly businesses can develop branding messages that empower audiences by creating Web sites that foster these new relationships.

Consumers are taking charge of the technology that intrigues them and know how to satisfy their daily needs on the Internet.

Empowered customers exercise their choices assertively. On the Internet, loyalty to the cyberbrand may just be a repeat visit to a Web site. In most cases, there's no exclusivity to any one product or service. Although visitors might be considered "loyal brand customers," chances are they also belong to the competition as well. Product purchases in the past were anchored with one well-known brand; Internet choices are vast, and consumers are apt to make purchases and receive daily information from more than one site. This is true when a visitor conducts a search on a popular search engine. The user might begin on Yahoo!, then travel over to Goto.com and try a Lycos or Hotbot search from there. A company's brand message should be complemented by a Web site that utilizes relationship-building techniques to capture and keep the attention of audiences that are taking control of the information that surrounds them.

OFFERING ADDITIONAL INFORMATION
TO BUILD RELATIONSHIPS

On the Internet, a closed system refers to a Web site that denies the existence of competitors and shuts out any additional information. This system does not work on the Internet. It's better to provide a customer with extra resources; after all, customers don't need consent to access another site. A better strategy is to provide users with more of the links they seek in their online excursions. However, an automatic reaction to the threat of losing a customer to the competition is to tighten the reins and gain more control. This is a natural reaction, but it contradicts the nature of the Web and an open system that allows users to have many choices and the ability to access them easily. Web sites designed to help **Web sites designed to help customers find additional information gain loyalty from their visitors.** customers find additional information gain loyalty from their visitors. Years ago, the holiday film *Miracle on 34th Street* was released with the familiar scene that depicts a type of open system. The character Kris Kringle offers a Macy's customer information on a product that Macy's does not carry. Kringle sends the customer to Gimbel's (a close competitor) to purchase the product. The open system is an informational system that points the consumer in another direction—even if that means a customer is satisfied somewhere else and a sale is lost. However, the open system gains the consumer's attention and respect, and is designed to satisfy his or her needs by going above and beyond the norm to supply relevant information.

Focusing back on the Internet, eMarketer.com, a daily newsletter for Internet marketing professionals, is well on its way to building solid relationships by providing additional information.

Marketers subscribe to the newsletter to receive the latest Internet news, reports, trends, statistics, and e-commerce information. The newsletter is a model example of the open system. Each article contained in the newsletter is either written by eMarketer or is from another Internet news source. Each "news daily" report contains articles that link directly to CNET.com, *Red Herring,* and the *Industry Standard,* to name a few. eMarketer.com is not concerned about losing an audience to another publisher of Internet news and information. Rather,

Companies that move beyond the threat of sharing resources have the cyberbrands that promote the natural and logical flow of information on the Internet.

this dot-com has formed strategic partnerships with other sites to gain improved access for its audience to valuable resources. As a result, the professional who subscribes to eMarketer has a stronger relationship with an Internet publication that goes above and beyond to provide additional relevant information. Companies that move beyond the threat of sharing resources have the cyberbrands that promote the natural and logical flow of information on the Internet.

PERSONALIZATION TO BUILD RELATIONSHIPS

Amazon started a trend of personalization on the Internet, and a host of companies followed suit. Today, more companies are making a concerted effort to design Web sites with personalized features to satisfy their audiences' needs. MSN's Hotmail.com recently launched its new calendar feature to provide Hotmail subscribers with a scheduling function that sets up their daily schedules and reminds users of important dates, meetings, and tasks. Another example of personalization to build a relationship is seen on Earthlink.net, with the user's ability to personalize a home page. Online users can design their pages to receive the weather in various areas of the country (perhaps where they live and where they travel frequently on business) and to obtain horoscopes, stock quotes, and news headlines.

Personalization is also seen on the popular teen site Alloy.com. The Web site allows teens to send in a picture to post online and receive a virtual makeover by Alloy.com. Alloy.com's Stylewise section manipulates a young woman visitor's "profile," based on her picture, telling her what type of "spring fling dress" would look best, how Local 212's Donna tank top is "comfy and stylish," and which color is "her" color.[2] Of course, all of the product recommendations are available for sale on the site, and the teen and her friends are sold by the personalization.

> **It's the personalization that creates a feeling of control over the information process and illustrates how cyberbrands recognize a consumer's right to make choices, which results in increased brand loyalty.**

It's the personalization that creates a feeling of control over the information process and illustrates how cyberbrands recognize a consumer's right to make choices, which results in increased brand loyalty.

CUSTOMIZATION TO BUILD RELATIONSHIPS

A Wall Street–type executive walks into a custom tailor shop for men. He goes in and is greeted cordially by the tailor, who introduces himself as the shop owner. First the man tries on his new suit for the tailor, buttoning it completely to begin the tailoring process. The tailor then pulls the suit taut and begins to take the man's measurements. First he checks the back of the suit and then starts to measure the length of the arms. The tailor finishes the process by checking the man's waist size and pants length. This is traditional customization. The man pays more for a suit that fits his physique perfectly. Customization is costly, but leads to a finished and preferred look (more than if the suit were just worn off of the hanger).

A woman walks into a small boutique in Soho and admires a lovely bangle with colored stones. The shop owner and designer of the piece assists her customer. They exchange pleasantries, and the woman compliments the bracelet, but mentions that she prefers yellow gold to white gold. The owner quickly tells the woman that she would be happy to design the same piece in yellow gold and also shows her the sketches for a complementary necklace that she is designing. The owner then counsels the woman on the best length of necklace that would complement her style of dress. And although the woman had no intention of making a purchase, she leaves the boutique that day with a receipt in her hand for the 50% deposit on her new matching jewelry set. The purchase was based solely on customization.

The practice of customization has been around for decades— giving the customer the ability to choose and tailor a product to meet the strictest criteria. Customization on the Internet is taking off as well. The new economy boasts a boom in e-commerce, and online customization lends a hand in the process, motivating customers to make purchases. When a customer makes a purchase from a catalog, there is no guarantee that the order will be exactly what the shopper has specified. Customization online shows consumers exactly what they are purchasing by involving them in the process and offering personalization at the same time.

The practice of customization has been around for decades—giving the customer the ability to choose and tailor a product to meet the strictest criteria.

Nike iD was introduced by Nike Retail Services to provide its loyal brand followers the ability to build their own sneakers. According to Nike, "It's all about participating in the design of the shoe. It's about the freedom to choose and the freedom to express who you are. . . . It's about time you had a say in what you're wearing."[3] Customization is working to capture the empowered audience. First is the customization strategy for the Nike brand lover to choose the perfect sneaker. Will it be a running shoe, cross training, or track-and-field? Then there's the choice of color and accent, too. With Nike iD, the user also gets to personalize an eight-character message that appears on the back of the shoe. The Web site technology allows the shopper to see how the style, colors, and personal ID message look by viewing the sneaker from different angles. This strategy has empowered the consumer to be a part of the decision-making process.

Customization is working to capture the empowered audience.

At Landsend.com, the company did not want to lose any time attracting female audiences wanting customization. Upon entering the site, customization jumps off the page. Swim Finder is the tool that locates swimsuits based on style, leg height, and body shape and even considers the female's "Anxiety Zone." The premise behind Swim Finder is to customize the search function for visitors to find exactly the type of bathing suit they need. The message is loud and clear: spend less time at a store trying on bathing suits and more time in swimwear on the beach.[4] There are three features highlighted in the Swim Finder. The Bathing Suit Sorter provides search features for style and leg height. The Anxiety Zone focuses on

. . . customization allows the consumer to take control of the shopping process . . .

any problem area a woman wants to camouflage and recommends the best styles for those problem areas. Last, Body Shape focuses on different shapes and sizes of women. All shapes and all sizes are listed for women to find the body shape that best fits their attributes. This is only the beginning of what technology has to offer on the Landsend site. The 3D model option is an advanced feature that constructs a three-dimensional figure to match the user's shape and characteristics. A detailed questionnaire asks specific questions regarding measurements of shoulders, hips, waist, and bust. Then, going a step beyond, Landsend.com gives the model a hairstyle, hair color, skin tone, and facial structure similar to the user's. When the "Build My Model" button is clicked on, within less than a minute a model appears to try on a swimsuit for the consumer. She may not be a perfect match but is at least a fair representation. The model can try on as many swimsuits as the user desires and rotates in different directions to help pick the most flattering suit. Again, customization allows the consumer to take control of the shopping process and create hands-on the swimsuit that best suits her taste and fits her figure. The site is customized and personal and aids any female in one of the most difficult tasks. Bathing suit shopping is an arduous process, in a store or otherwise, but Landsend.com attempts to make the process easier through customization. Loyalty is gained for the brand that accomplishes this task.

BUILDING RELATIONSHIPS THROUGH INCENTIVE PROGRAMS

Continental Airlines has its One Pass program for frequent flyers to accumulate miles for free airfare. American Express has a frequent buyer program that turns into "membership miles," and the Discover card is famous for giving back a percentage of purchases to its card carriers. It's all about rewarding the loyal consumer for a faithful relationship with a brand. This is the well-known incentive or reward program that is also illustrated in the form of sweepstakes, giveaways, contests, and freebies. Incentive programs have made it to the

Incentive programs have made it to the Internet, and cyberbrands are rewarding online consumers for frequent visits to Web sites, answering surveys and polls, participating in contests, and, of course, purchasing products.

Internet, and cyberbrands are rewarding online consumers for frequent visits to Web sites, answering surveys and polls, participating in contests, and, of course, purchasing products. At ClickReward.com the brand message is clear: "Shop Here. Earn Miles."[5] The Web site focuses on rewarding the customer. The site is able to facilitate this effort by providing shoppers with an attractive reward program. They receive free ClickMiles for shopping and donating to charities. When users visit partnering e-commerce sites, such as PlanetRx, Selfcare.com, and MCI Worldcom, they receive ClickMiles for joining as members or for making a purchase. The partnerships add to the value of the incentive program by bringing different shopping resources to the site. The object for the consumer is to purchase enough products to be rewarded from the Rewards Catalog. All of the rewards require specific ClickMiles amounts. So, for example, a Casio 2.3-inch color LCD TV is 5600 ClickMiles (that's not bad, considering that the shopper gets 200 ClickMiles just for subscribing to a free online publication). The premise behind the brand is to promote shopping on the site and have users become frequent buyers to receive bigger and better prizes. The brand builds the incentives and loyalty into its message. Consumers equate shopping with rewards. Thus, the brand experience is a rewarding experience.[6]

ZDNet.com also relies on "freebies, bargains and contests" as a daily practice to attract brand followers. "Whoever said 'you can't get something for nothing' never went online. Everyday we bring you something free, something cheap and a chance to win big." This is a statement on ZDNet's home page. Incentives are up front and unmistakable. They are integrated into the daily design of the site. And, based on the quote, if ZDNet says that users will find something free and something cheap and will win big, then that had better be true. It is because of these very factors that consumers will check back to the ZDNet site to see if it's a free sample of perfume from Calvin Klein or $10.00 off a product. Contests are also a main attraction for users who want the chance to win big with a shot at a BMW Z3. Incentives and rewards keep audiences "stuck" to the ZDNet site.

Another site fully loaded with consumer incentives is AltaVista Shopping.com. AltaVista launched its Web-wide incentive program to reward shoppers for "their everyday shopping activities on AltaVista's Shopping.com."[7] This is a tremendous advantage AltaVista takes over other portal sites, such as AOL, Excite, Lycos, and Yahoo!

(none of which established a point-earning system for visitors). As of May 2000, AltaVista's program was up and running. Immediately it gained attention from audiences who took advantage of "double points" for any activity from product searches to visiting AltaVista's partner sites. As a kickoff program, AltaVista also enticed Web site audiences with a sweepstakes promotion that offered a Mercedes SLK 230 convertible as the grand prize and spectacular vacation experiences.[8]

However, what happens to the Web site that is more content- or product-specific and is not based on an incentive program? These Web sites should integrate contests, giveaways, bargains, and free items into a site's content as often as possible. So, for instance, if users are asked to fill out questionnaires, they should be rewarded for that participation on the site. If it's a poll they have to answer, they de-

> **... Web sites should integrate contests, giveaways, bargains, and free items into a site's content as often as possible.**

serve a free gift or a percentage off their next purchase. On efloralz.com, a virtual floral department store, wholesale shopping attracts businesses and consumers that want to purchase in bulk. Visitors on this site expect to find weekly bargains, featured discounted products, and seasonal contests and sweepstakes. From the reward-strewn Web site that screams "incentive" to the lightly clad site with weekly, monthly, or seasonal rewards, this is the highly accepted Internet practice and a recognizable sticky relationship-building technique in the new economy.

Here's the catch. Yes, new relationship-building techniques are gaining attention—positive attention when the technique works from a technological aspect and from a fulfillment standpoint as well. However, when new techniques are introduced and don't function properly, the brand image suffers. Although Landsend.com has advanced technology, it has to be available to all online customers and not frustrate shoppers who have slower connections. At the same time, with respect to the 3D model questionnaire,

> **When the technology is successful and brings the user more information, customization, personalization, and incentive programs, loyalty to the brand is quickly realized.**

these must be as simple as possible and have specific tips and guidelines concerning measurement procedures to walk the female shopper through the measurement process.[9] When the technology is successful and brings the user more information, customization, personalization, and incentive programs, loyalty to the brand is quickly realized.

BUILDING CUSTOMER RELATIONSHIPS: DRUGSTORE.COM™

The drugstore.com Web site is the leading online drugstore and information site for health, beauty, wellness, personal care, and pharmaceutical products. In an interview, Judith McGarry, Vice President of Strategic Partnerships, discussed the company's brand promise as "a very healthy way to shop," and how the company prides itself on valuing customer relationships by building the best replenishment shopping experience on the Web. According to McGarry this is achieved through optimizing its great technology to establish and maintain customer relationships, demonstrating responsiveness to customers' feedback and needs, and, finally, rewarding customers for their loyalty with value-added services.

Background

drugstore.com, Inc., was founded in July 1998 and launched its Internet e-tail store in February 1999. The company's mission is to become the leading online drugstore by providing a means to healthy shopping, with convenient, timesaving features and value-added services.

"We provide our customers with the information they need to make educated purchasing decisions for their health and well-being and that of their families. We also make it really easy for our customers to buy the products they need and check out fast, so that they can spend more time doing the things they enjoy," states McGarry.

Establishing customer relationships is a top priority of the drugstore.com team, and by using great technology the company is able to pioneer new ways to interact with customers in the newly emerging Internet landscape. The Internet creates an entirely new paradigm for customer relationship management, enabling extensive consumer-brand contact beyond the storefront. The drugstore.com Web store optimizes this paradigm by focusing on every touch point of the customer's shopping experience, including browsing, purchasing, e-mail order confirmations, fulfillment, e-mail order status updates, packaging, live customer service, and HTML e-mail newsletters. The company's holistic approach to the customer experience is its key success factor. Furthermore, being able to maintain contact with customers—even after they've made their purchase—enables the drugstore.com Web site to turn a first-time customer into a loyal drugstore.com shopper.

Great technology makes the customer relationship-building process a reality, and recognizing and greeting repeat customers through personalization is the second essential piece in the drugstore.com customer relationship management strategy. For example, as a new customer browses the site, drugstore.com technology learns more about the user's behavior and uses that to cross-promote additional products, based on his or her selections. The drugstore.com Web store has also developed "Your List," which automatically stores a customer's purchases to create a personalized shopping list that makes repeat purchasing easier and more efficient. This feature allows customers to sort and organize their personal lists by category, order date, and product type; set up e-mail reorder reminders; and order directly from their custom list. "Your List" enables the drugstore.com Web store to make the consumer's next visit more relevant, with messages that direct him or her to specific products or product sales, or with reminders that

the products on "Your List" may be running low. In addition, the drugstore.com newsletter is targeted toward individual consumer preferences. McGarry mentioned that the online drugstore is excited about a new, targeted sampling program that allows sample products, targeted to the consumer's preferences, to be shipped with every purchase. For example, if a consumer is a frequent makeup user, the drugstore.com Web store encloses samples of make-up for the user to try and later purchase on the site. By maximizing customer-brand touch points and by personalizing each customer's experience, the drugstore.com Web store is optimizing technology and a new space to build customer relationships at Internet speed.

According to McGarry, all areas of the drugstore.com Web site are doing well with increased traffic every month. The company attributes its strong growth to its success in developing strong customer relationships, by responding to and incorporating customer feedback. The online drugstore has several programs that enhance the relationship-building process. One of these is the "Test Drive" product review program, which provides consumers with an opportunity to try and then write reviews on over 1000 products on the Web site.

Each week, the drugstore.com Web site recruits prospective reviewers while they are browsing for products. Interested customers sign up on the site, receive free samples to test at home for one to two weeks, and then complete a detailed evaluation. Verbatim opinions from these home assessments are posted on the site. The program is so successful that more than 8000 customers have participated in the Test Drive product review program. Plans for the coming year include doubling the number of reviewed products by adding another 1000 product reviews.

The Future

Proactively seeking customer feedback, through formal survey research and focus groups, is essential to the drugstore.com customer relationship-building strategy. Listening to customers articulate their likes and dislikes prompted the Internet category leader to redesign the site in March 2000. After a great deal of qualitative and quantitative research, the e-tailer changed the look and feel of the drugstore.com Web site and added new features to better suit the needs of its customers. The company felt that the Internet, in general, is still somewhat difficult for consumers to navigate and wanted the redesign to offer the easiest way for consumers to navigate the site while optimizing its visual aspects, for a more enjoyable and more rewarding shopping experience. The redesign of the site showed consumers that the drugstore.com Web store values customer suggestions and feedback, and is motivated to continuously improve, in order to benefit consumers.

Determining and meeting the needs of the drugstore.com consumer is also essential to the drugstore.com relationship-building strategy. The targeted consumers are busy women, aged 25 to 54. In fact, women make the majority of health care decisions and overall purchases in the family. Research uncovered four primary need states for drugstore.com consumers:

- *Productivity:* Often, women go to the drugstore.com Web store to get in and get out as quickly as possible. Their main objective is to purchase all of the items on their list quickly and easily without complication. In addition to offering easy navigation and relevant content, drugstore.com provides consumers with "Your List," which allows customers to quickly reorder their replenishment items from a personalized shopping list.

- *Information seeking:* Women also come to the drugstore.com Web site seeking information about products in order to make more informed purchase decisions. The drugstore.com online drugstore provides consumers with relevant information and buying guides which help them make educated health care decisions for themselves and their families. For example, a mother shopping for cold medicine for a sick child often doesn't know how one cold medicine stacks up to the next, let alone which one is right for her child. The drugstore.com Web store offers concerned moms buying guides and advice from child health experts, in addition to information from the product manufacturers. The drugstore.com pharmacy also has licensed pharmacists available by phone or e-mail to answer any additional questions customers may have.

- *Empowerment:* At other times, consumers seek assistance in devising a regimen for healthier living. For example, consumers can gather advice from the drugstore.com Web site on how to eat a healthier diet, and can frequent the site for additional up-to-date information to help them achieve their goals.

- *Reward and enjoyment:* The leading online drugstore knows and understands that consumers want to be rewarded for caring for their families. The company strives to inspire its consumers and create an enjoyable shopping experience at the drugstore.com Web store with products, services, and features that support them and their lifestyles.

McGarry's final thoughts: The drugstore.com site was redesigned with these need states in mind, adding new editorial features such as shopping guides, product comparisons, related articles, and additional product content into the site architecture, so that content is more closely aligned with the products themselves. Content in context provides customers with the information they need to make the right purchase.

9

Cyberstrategies to Optimize Audience Response

Objective:

Marketers need to understand the changing dynamics of cyberbranding strategies. From search engine optimization strategies to "viral marketing," the new economy supports advanced marketing techniques. Audiences are actively engaged in cyberprograms that are far more attention-grabbing than the programs of the twentieth century. These marketing campaigns drive traffic to Web sites and optimize audience response because the "cyberbranders" behind the campaigns recognize the need to do the following:

- Move beyond search engines
- Institute contagious (viral) marketing campaigns
- Get serious about e-mail with opt-in programs
- Exhibit sensitivity to online audiences and privacy issues

MOVE BEYOND THE SEARCH ENGINE

Empowered employees communicate a cyberbrand with "proud" communication. Empowered audiences embrace the cyberbrand that involves them in the decision-making process. Relationship-building techniques further support audiences' needs to take control. However, it's the cyberbranding strategies that enhance the message of the brand, drive the traffic to the Web site, and optimize audience response. The outcome: an Internet audience closely connected to the brand and interacting with it on an intimate level.

> . . . it's the cyberbranding strategies that enhance the message of the brand, drive the traffic to the Web site, and optimize audience response.

In the beginning there were search engines. In the 1990s, popular brands concentrated on search engine optimization. Two concepts prevailed:

- Cyberbrands bought precious real estate as an advertising strategy.
- Web site specialists were hired to build sites with programming language easily recognized by search engines that would identify metatags and key words (key words and key phrases inside of HTML tags).[1]

For the cybergiants, search engine optimization was as simple as that. Mega banner advertising dollars were expended on the search engine site pages, and other considerations ranged from "designing, writing, and coding a web site or some of its pages so that there is a good chance that these pages will appear at the top of the search engine"[2] to researching how an audience will react to certain key words in their search process.

But leaving the fate of a Web site's traffic up to search engine optimization is not realistic in the new economy. The practice of building cyberbrands by driving traffic, and engaging audiences interactively with the brand, is moving in a new direction. Again, it's the cyberstrategies that personalize, customize, and engage users with information tailored to their specific needs.

> **. . . leaving the fate of a Web site's traffic up to search engine optimization is not realistic in the new economy.**

INSTITUTE CONTAGIOUS VIRAL MARKETING CAMPAIGNS

When it comes to cyberstrategies, viral marketing (*viral* in a positive sense, meaning a way to spread the word, not to be confused with the negative connotation of "infectious") is "catching" on in the new economy, states Karen J. Banner in her article "It's Catching," which appeared in *Adweek*

> **When it comes to cyberstrategies, viral marketing (*viral* in a positive sense, meaning a way to spread the word, not to be confused with the negative connotation of "infectious") is "catching" on in the new economy, . . .**

magazine. In keeping with its name, viral marketing spreads quickly and is contagious on the Internet.[3] Viral marketing is the strategy that extends messages via a brand's own users who, on behalf of the brand, forward e-mail messages to friends, family members, and colleagues.

At one time, viral marketing was just occurring, without marketers' even realizing the strength of its presence. For instance, a consumer on the Internet would find an interesting Web site, a product or a service, or a piece of information that was too interesting not to share with someone else. The information was valuable enough to pass along. MSN's Hotmail developed an earlier viral marketing strategy in the body of its e-mail system. When a registered user e-mailed another party, the bottom of the recipient's e-mail message stated, "Get your private, free E-mail from MSN Hotmail at http://hotmail.com"[4] (with a link to the hotmail site for new users to register). This was an extremely effective tactic to pass on information

The most common form of viral marketing is the "tell a friend" option on a web site. Word of mouth and recommendation or referral from a friend is one of the easiest marketing strategies.

through brand users at no cost or inconvenience to the user or the company. Banner's article further describes how viral marketing is becoming commonplace with advertisers looking to optimize marketing campaigns. The most common form of viral marketing is the "tell a friend" option on a web site. Word of mouth and recommendation or referral from a friend is one of the easiest marketing strategies. Consumers make choices based on referrals and have more faith in the credibility of the referral.

Etour.com is a Web site that assists online audiences in finding Web sites that interest them and allows them to share the newfound information through a viral marketing campaign. Etour touts itself as the personal Web tour guide. The brand message: Discover sites you like, one click at a time, with a Web site that guides the consumer every step of the way. Etour equates Web site clicking with television channel surfing (an interesting comparison, as television and the Web are coming together to reach larger audiences with digital and interactive television). Web site editors are hired to review and add new sites daily to Etour's spectrum of offerings for users to enjoy free of charge. Any profitability on the site is strictly from advertising revenue from the site's sponsors. Consumers enjoy Etour for free. The user is required to fill out a lengthy questionnaire (an example of personalization to target the campaign) that delves into matters of education, profession, income level, residential status, and detailed personal interests (from business and finance to shopping and hobbies). After completing the questionnaire, the user is officially registered (and has entered enough demographic information for the cyberbrand to target specific interests, site content, and advertising messages that will spark the user's interest and make the site sticky).

As an illustration of the tour aspect of the site, if a consumer fills out the questionnaire with health as a topic of personal interest, Etour provides several health-related Web sites for the user to view and "tour." On the bottom of the page, located next to the "Next Site" button that advances the user to browse a new Web site, is the "Send to Friend" option. The user clicks on the Send to Friend option and then indicates one or two e-mail addresses of friends, accompanied by a message regarding the site referral.[5]

In September 1999, Asimba.com, a health and lifestyle Web site, instituted a viral marketing program that saved the company significant marketing costs. Believing in the power of viral marketing to spread the word via the site's own consumers, a company with inadequate funding needed to embark on a new strategy. Asimba.com set up a link on its site for what it called the "Friends and Fleece" viral marketing program. The program itself was a takeoff on MCI's "Friends and Family" campaign.[6] If an Asimba.com user recommended the site to 10 friends, then when the tenth friend registered with Asimba, the person who "spread the word" received a new fleece as a free gift. The vice president of marketing, Adam Roth, was pleased at the overwhelmingly popular response of the program. In June 2000, as a result of the Friends and Fleece program, Asimba had over 500,000 users, and the cost per acquisition of users was only $3.00. This is a tremendous savings for a company, compared with the $300 per acquisition that would have been spent should the company have opted for a television advertising campaign.[7] For Asimba, viral marketing was fast and effective, and the company's ability to combine the strategy with a reward program optimized audience response significantly.

GET SERIOUS ABOUT E-MAIL WITH
OPT-IN PROGRAMS

According to Jupiter Communications, e-mail marketing has taken off mostly because of high response and low cost. By 2005, the e-mail marketing category is predicted to grow to $7.3 billion, up from $164 million in 1999.

By 2005, the e-mail marketing category is predicted to grow to $7.3 billion, up from $164 million in 1999.

In addition, Jupiter also reports that by 2005 approximately 268 billion commercial e-mails will be sent annually, a dramatic increase over the 3 billion e-mails sent in 1999.

Another e-mail marketing strategy that is capturing the attention of cyberbrands is opt-in e-mail programs. A recent survey conducted by FloNet, an online marketing application service, and NFO Interactive revealed positive attitudes toward opt-in e-mail based on responses of approximately 1000 Internet users. Of those 1000 participants, 94% had signed up for opt-in permission-based e-mail programs. In addition, 89% of the participants believed that e-mail is an effective way for consumers to learn about Internet products, services, and information that interest them. In general, the survey revealed that e-mail is an excellent means of communication with brands online, and more than 50% of the survey respondents chose to trade private information for personalized service. Other interesting statistics were that 95% of the participants enjoy communicating via e-mail, 69% think e-mail is the Net's most powerful tool, and 71% of opt-in e-mail recipients opt to click through to view a company's Web site.[8]

"Personalized, targeted and as graphically sophisticated as the customer's computer will allow . . ."—this is what technology has to offer in the new economy, according to *Internet World*'s article "Spam's Good Twin." The article focuses on e-mail done right—the way consumers want to receive information. Not invasively, always permission-based. Opt-in e-mail is the opposite of spam; it's the good twin that users do not mind receiving.

Opt-in e-mail is the opposite of spam; it's the good twin that users do not mind receiving.

The article also discusses the elements of a good e-mail pitch, which include the following:[9]

E-mails must be permission based. *Users have to agree to receive messages; that is, e-mail marketing must consist of permission-based marketing.* Companies need to ask users to sign up for an opt-in newsletter or ask whether they would like to receive timely Web site updates and reminders. Most opt-in programs notify the user at the beginning of the e-mail with the following type of message: This mail is never sent unsolicited. This is not "spam." You agreed to receive this e-mail.[10]

E-mails should provide links for consumers to unsubscribe. Making it easier for the consumer to opt out may just be the difference between a successful and an unsuccessful program. With this type of option prominently displayed to cancel the e-mail subscription, a certain comfort level is established and maintained between the brand and the consumer. Examples of opt-out messages:

> **Making it easier for the consumer to opt out may just be the difference between a successful and an unsuccessful program.**

- Click on the link below to be removed from this "ezine" list.[11]
- If you do not wish to receive future e-mails, reply to this e-mail with the word "remove" in the subject line and your name will be promptly deleted from our database.[12]

Either option gives the consumer a way to cancel an e-mail marketing program. In most cases, just because they know they can cancel their subscription, users do not generally end a program.

Use the e-mail to communicate the cyberbrand message. The e-mail message should remind recipients that they chose to hear from the cyberbrand. The body of the e-mail should include the name of the company, logo, tag lines, and any visual representations of the company (if the e-mail is in an HTML format with graphics). The e-mail should also contain a hyperlink to the brand's site. Even a newsletter in plain text should contain the name of the company in the subject line and a hyperlink.

Personalized messages make a difference. Users opt to receive the e-mail, but pay more attention to the message when it is personalized and targeted. Stating the customer's name in a greeting message and forwarding relevant information is more meaningful. In addition, messages should be timely. If a consumer purchases a product from a Web site, waiting approximately one month to forward an e-mail message for a special offer on a

Users opt to receive the e-mail, but pay more attention to the message when it is personalized and targeted.

related product is effective (e.g., after the purchase of a television set, a special offer on a VCR is appropriate 30 days later).

Use results to guide the marketing campaign. Tracking e-mail marketing results is a must. Regina Brady, vice president of strategy and partnerships, FloNetwork, believes that analyzing this information will assist the company in customizing future marketing efforts. In addition, understanding sales volume and total purchases will also guide the company with its strategic planning, allowing the company to budget properly for programs that were successful and to observe any breakdowns or failures of previous e-mail efforts.[13]

BE SENSITIVE TO ONLINE AUDIENCES AND PRIVACY ISSUES

Optimizing audience response through cybermarketing strategies is only as good as the audience that allows the program to be successful. As companies strive to create these programs, it is imperative to consider how consumers view and value privacy on the Internet, and have the power to eliminate, from their cyber regimen, any brand that infringes on their Internet privacy rights. In other words, the cybermarketing program is in the hands of its audience. An article called "Gauging Attitudes about the Internet," by Jeri Clausing, discusses the results of a research study that involved 10 two-hour sessions with groups of consumers to find out how people really feel about the Internet and if they trust businesses online. The six-month study un-

Optimizing audience response through cybermarketing strategies is only as good as the audience that allows the program to be successful.

covered several interesting findings including the following quotes from its participants: "It should be buyer beware or user beware," and "I think we should know where personal information is going. I think we should be protected so not anyone could know where I live, [or] how old I am."[14] These issues are still quite present on the Internet, and businesses need to address the manner in which information is targeted and used for marketing purposes.

Take IBM, for instance. The company decided that it would not advertise on any Web site that did not clearly state an up-front privacy policy for its users. IBM's logic behind the decision was that any cyberpartner associated with the IBM name must have the same respect and concerns for privacy on the Internet. Any Web site that did not adhere to this reasoning would mar the IBM reputation.[15] In Washington, policy makers are closely watching Internet information-gathering practices. As of June 2000, more than 20 companies and groups had opted to work together to find solutions for privacy issues that would benefit consumers and soothe Internet fears. The effort, which comprises companies such as AT&T, Dell Computer, Ford Motor Company, and IBM Corporation, is called the Privacy Leadership Initiative. The results will be the implementation of basic privacy rules on the Internet, with Web sites adhering to spe-

In the long run, audiences will share with cyberbrands what they want to share, when they want to share it.

cific practices that will respect the right of the online consumer. A further initiative is the new privacy technology, the Platform for Privacy Preferences (P3P), that took its first test drive in June 2000. Specifically, this type of technology permits computer users to come to a decision as to the amount of personal information they want to divulge online.[16] It's evident that attitudes toward privacy range from consumers who may not care much about the information they reveal, to others who feel betrayed by brands that use information improperly. Cyberbrands are quickly realizing that it is better to be ultrasensitive to the issues that consumers have about privacy and targeting information. In the long run, audiences will share with cyberbrands what they want to share, when they want to share it. Those brands that have respect for consumer issues, and those that use targeting methodology and information-gathering techniques properly, will benefit in the twenty-first century.

OVERCOMING INTERNET CHALLENGES AND OPTIMIZING AUDIENCE RESPONSE: ATT.COM

In January 1999, AT&T launched Personal Network, a Web site with online ordering, which allowed customers for the first time to select different communication packages online and configure a bundle of AT&T services in a one-stop shopping effort. An interview with Maritza DiSciullo, director of consumer research, provides insight into the program's awkward start and how the company strives to overcome Internet obstacles. AT&T anticipated that customers would embrace using the Internet to choose services and get customer support. However, customers were more likely to call in to place orders and receive support. This resulted in call centers' being overtaxed with sign-ups, which, though good for AT&T, was frustrating to many customers who wanted to receive these services.

Challenge

"AT&T's idea was ahead of its time," states DiSciullo. She explained that the launch of the Personal Network occurred at a time when AT&T customers were not completely confident about online telecommunications. As a matter of fact, AT&T experienced several challenges at that time, including the following:

- Though they could sign up on the Net, when people had problems with services they did not always turn to the Internet or the AT&T Web site.

- AT&T provisioning centers were still overtaxed in dealing with the response rate, which led to lost sales and disappointed customers.

- AT&T realized that building a Web site was not only about offering services online but also about changing AT&T customers' behavior.

- AT&T offered the best incentives, but that had little meaning if the behavior did not alter.

Solution

AT&T's primary audience was its high-paying ($75-plus) customer, or the customer who selects multi-communications from AT&T (who orders Internet access through AT&T as well as a long-distance plan and a cellular telephone). This group was the initial target of AT&T's e-based services.

Since the launch of the site, AT&T has offered its customers more incentives to take advantage of its online billing program. AT&T is positioning online customer service as a program that benefits customers, allowing them to enjoy several advantages, including:

- The ability to view an online statement and have the convenience of automatic bill payment from a credit card or personal checking account
- The capability to sign up and receive free minutes of calling (an incentive that is not offered traditionally)
- An automatic payment system with no more paper bills
- The convenience of online customer service

The program stresses to customers that online billing is "not like their average bill."* Instead, it's easy to read and friendly and allows the customer to review telephone calls, charges, and more with a click of the mouse. The customer can also access online customer service representatives quickly and easily. Even with incentives, the online billing program is about changing customer behavior. "For example," DiSciullo says, "BMW has a great reputation, but consumers are not

*www.shop.att.com

purchasing cars online as a daily practice. Their customers still want to see and touch the product."

AT&T has employed extensive research to find out why customers are hesitant to take further advantage of online services and how the functionality and design of att.com increases or decreases customer participation on the site. AT&T conducts usability studies regularly (DiSciullo coordinates them, and analyzes the research findings) to test whether customers know and understand how to use the AT&T site properly. DiSciullo explained that if a site is not designed appropriately, then customers will not know if a transaction has taken place. This leads to confusion and frustration. The usability studies are in a one-on-one setting, with the AT&T customer at a computer terminal. A series of tasks and functions are performed on the AT&T Web site with the moderator timing and measuring the number of mouse clicks to perform each task. Following the exercises, the participant is given a qualitative interview to elicit responses regarding preferences, likes, dislikes, and opinions about the site.

Through extensive research, AT&T has overcome several obstacles and has seen the following results:

- More successes online with the billing system.
- Wireless Web sites have improved tremendously.
- The site has been redesigned to become neater, slicker, and easier to use (with respect to design, AT&T found out that less is more).
- AT&T is working to integrate a central theme and design for all of its Web sites and be consistent with brand messages.
- AT&T is able to offer a la carte services for one-stop-shopping.

According to DiSciullo, with respect to e-commerce, "consumers have gotten their feet wet with companies like Amazon and the ability to purchase a book." She further stated, "This is the safe way to test the waters and then move on to larger purchases, such as airline tickets and getting involved with real estate and banking online (which was rarely heard of 5+ years ago)." When asked to discuss how AT&T fits into the picture, she explained that telecom is coming through slowly and that it requires a great deal of commitment and trust. AT&T customers tend to research and investigate the various rate plans on att.com but still order the service over the telephone with a customer service representative. They tend to add in that extra unnecessary step offline, instead of just clicking the mouse and ordering online. This has absolutely nothing to do with the brand; it all about the Internet as a medium—a company could offer the best incentives, personalization on a site, and customized products, but that is irrelevant if the Internet does not have the complete trust of its consumer users.

10 Persuasion in Cyberspace

Objective:

Persuasion on the Internet ranges from the most creative branding communication endorsed by celebrities to the simplest e-mail marketing and banner ad programs. From rich interactive media to straightforward HTML text messages, persuasion online urges consumers to try new products and services. The objective of this chapter is to reinforce how the Internet has varying levels of acceptance of persuasion and to gain a clear understanding of the following:

- Powerful persuasive tactics
- Persuasion in its infancy stage
- Beyond the traditional endorsement
- How technology intensifies persuasion
- The fine line between persuasion and invasion
- Varying levels of acceptance

POWERFUL PERSUASIVE TACTICS

Television, radio, and print media have seen their share of celebrity endorsements—a powerful and persuasive branding technique popular with both the brands that seek to develop everlasting life and the star personalities who want their unique personas to be associated with more than a movie, a hit sitcom, or a Broadway performance (and, of course, for the sake of maximum exposure too).

Quick Test:

Which products are associated with these celebrities—Jerry Seinfeld, Candice Bergen, Paul Reiser, Phil Rizzuto, Sarah Michelle Gellar, Ricardo Montalban, and Dan Marino?

Answers:

American Express, Sprint, AT&T Long Distance, The Money Store, Cover Girl, Chrysler, and Isotoner.

For the brand, a celebrity's name translates into product recognition and increased brand awareness. For the star, endorsements mean life beyond immediate stardom. For this very reason,

For the brand, a celebrity's name translates into product recognition and increased brand awareness.

Joe DiMaggio, famous for his record-setting career in baseball, will always be remembered in the Mr. Coffee advertisements. And as the Internet transforms brands into cyberbrands, the same persuasive star power is present.

However, celebrity endorsements online have started on a smaller scale—although, according to the *New York Times on the Web,* Hollywood has found a new status symbol: it's celebrities online with "official" Web sites that offer fans a means to communicate and interact with stars, allowing the stars to ". . . reach their fans directly, skipping past press, promoters and movie studios."[1] Now, there's more to the persuasive presence of stars online. When sports celebrity Shaquille O'Neal appears in a *Business Week* advertisement (June 2000) endorsing Digex.com, he also has his own Web site address and logo displayed in the ad (dunk.net). Both cyberbrands and tal-

Both Cyber brands and talented personalities are looking to team up to make the most impact in Cyberspace.

ented personalities are looking to team up to make the most impact in cyberspace. There are many popular personalities taking a stab at Internet endorsements: William Shatner and his unmistakable singing for Priceline.com, Whoopi Goldberg for Flooz.com, Sophia Loren affiliated with Giftcertificates.com, and Florence Henderson endorsing Carpetone.com. As a channel of persuasive communication, how does the Internet rate in comparison with offline endorsements and persuasion?

PERSUASION IN ITS INFANCY STAGE

Persuasion on television is the same as persuasion on radio, which is the same as persuasion in magazines, which is the same as persuasion on the Internet. Persuasion is persuasion is persuasion is persuasion.

Persuasion is persuasion is persuasion is persuasion. Not so. The effects of persuasion depend upon the audience's reaction to the medium that communicates the persuasion.

Not so. The effects of persuasion depend upon the audience's reaction to the medium that communicates the persuasion. A common, traditional definition of *persuade* is:

> To cause [someone] to do something by reasoning, coaxing, urging, etc.

The act of persuasion depends upon the recipient of the action. Consider this scenario and how several tactics come into play. A 40-year-old woman owns a cell phone and is not necessarily in the market to buy a new one. She's satisfied with her current AT&T telephone and its accompanying plan. However, the woman hears an advertisement on the radio offering a new Verizon plan with a Nokia cell phone and 60 free minutes of telephone time on weekends. The advertisement comes on when she's listening to her favorite radio station, and it's not the first time she's heard the commercial. As a matter of fact she's heard it at least six times during her morning commute to work. The woman decides to memorize the 1-800 number that is aired in the advertisement. A few things have occurred in this situation. The woman is persuaded by a repetitive commercial that airs on a radio station that she trusts and, therefore, will consider researching the Verizon plan and the Nokia brand.

In this example, persuasion is only as effective as the channel that communicates it, the amount of trust consumers place in that communication channel, the clarity of the message and the number of times the persuasive message is communicated. When it comes to the Internet, persuasion is still in its infancy stages. On the contrary, persuasion in print and broadcast is much more mature, with research studies and statistics to prove its effects on consumer behavior. At this stage of Internet development, persuasion may not necessarily result in a product purchase or use of service via e-commerce, but may simply amount to holding an Internet audience's curiosity. What does William Shatner sing about for Priceline.com, or what will happen when the consumer puts that

> **. . . persuasion is only as effective as the channel that communicates it, the amount of trust consumers place in that communication channel, the clarity of the message and the number of times the persuasive message is communicated.**

AOL CD-ROM into the computer disk drive? And although the Internet has penetrated more homes in a shorter time frame than television

or radio has in the past, there are still significant consumer privacy issues and concerns that hinder the effects of persuasion on a consumer's product purchase or use of a service online (even if the consumer's favorite celebrity is the spokesperson for the brand).

However, as companies and the government band together to address privacy issues—and especially as more and more consumers put their trust into this interactive and highly engaging medium—persuasion on the Internet will grow and surpass any other communication channel. The Internet is the only medium that affords the cyberbrand constant persuasive power, interacting with the consumer with a broader reach than any other communication channel.

> **. . . as companies and the government band together to address privacy issues—and especially as more and more consumers put their trust into this interactive and highly engaging medium—persuasion on the Internet will grow and surpass any other communication channel.**

BEYOND THE TRADITIONAL ENDORSEMENT

Famous personalities, or agents on their behalf, are actively seeking opportunities to assist companies to promote their brands for the sake of constant interaction and exposure by employing persuasive celebrity appeal. The mixing together of Internet reach, constant interaction and exposure to the consumer, and celebrity charm is known as the convergence of high technology and celebrity culture, with a branding potential that is tremendous for all parties involved.[2] What happens when venture capital looks to the stars? Apparently, "big" deals are being made between dot-com start-ups that need to rise above the clutter and celebrities looking for more than just a paycheck for an endorsement. Hollywood on the Internet is no longer the same promotional game. Stars are looking for not only more exposure and larger paychecks, but also a piece of Internet action. Celebrities are being offered stock options worth millions of dollars and opportunities to sit on the boards of directors of start-up ventures. William Shatner received 125,000 stock options from Priceline.com, and Cindy Crawford was offered a stake in estyle Inc. and the opportunity to sit on its board of directors. Traditionally, these options were not available to Hollywood. The Internet takes persuasion to a new level for celebrities and for companies that are trying to rise above the dot-com noise that has saturated print and broadcast media channels.[3]

> **The Internet takes persuasion to a new level for celebrities and for companies that are trying to rise above the dot-com noise that has saturated print and broadcast media channels.**

The effect of persuasion on online consumers (from star endorsements) is undetermined. However, the possibilities are limitless. Consumers buy Nike golf wear and equipment because Tiger Woods wears and uses that brand. After the equipment is purchased, the only connection the consumer has to Tiger Woods is the memory of his television advertisement. The Internet takes celebrity appeal to a new level of interaction for the consumer and a new level of exposure for the celebrity.

Voxxy.com, a Los Angeles start-up that targets a teen audience, has chosen Jennifer Aniston as its "spokesgoddess." According to Aniston, "Voxxy will let me cut through the hype and allow me to speak honestly with teens about anything from self-image and social politics to family and friends—leaving little room for misinterpretation by the mainstream media."[4] Voxxy.com believes that Aniston's star power will go a long way on the Internet. And on the Internet, teens will hear personal messages from Aniston that will draw them closer to the cyberbrand. Aniston's celebrity appeal will be constant and extends far beyond the memory of a television commercial. It can be reinforced every time the teen logs on to Voxxy.com. The ability to reach the teen one-on-one is extremely persuasive and engaging for this audience. Persuasion on the Internet will be an ongoing effort for the cyberbrand. The Voxxy brand has the opportunity to continuously reach teenagers, on a 24/7 basis, with persuasive messages that cause them to respond to the brand with one or more of the following reactions:

- *Association:* Always making the connection between the Voxxy cyberbrand and Jennifer Aniston, who is well known and well respected as the likable character Rachel on the hit television series *Friends.*

- *Familiarity:* Remembering the Voxxy name and URL address and feeling comfortable with a cyberbrand that Aniston is involved with and contributes to daily, compelling teens to talk about Aniston as if she were a personal friend.

- *Credibility:* Celebrity appeal also translates into instant credibility—if the teen likes Aniston and her friends do too, the teen will like the Voxxy cyberbrand.

- *Notoriety:* The feeling of self-importance that comes from using a brand that Aniston supports and believes in herself. Teens will feel as "popular" interacting on Voxxy as Aniston is on television.

TECHNOLOGY INTENSIFIES PERSUASION

The Internet has the ability to take every consumer reaction and intensify it because of the constant interactive quality of the medium and the steady reinforcement the Internet provides for the brand. Beyond star endorsements, persuasion on the Internet also appears in other forms, including these increasingly popular types of persuasive tactics:

> **The Internet has the ability to take every consumer reaction and intensify it because of the constant interactive quality of the medium and the steady reinforcement the Internet provides for the brand.**

- Treeloot.com's punch-the-monkey banner ad is persuasive since it challenges the user to "punch" or "click" the monkey to visit the Treeloot site and win a prize. Challenging banners evoke interest and tempt consumers to click on ads.

- Interactive rich media banner ads with movement and Flash programming use recognizable symbols to entice users to click on banner ads. For instance, Trappolotto.com has bold flashing dollar signs letting users know there are opportunities to win money. Banners that imply money and prizes entice consumers to enhance their chances to win.

- CDnow.com urges audiences to take advantage of great music deals both in banner ad text and on the site itself. The opportunity to receive a discount is appealing to the consumer.

- J. C. Penney e-mails consumers in HTML text (plain and simple) alerting them to sales and holiday bargains (e.g., Fathers Day—25% off items for dad). Consumers appreciate receiving the same type of deals that are available at J. C. Penney brick-and-mortar stores without having to make the trip.

THE FINE LINE BETWEEN PERSUASION AND INVASION

When does persuasion on the Internet go too far? A 62-year-old woman has been on the Internet for about six months. She has recently purchased a laptop computer and enjoys the Internet for research and the ability to communicate via e-mail with friends and family. The woman definitely has "issues" with the Internet about privacy and is not willing to purchase from just any Web site (even if it appears to be a good deal). She logs on to CompuServe twice a day (morning and evening) to check her e-mail. Since the merger between CompuServe and AOL, the woman receives the same message on her screen over and over again: "Learn more about AOL. Click here for details—try 500 AOL hours free." The woman clicks the "x" to close the window (every time the message appears) and finally says, "Maybe if I just keep ignoring this annoying message, it will eventually go away." An annoying, repetitive message is how the woman views the CompuServe/AOL message. Sooner or later she will equate the annoying message with the brand. Persuasive? No. Why? Because persuasion has crossed a fine line between reasoning, coaxing, and urging to invasive and bothersome. And because the

There has to be a limit to persuasion, a program that discontinues a series of messages or the same message delivered over and over again if the consumer does not respond after a certain amount of time.

woman is a subscriber to CompuServe, she automatically receives the message with no option to cancel it (on television she would turn the channel, and on the radio she would change the station). There has to be a limit to persuasion, a program that discontinues a series of messages or the same message delivered over and over again if the consumer does not respond after a certain amount of time. Otherwise, the persuasive tactic becomes invasive and tarnishes the brand.

There are two traditional marketing terms, "Adspeak" and "Marketing Speak," both used in reference to a style of communication that addresses mass audiences with manipulation and persuasion (treating all of the members of the audience the same). At one time both Adspeak and Marketing Speak worked well over traditional communication channels. The Internet is not about Adspeak or Marketing Speak. It is a one-on-one, permission-based medium—even when it comes to the art of persuasion. What is the consumer looking for in a cyberbrand? From the consumer's perspective: If you want to reach me, speak to me like a unique individual. Do not try to persuade me the same way you (the cyberbrand) try to persuade thousands of other prospects on the Internet. I am a real person and I want you to communicate to me in this fashion.[5]

VARYING LEVELS OF ACCEPTANCE OF PERSUASION

Different audiences accept varying levels of persuasion on the Internet. Groups that are technologically advanced and Internet-savvy, such as children, teenagers, and young adults, and who are exposed to the Internet and computers through school programs are more likely to be persuaded online than a senior citizen on the Internet who is just beginning to research available information and services. For instance, a 24-year-old male is easily persuaded to bank online by PNC Bank because of its Account Link program. By registering on the PNC Bank Web site, the young man has the opportunity to win one of

Different audiences accept varying levels of persuasion on the Internet.

five "great prizes" every week simply by using the Account Link banking service. PNC Bank offers its customer the chance to win a new Dell PC, a Palm Pilot organizer, a digital camera, a CD rewriter, or a color printer. For the 24-year-old, navigating the Internet and using the Account Link program is trouble-free. He has grown up with computers and has attended Internet classes in college. The young man believes in the Internet and is not threatened by the medium. He is therefore easily persuaded by his bank to take advantage of Account Link.[6] The earlier example of the 40-year-old woman who heard the radio commercial signifies another level of acceptance. She not only memorizes the 1-800 number, but also realizes she can log on to the Verizon Web site or Nokia.com to find out about the brand and to get a better cell phone deal. She is extremely accepting of persuasion online (females age 30+ are a large Internet shopping audience) and will not hesitate to order services for her new cell phone.

According to an Internet study of approximately 2000 Internet users that was conducted by PeopleSupport, an Internet customer service provider, 63% of those who shop online more than once a week are women.[7] However, the 62-year-old woman who logs on to CompuServe and receives annoying e-mails

> ...63% of those who shop online more than once a week are women.

has an extremely low tolerance for persuasion. The Internet is not reaching her, because it lacks the human element she needs (the persuasive salesperson in a boutique who tells her she looks wonderful in her dress, or the telephone customer service representative who assists with a product return). Because the woman has not completely grasped the technology, she does not fully understand what Web sites have to offer and how they can satisfy her shopping needs. Therefore, the woman does not allow herself to be persuaded online. Without enough knowledge of or respect for the Internet, any offer that a cyberbrand makes is absolutely useless to the woman. It might not even matter if Robert Redford, her all-time favorite celebrity, addressed her personally and asked her to accept a discount coupon (unless, of course, it was Robert Redford

> Lack of knowledge on the part of the consumer is a dangerous thing for the cyberbrand. Cyberbrands will be most successful with persuasive tactics when all audiences accept the Internet as a viable, safe, and secure place to shop and exchange information.

making an "indecent proposal" as in his movie). Lack of knowledge on the part of the consumer is a dangerous thing for the cyberbrand. Cyberbrands will be most successful with persuasive tactics when all audiences accept the Internet as a viable, safe, and secure place to shop and exchange information.

The results of a recent study aired on CBS Radio's MarketWatch discussed how the Internet lacks the "human element," a Web strategy that would result in an increase in e-commerce sales and further acceptance of e-commerce programs among larger groups of consumers.[8] CBS Radio talked about how Web sites will be equipped to handle more interactive conversation and how they need to be operational with technology that allows consumers to roll their cursors over a product and receive an audio message that states, "May I help you" or with the capability of immediate response and feedback to answer consumer product and service inquiries. This study concluded that brands on the Internet will lose 60 to 70% of their e-commerce sales if the human element is not incorporated into Web site design and technology.

There are programs being developed to add in the human element. For instance, Instant Call by Global Online Telephone is an e-mail application that allows the online consumer to receive a telephone call from the cyberbrand. For example, the software allows the user to input a name, an e-mail address, a telephone number, and whether or not the user wants to be contacted in one minute, five minutes, etc. The program requires Netscape version 3.02 or Internet Explorer version 3.02 or higher and is an excellent means for the user to experience the human element that is missing from most cyberbrands. Incorporation of these human elements will make audiences more receptive to persuasion on the Internet. Thus, groups that normally would not be as affected by persuasive Internet tactics will soon be exploring cyber opportunities based upon newfound trust and the nature of the persuasive messages they receive from cyberbrands. Remember, persuasion is as effective as the medium that communicates the message.

INTERVIEW: THE HUMAN TOUCH HAWAIIAN STYLE: SURFWEARHAWAII.COM

The Internet is the only communication channel that allows an audience to experience and interact with Hawaiian culture from anywhere in the world. SurfWear-Hawaii.com, an international e-tailer of surf products including Gotcha, More Core Division (MCD), Faith Riding Co., XCEL, North Shore Underground, and other popular Hawaiian brands, sells contemporary Hawaiian culture and shows its audiences worldwide what it is really like on the Hawaiian Islands—the weather, the culture, the people, and the products. With trendy surf wear and a strong Hawaiian brand, the company is growing rapidly to facilitate markets in the United States including Florida, Texas, Chicago, and California, and also international markets including parts of Europe, Hong Kong, and Singapore.

Background

Rick Tuteur, president and founder of SurfWearHawaii.com, launched the site in November 1998. In an interview, Tuteur discussed how he left a "good" paying job in the corporate world to pursue an Internet venture and his dreams of educating the mainland about contemporary Hawaiian lifestyles. Surf-WearHawaii's primary audience is college students and people aged 20 to 30. Secondary markets include those 13 to 18 years of age. To date, an existing customer's average purchase is approximately $75. "Because the Internet is still educational for most, our shoppers tend to order $25.00 in product the first time around, and then usually increase orders to over $100 for second purchases." According to Tuteur, repeat business is a lot cheaper than trying to win new customers. SurfWearHawaii.com focuses on "growing" repeat visitors, utilizing the following persuasive techniques:

- *Freebies for customers:* SurfWearHawaii gives away free surf stickers, calendars, and Lolo postcards to send to a friend or relative.

- *Discounts for customers:* As an incentive to purchase more products, programs such as "Mr. Big Buy" discount customers 15% on their purchases of $250 and more.

- *The human element:* The human element is critical for customer service: "Talk to Us" on the SurfWearHawaii site prompts customers to order by telephone or to e-mail any one of four people for their customer service and Web site inquiries.

"Having a customer service representative's e-mail address available [e.g., susan@SurfWearHawaii.com] gives customers the opportunity to receive real-time feedback from a live Hawaiian representative," states Tuteur. He goes on to discuss that the human element is the single most important aspect of the SurfWearHawaii.com site. The company has gone to great lengths to find out from customers what they need and what they enjoy on the site, and the company uses this valuable information to build a better customer service program. SurfWearHawaii.com believes in personal response, from the real-time e-mail replies, to the personal Mahalo (thank you) letters from Tuteur himself, signed in bright-red ink, on yellow paper with an Astrobrite envelope—completely personal and completely customer-friendly. Even the FAQ section on the site is updated frequently to display questions posed by customers. Most Web sites forget about updating FAQs to reflect new customer service issues or even new Internet issues. SurfWearHawaii.com pays close attention to customer inquiries. "Customers willingly offer us feedback. They love to discuss what they like and dislike on the site including the easy navigation and the 'cool' Hawaiian theme," explains Tuteur. Research of this type is also obtained through SurfWearHawaii.com's suppliers, who keep Tuteur updated on the hottest colors, what products sell the most, what their core products are, and in which areas they do well. "Suppliers are only too happy to contribute. Between supplier and customer feedback, we have been able to move forward with a site redesign utilizing brighter colors (as preferred by audiences) such as yellow and red which are also considered traditional Hawaiian colors," states Tuteur. The company moved away from blacks and blues toward happy, splashy colors that please its youthful audience and reinforce the Hawaiian culture.

The Future

Even with the business growing at a rapid rate, SurfWearHawaii.com faces its Internet challenges. The company was born online and, like any dot-com start-up, wants to see return on investment. According to Tuteur, the company doubled its traffic and sales within the first year (he jokes how *every* dot-com doubles traffic and sales, considering where most start off!). In any case, Tuteur attributes 40% of site traffic to the search engine listings and 60% to other Web sites (and SurfWearHawaii.com's upgrade to an associate program). And, yes, they too follow the Amazon Associate Program model.

Tuteur's final thoughts on the direction of his company are to have an entertaining site that is rich with local Hawaiian culture. Currently, SurfWearHawaii.com has Web cams for customers around the world to check out the weather and beaches in Hawaii—Kauai, Maui, and Waikiki; only the Internet makes this possible for SurfWear-Hawaii.com. The ability to reach out to mainstream communities around the world and expose them to contemporary Hawaiian lifestyles was never attempted pre-Internet. The Internet allows SurfWear-Hawaii.com to spread the hospitality and friendliness for which Hawaiian culture is so well known.

Full-Case Study

IBM AND CYBERBRANDING

In the new economy, IBM has managed to stay in the vanguard of marketing communications both on- and offline, by harnessing the unique capabilities of the Internet to better communicate with and serve its vast range of customers. It has done so by focusing on three different functional perspectives: technology, organization, and culture. The outcome is a brand that maintains its historical promise but at the same time emphasizes its evolving focus on providing one-to-one, increasingly customized "e-interactions" with its customers.

According to Todd Watson, digital brand manager with IBM Corporate Marketing, the reach of the Internet across traditional organizational functions forces companies to begin focusing on holistic customer relationship management, or CRM, as it has come to be known. Watson, who has been involved with the IBM Web since September 1994, and who is a passionate and energetic advocate for sound digital brand management, suggests that making this transition requires an especially sensitive understanding of the issues surrounding consumer privacy and customer data protection, which will increasingly impact Internet marketing communications.

Watson explained that for IBM, branding is an experience, and must increasingly be looked at and treated with a cross-functional approach, tying together all a company's organizational vacuums and adopting a customer-centric "e-perspective." While such efforts may begin with online marketing communications— say, with an interactive banner or pop-up window featuring a company's product or service—with the move toward increased bandwidth and device portability, it will increasingly begin to force other functions to become an integral part of the interactive food chain, including customer support (before and after the sale), financing, product development, etc.

The Internet has forced companies to learn more about their existing markets and to branch out into new markets. Watson discussed how IBM increases the brand experience through an understanding of its customers and the nature of their needs. "Data is critical for the new model. If you don't know your customer, you will lose them," explains Watson. Companies focused on creating an effective cyberpresence will increasingly have to take the steps to identify customers—whether they're a group that spends $100,000 or

$1 million—and their needs and, more important, cultivate ongoing, mutually beneficial relationships with existing customers. Despite the recent dot-com fervor, reality is hitting home, and companies are realizing they must move beyond simply focusing on Internet acquisition and instead begin to focus on long-term retention. Simply put, the Internet has forced companies to learn more about their existing markets and to branch out into new markets.

Challenge

Companies need to understand existing markets and branch out into new markets by better understanding their customer needs and preferences while at the same time ensuring that their business intelligence is both permissioned and sensitive to consumer privacy concerns.

Solution

There's evidence that reveals people are revisiting how to use data—responsibly, placing information back into the product and service development cycle. All of this suggests that effective cyberbrands moving forward must learn how to more intelligently and responsibly gather and analyze customer data and information. How-

ever, the foundation of any relationship is mutual trust. E-businesses must understand this relationship and realize that customer data and privacy will prove to be the single most important issue in the new economy. The ability to receive customer data is a privilege and should be treated as such. A business asks questions because it is looking to find out what the customer needs and wants, and everything it does from there out should be based on that permissioned business.

IBM employs research before, during, and after to test for the effectiveness of a campaign's results, which ultimately begins to pave the way for a better service relationship with its customers. "A company that goes out of its way to service its customers is well on its way to building long-term loyalty. Building that loyalty begins with the customers' first touch-point, no matter whether that's via a conversation with a customer service representative at your call center or via an interactive communications experience via the Internet." Increasingly, respecting that customer's privacy in the cultivation of your ongoing business relationship is going to become a competitive advantage. Customers want to feel in control of an

(continued...)

experience, which, in turn, leads to increased interaction. Opt-in e-mail, for example, is a way of saying, "I have full permission from a customer who is willing to engage in an interaction with my cyberbrand." However, some companies are not respecting privacy issues and are being hammered for selling online customer data. Companies need to be responsible with how data is handled.

IBM creates a brand experience for its customers by "energizing" the brand and focusing on more than the mere message. The communication should be useful at all times. "Take Amazon.com, it can send me an e-mail any time," says Watson. His explanation:

- Amazon knows its visitors. (How? Because it asks and remembers the user's likes and dislikes.)

- Based upon information, Amazon makes useful recommendations.

- Amazon makes it easy to purchase and easy to complain.

- Amazon also knows that if the brand experience is not pleasurable, www.bn.com is 10 keystrokes away.

Challenge

Marketers need to create this service brand experience online in order to build long-term customer loyalty.

Solution

Through gathering data and research information, cyberbrands will provide users with better brand service experiences. As a result, communication will be useful at all times and interaction will be informational, educational, entertaining, and even humorous.

Watson's final thoughts focused on the IBM brand experience. "We've come a long way. Every brand needs to take that extra, one-step-further approach to know each individual customer. It's the only way to achieve long-term customer loyalty," he states. For all companies, especially the brick-and-mortar establishments with existing infrastructure, it's a challenge to get over the organizational dysfunction. However, success lies in the ability to provide Web audiences with positive brand experiences every time there's contact with the brand, which means those disparate functions must be brought into closer alignment.

Tips to Remember

- The Internet forces companies to wrestle with providing effective and holistic customer relationship management (CRM). Accept the challenge and gather as much information on the customer as permissible with the objective of providing better service relationships.

- All of the touch points in a company need to be in place for a complete brand experience. One bad brand experience can frustrate the customer and mar the brand.

- Cyberbrands effectively gather and analyze customer data so that they can better understand their audiences. The foundation of any sound business relationship is mutual trust. The ability to gather customer data and the privacy issue will prove to be one of the most important concerns in the new economy. Having a solid understanding of consumer privacy issues and respecting those concerns will build confidence with your customers, which, ultimately, translates into profits.

3

Market Research
for Effective
Cyberbranding

11 Traditional Research Aids in Cyberspace

Objective:

To reinforce traditional research is at the heart of a marketing campaign and the life of the brand. Research is the key element that allows a company to understand the customer's needs and, as a result, optimizes audience response. Research methods will always exist, whether they are offline for the brand or taken to a new level and implemented in cyberspace. Focusing on the newer online techniques, they are becoming increasingly popular, not only because they work successfully, but also because they are quicker to execute. Cyberbranders will benefit by paying attention to:

- The value of market research
- Traditional research and the cyberbrand
- Cyberbrands and research beginnings
- Transformation of the traditional method—questionnaires
- Transformation of the traditional method—focus groups

THE VALUE OF MARKET RESEARCH

Optimizing audience response takes more than a team of executives brainstorming around a boardroom table. It means more than just applying popular strategies, such as customization, personalization, and the incentive programs that are surfacing with the development of new cyberbrands. It's even more **Call it traditional research or take it online; either way, it's the research that is crucial to the brand.** than the technology that launches the brand into cyberspace. The key element missing, the one that drives the executives to strategize, identifies the necessary customization, personalization, and incentive programs, and makes the technology highly interactive and effective in changing audience behavior, is *research*. Call it traditional research or take it online; either way, it's the *research* that is crucial to the brand. It's the *research* that determines how audiences feel and how they react to the brand at the time of its birth and at every intersection and crossroad of the brand's life. It's all about research—from the beginning to the middle to the end.

Research supplies data, which, when analyzed, leads to better, more powerful strategies and brands that entice and evoke audience response. With traditional research that is applied offline, the first step in the process is to recognize the problem or the situation. The company then identifies what or who needs to be researched to draw an accurate conclusion. Next is the decision as to which method is appropriate to elicit true responses and valuable information. Survey research, focus groups, in-depth interviews, content analysis, and usability studies were all methods frequently used and relied upon pre-Internet. After the research is observed, measured, and analyzed, the most critical step in the research process is implementing the results to benefit the brand and optimize response

Companies have been employing these research strategies for years. Just because the digital revolution turns the world upside down, this does not mean that any traditional strategies should be abandoned.

to the brand. Companies have been employing these research strategies for years. Just because the digital revolution turns the world upside down, this does not mean that any traditional strategies should be abandoned. As a matter of fact, because the World Wide Web has been thrust upon brands in the new economy, there is more of a reason to employ traditional research in the marketing mix.

TRADITIONAL RESEARCH AND THE CYBERBRAND

Research is classified as either primary or secondary. Primary research, for instance, comes directly from the audience whose behavior needs to be altered. Secondary research comes from a reliable source about the audience whose behavior is being studied. The reliable Internet research sources, mentioned daily in both broadcast and print news, are Jupiter Communications, Forrester Research, The Gartner Group, and Nielsen Net Ratings, to name a few. These companies are among the leaders in Internet information with in-depth studies and analysis. Jupiter Communications (www.jupitercommunications.com), for example, offers a comprehensive view of Internet commerce. The company provides expert analysis of broad strategies online as well as market strategies that are region-specific.[1] Jupiter offers its clients the ability to assess research on market trends, analyze competitive landscapes, and evaluate success criteria as well as a host of services to best suit a client's informational needs.

As for primary research, the ability to question audiences directly will always be a key strategy to understand the needs of an audience. Perhaps this is one of the reasons why traditional face-to-face research is crucial and should be used throughout the life of the brand. For instance, one well-known method, the focus group, is designed for conversation between participants and the moderator of the group with researchers and clients behind a one-way mirror to view the interaction of the group. Typically, focus group participants represent different publics and are valued for this reason. But one of the true values of focus group research is the *nonverbal communication* that is observed by the client and the researcher behind the one-way mirror. This type of communication might be anything from eye rolling and a grimace to crossed arms and tapping pencils at the session table. Body language reveals a great deal about how a panelist truly feels with respect to a particular question or subject that just cannot be measured through an online research method. This theory holds true for in-depth personal interviews, survey panels, and usability studies as well. Nothing will ever replace the body language or the true value it holds in research for the brand.

Cyberbrands are out there employing traditional methods. For instance, one of New Jersey's largest newspaper groups needed to take its 26 print brand newspapers and move them online with news

Cyberbrands are out there employing traditional methods.

and information for its North Jersey audience. Sales representatives were asked not only to sell traditional advertising to their faithful print brand clients, but now also to give a sales pitch about online advertising in the form of directories, classifieds, banner ads, and sponsorships. This was a tremendous undertaking and required traditional research methods at the onset of the project. The first step was to find out from sales representatives and managers how they felt about pitching Internet advertising and their level of understanding of the Internet. Did they believe that their client advertisers would see the online advertising as an opportunity, or an unnecessary expenditure that was not valuable enough to be included in their advertising budgets? In addition, the newspaper group needed to find whether or not their sales representatives and managers would actually buy into the online ad program and what incentives would make them eager to push the Internet advertising along with the print advertising opportunities. The Internet division of the newspaper group held a series of videotaped focus groups with its sales representatives and managers of the various newspapers. This type of method was extremely valuable for the brand to see that there were extensive concerns regarding the sales representatives and their ability to pitch Internet advertising confidently. Issues were raised immediately regarding the representatives' lack of understanding of the Internet and concerns of not having the proper materials to present to clients to interest them in an online advertising program. After careful review of the videotapes, a report was submitted to the head of the Internet Division suggesting that the sales team be presented with an internet advertising kit that would enable them to have a comprehensive guide to Internet advertising on the Web sites. The kit included Internet statistics on the North Jersey area, Internet rate cards, presentation materials to show advertisers, frequently asked questions (FAQs) that advertisers might ask, benefits to Internet advertisers, and benefits and incentives to sales representatives who participated in the program. The company also went a step further and provided sales teams with the opportunity to attend cyberbranding conferences and to ask cyberbranding experts questions about the Internet and discuss the concerns about Internet advertising. This effort could not have started without traditional research to gain a better understanding of the sales teams' concerns. The information from the focus groups proved extremely valuable to the company's cyberbrand vision.

OnlineBoardwalk.com, the virtual boardwalk in cyberspace, planned a Labor Day 2000 launch of its site. The site is positioned to become a model or field leader of online gaming. It carries a boardwalk/amusement pier theme with carnival-type games for children and teens, and more challenging parlor games such as trivia, chess, checkers, concentration, and keno for older audiences. Eventually, the site, through extensive development postlaunch, will expand with a new game a month to become an exclusive online gaming community. OnlineBoardwalk employed traditional research methods during the development of its site to fully understand the nature of its competition and to find out what target audiences felt about other popular game sites. The company performed a series of usability studies, with children (ages 6 to 12), teens (ages 13 to 19), young women and men in their twenties, and women aged 30+. The usability studies were conducted at a computer terminal with each study participant logging on to competitive Web sites including Uproar.com, Nabiscoworld.com, Boxerjam, and a host of other game Web sites. The users were observed as they accessed each different competitor and had to figure out how to play various games on each site. The users were timed for their ease of use on a site and their ability to navigate quickly, and observed for their level of frustration with game playing, etc. Facial expressions were monitored, as users were irritated when games did not download quickly and were also difficult to operate. These findings were extremely significant to OnlineBoardwalk.com during the developmental stages of its Web site. From the usability studies, the company was able to develop its site with a quicker download time and an easier navigation system to "walk" the Boardwalk and find the game of a user's choice, and to develop games with easy-to-read instructions that do not frustrate users before they begin playing. These strategies were incorporated into the Web site based upon the initial market research findings. Usability studies will continue, as the site develops to provide OnlineBoardwalk users with the best possible game site on the Web.

CYBERBRANDS AND RESEARCH BEGINNINGS

Jeffrey Graham, e-marketing director of Novo, discusses in his article "Building a Research Mosaic" how research is not static. When research is used correctly, it becomes the driving force behind a marketing campaign. "That's why you must work closely with the client and the account team to create a comprehensive research plan that starts from day one of the investment online," states Graham.2 He explains that unplanned research is much less effective. Indeed, the companies that are online with successful brands are the companies that utilize research as the critical "building blocks" in the planning phase. Cyberbrands such as the newspaper group in New Jersey and OnlineBoardwalk.com are off to a good start with initial market research to guide the marketing effort and Web site development. Market research, both qualitative and quantitative, has been around traditionally to study brand success. Research must be conducted, whether it is by the "good old" traditional method or the traditional methods extended to the Internet, which provide rapid results. Brands that do not constantly test target markets and use research to segment customer bases will not survive—especially on the Internet. In cyberspace, competition is fierce and brands need to employ the findings of research in order to rise above and stand apart from the competition.

> **Indeed, the companies that are online with successful brands are the companies that utilize research as the critical "building blocks" in the planning phase.**

TRANSFORMATION OF THE TRADITIONAL METHOD—QUESTIONNAIRES

There's a great deal of discussion about research online and whether it's truly effective. Of course, with every method employed there are "best practices" to consider (and best practices for online measure too). For example, what's the difference between the way to formulate a traditional offline questionnaire and the way to construct an online template? Questionnaires that are developed for offline audiences tend

A questionnaire on the Internet created for an online audience must be precise, considerably shorter with only the information that is necessary and relevant for it to be filled out accurately.

to be longer and more comprehensive, with several parts for users to complete. A questionnaire on the Internet created for an online audience must be precise, considerably shorter with only the information that is necessary and relevant for it to be filled out accurately. With the average online consumer having an attention span equivalent to that of a toddler (just a judgment based upon the amount of Web surfing going on out there), a questionnaire that is not short, sweet, and to the point will not receive a large number of willing responses. Among other helpful hints for online questionnaires, questions should be targeted toward a specific audience (general questions that

. . . participants who answer questions want to be rewarded. Let's rephrase that: they *expect* to be rewarded. That's the nature of the Internet: it's all about immediate response and reward.

ask for broad audience responses are less effective) and easy to read and interpret. And as in traditional questionnaires, questions should avoid jargon or business-type language (unless it's a specific group that will identify with the language being used, such as lawyers on a legal site). Last, participants who answer questions want to be rewarded. Let's rephrase that: they *expect* to be rewarded. That's the nature of the Internet: it's all about immediate response and reward.

Established brands have also figured out the benefits of online surveys—fast, cost-effective, and easy to tabulate. They are employing Internet research daily. Bonne Bell, the company known for preteen and teen cosmetics, recently utilized a short Web site survey entitled "A Fun Little Fragrance Questionnaire." With only seven questions on the survey, Bonne Bell was able to enlist the help of its online brand users to determine that a necklace with fragrance would not be a popular item for its teen audience. The simple question "If you had a perfume or a fragrance that could be attached to a necklace or a clip-on key ring so that you could wear the fragrance, which one would you choose?" led Bonne Bell to develop the clip-on key ring with a fragrance.[3] According to Buddy Bell, executive vice president of the company, the survey was completely voluntary and Bonne Bell would never force anyone to participate. Bonne Bell's young audience was more than willing to cooperate. The ease of use of the Web makes compliance higher than traditional methods.

TRANSFORMATION OF THE TRADITIONAL METHOD—FOCUS GROUPS

It's been said that on the Internet "everyone is the same."[4] The ability to give an open and honest answer when an online participant does not have to look someone in the eye is valuable research—finding out exactly how someone feels "no holds barred." Subjects that are sensitive in nature—for instance, medical and health-related topics, workplace relations, and, of course, Internet-related subjects—are a natural for online discussion.[5] Thus, the focus group online appears, with companies and researchers asking probing questions and monitoring typed-in responses.

Companies are figuring out how to emulate face-to-face research methods. VRRoom, a New York–based company, gathers people together for what it calls a "specialized chat room." As in traditional focus group research, there is a moderator to ask the questions for the participants to answer; however, all of the Q&A is done via the computer. The company that contracts for the research study is able to review the chat sessions in progress at a separate computer terminal (one that is set up to allow clients to see the transactions in real time and which allows them to redirect the line of questioning, if desired). They are also able to walk away that day with a transcript of the focus group discussion for further analysis.[6] The assumption of the online focus group is that participants all have access to a computer with Internet connections

... the future of online focus group research is moving toward videotaped chat sessions that film participants as they type in their answers to online focus group questions.

either at home or at work. And although currently the nonverbal communication aspect is removed from the research method, the future of online focus group research is moving toward videotaped chat sessions that film participants as they type in their answers to online focus group questions. This will provide visual images to companies in real time and combat the threat of losing the nonverbal communication.[7]

George Paap, manager of e-business intelligence for Motorola Semiconductor Products, gives his interpretation of the coming together of the online focus group. He describes the convergence as an encounter similar to that of guests meeting for the first time at a cocktail party.[8] This is an interesting analogy—it appears that the same type of "small talk" takes place in both situations as people discuss the weather and find common ground with one another. As the people in the focus group session become more comfortable, they realize the advantage of being in this situation. It's the ability to answer questions whenever they want without having to stop and wait for another participant to finish. Traditionally in the focus group, one participant speaks at a time. In the online sessions, everyone types at the same time. This eliminates one party from dominating the session (which often occurs in traditional surroundings and can be intimidating to other group members). The nonstop participation from all members creates communication that flows in a much less stifling environment.

Research and data-gathering techniques are the keys to customer relationship management. The ability to compile information from audiences, analyze the information, and then put it back into the product or service development cycle is the differentiating factor between the companies with cyberbrands that survive and the companies that come to life with a burst of energy and a flame that fizzles out quickly. It's more than the cyberbrand vision; it's more than the technology; it's more than the executives at the boardroom table—and the list goes on. There's only one thing that ties the components of the marketing mix together—it's the research

> The ability to compile information from audiences, analyze the information, and then put it back into the product or service development cycle is the differentiating factor between the companies with cyberbrands that survive and the companies that come to life with a burst of energy and a flame that fizzles out quickly.

that is analyzed and recycled to keep clients satisfied and with which better products and services are built. With research, brands are able to have one-on-one interactive relationships with customers. As a result, these relationships will be more than just marketing-based. On the contrary, they will be service relationships that increase customer loyalty and trust of the cyberbrand.

Interview: Academia Embraces Online Research

Is it easy for traditional researchers to make the transition online? According to Dr. Hairong Li, a professor at Michigan State University (MSU), the traditional principles of research, focusing mostly on survey research and focus panels, are still utilized in the online forum. Online research is not that much of a break from the principles of the past. Chat sessions, focus panels, and Internet polls are assembled in the same manner. Dr. Li, who instructs doctoral seminars on Internet research methods at MSU, works with students and professionals who are learning to use the Internet as a tool for social research in cyberspace. Dr. Li has a background and area of expertise in traditional and new media research. His courses focus on survey research, content analysis, experimentation, and focus groups, all via the Internet. Dr. Li conducts hands-on workshops for students to test and analyze new online research software and fine-tune research online. "Students are very knowledgeable and really know their way around the Internet. My courses show them how to take the existing re-search principles, coupled with good Internet knowledge, to reap the benefits of an online research forum," states Dr. Li.

Dr. Li is a firm believer in the potential of online research and discussed the many benefits for researchers. Provided the research methodology consists of assembling a "good" sample, online research will produce a "good" response rate. Dr. Li discussed how (1) online research is convenient to use and elicits a quicker response rate since a poll or survey can be completed and e-mailed back to a researcher in a moment's time, (2) the cost of online research is considerably lower (online eliminates the cost of mailings and prepaid stamped return envelopes) regardless of whether there are 10 or 10,000 respondents, (3) online research is becoming familiar to a society that is grasping technology with ease, and (4) it is also a forum that allows people who would not normally contribute to a group discussion to become actively involved, to voice their opinions and be heard.

There are similarities and differences between the offline and online research methodology. Dr. Li discussed that surveys, for instance, on the Web are constructed following some of the same principles for a mail survey. Specific to both traditional and new media is the way professionals need to apply the same amount of social, ethical, and legal responsibility when conducting research online. On the other hand, online surveys should be easier to read and have short questions. Last, the use of random digital dialing (RDD) when assembling a survey still applies to both forums. There are, however, slight differences that researchers need to address when moving research methodology online. Consumers are familiar with traditional research methods. They know what a survey looks like and can identify with the research process. Therefore, it is important to construct questions and research models that people can recognize. With online research there is a missed opportunity with respect to reading the participants' body language and facial expressions. Also, when conducting online focus panel sessions, certain nuances are lost when respondents are typing answers compared with a face-to-face discussion with a mediator. Last, with online research, Dr. Li has discovered that the size of focus panels needs to be smaller and condensed to six to eight people for maximum results.

Dr. Li's final thoughts are that online research is here to stay. The traditional principles and confirmed methodologies are being integrated into a forum that is quicker and more cost-effective and enables participants to take part with ease. The result is a society that steadily embraces new technology and moves in the direction of the online forum to increase response rates and accurate findings.

12 Online Research—Leave It Up to the Technology Experts

Objective:

Brands are making the cyber transition by utilizing fast and accurate online research. As this occurs, it is important to realize that there are varying degrees of control of the online services available. From the simplest survey to more sophisticated techniques like online focus panel discussions and competitive analyses, the Internet is becoming an effective medium to facilitate the research process. Cyberbranders must determine when to move away from the "homegrown" research techniques (the do-it-yourself methods resulting from low budgets and plain, old traditional habit) and embrace the methodologies of the new economy. This chapter highlights the different types of online research, with an in-depth discussion of the following:

- When to turn to online methods
- Tradition and the Internet—the best of both worlds
- Benefiting the brand and the consumer
- Extending beyond offline limits
- Research—finding the middle ground

WHEN TO TURN TO ONLINE METHODS

The Internet facilitates online research techniques that were not even possible 10 years ago. The methods used today are considerably less expensive, are flexible, and most of all are timely with same day analysis and results. And with every question that surfaces regarding traditional methods, the same questions and more revolve around online techniques. How do you know the numbers supplied actually add up? How well does the sample match the desired population? Will one method of data collection greatly influence a response over another method?[1] A word of caution: When it comes right down to sophisticated technology and credible online market research, companies reaching out to target audiences should leave the research technology to the "online research experts." Yes, there are those methods that are referred to as "home-grown." This process might simply be asking customers, friends, and family members to reply to an uncomplicated online questionnaire (created in a word document, of course). However, just as technology enhances the brand (let's not forget the meaning of the optimum cyberbrand), it also enhances a company's ability to retrieve information and data with respect to a cyberbrand.

Kozyhome.com had to decide whether or not it would use its own homegrown research or online research from the experts. The Chicago, Illinois, company launched an online retail furniture Web site in January 2000. It went the homegrown route first (as many start-ups do) by utilizing in-house focus groups and then advanced to word document surveys. Unfortunately, the homegrown methods had a low response rate, with the company gaining little feedback. Kozyhome.com approached an online market research expert (enter Vividence.com into the picture).[2] The San Mateo, California, firm specializes in "Web experience evaluation."[3] A visitor entering the Vividence Web site is greeted by many questions including: What critical business questions keep you up at night? How effective is your company's Web site? Are you meeting and exceeding the expectations of online customers? And, How do you outperform the competition?[4] These questions are right on target. Not only is it the cyberbrander's quest to obtain the answers to these questions, but it is also the cyberbrander's job to search out the answers to these questions, even if it takes going to great lengths to get the job done. Vividence is successful answering these questions as evidenced by the endorsements on its site that include companies such as Compaq and drugstore.com. Both click and mortar and e-brands are praising Vividence for the new found ability to better recognize the needs of online audiences.

Vividence came aboard the Kozyhome.com research project to conduct a study of 500 people nationwide. Kozyhome.com saw the difference immediately between the homegrown, word document survey and the large-scale effort

Homegrown research just cannot compare and should not be considered in the same league as what the experts can do in terms of sophisticated online research technology.

implemented by Vividence. Homegrown research just cannot compare and should not be considered in the same league as what the experts can do in terms of sophisticated online research technology.

OK, next question: What about research budgets? Yes, money is a factor, and that goes without saying, with both traditional offline methods and cyber research. But Kozyhome.com realized that without Vividence, its research effort was "the poor man's version"[5] of the type of research necessary. With a growing cash pool of approximately $30,000, Kozyhome.com was able to step up to a higher research plateau and have Vividence apply techniques that actually guided the direction and development of the Kozyhome.com cyberbrand.

Through Vividence's research techniques, Kozyhome.com was able to confirm what it originally suspected regarding the company's Web site. Vividence employed consumers in an e-tour of the furniture site and then followed up with the consumer with an online survey. The analysis and results of the tours and surveys prompted a drastic change to Kozyhome.com's Web site including its shopping cart procedures.

Vividence has assisted companies with online research since the site launched in February 2000. According to *Internet World*'s "Company to Watch" section, Vividence is creating quite a "media buzz." The 100,000 Web site testers, located around the United States, are the company's secret weapon. According to *Internet World*'s review, "Vividence uses demographically selected consumer recruits to evaluate a site's search functions, registration and navigation."[6] Vividence's clients are well-known companies including Compaq, Excite@home, drugstore.com, and Nordstrom (Vividence attracts large companies that can easily afford its customizable research programs that begin at $20,000+).

TRADITION AND THE INTERNET—THE BEST OF BOTH WORLDS

When it comes to online research, there's an automatic assumption: all research participants need to be wired with a PC in their homes. Guess again. Actually, companies such as InterSurvey.com are becoming increasingly popular with cyberbranders for the following reason. InterSurvey (www.intersurvey.com), of Menlo Park, California, uses households (up to 250,000 households by 2001) whether they are connected to the Internet or not.[7] The company

When it comes to online research, there's an automatic assumption: all research participants need to be wired with a PC in their homes.

does a random sample of telephone numbers (they refer to it as random digit dialing, or RDD) to provide an unbiased list of possible research candidates. These potential respondents are selected regardless of Internet use in their homes. InterSurvey uses a trade-off or barter program for research participation. Participants are offered free Internet hardware and the ability to be wired for their involvement with InterSurvey. Usually, participation from any household amounts to one survey per week. The candidate is prescreened to obtain demographic information—profile data is maintained for all respondents. Any household that chooses to partake in a research study is shipped the necessary hardware, and receives a free Internet connection, on a monthly basis.[8] InterSurvey touts itself as a unique consumer research organization that combines the strength and broad reach of the Internet with the statistical reliability of traditional sampling methods. InterSurvey satisfies both worlds—the traditional and cyber—coming together in a harmonious union. This online research firm certainly proves that cyber research service providers work harder to tackle the obstacles that would get in the way of a company investing in an online research firm. InterSurvey is establishing new ground through innovative techniques by placing the proper equipment in a research participant's home. The benefits are significant: better random sampling of participants, increased compliance by respondents, and higher levels of accuracy and detail in the participant information collected. Other benefits from this type of online research include:

- With a Web-based platform, various forms of content that were considered too expensive previously can now be reviewed.
- Research studies have participants observe panoramic images, three-dimensional images, high-fidelity audio, and TV-quality video.
- The hardware or equipment installed captures the visual and audio stimulus that is crucial in measuring attitudes.
  www.InterSurvey.com[9]

InterSurvey takes the traditional research (probability sampling) and mixes it with the power of the Internet, to get the resulting right groups of people answering the right sets of questions. Again, *when tradition meets technology, the outcome is a powerful cyberbrand.*

BENEFITING THE BRAND AND THE CONSUMER

The Internet is transforming not only the way that companies are utilizing research but also the methods in which groups of consumers participate. Two factors need to be acknowledged: (1) the extent to which companies are moving toward online research

The Internet is transforming not only the way that companies are utilizing research but also the methods in which groups of consumers participate.

to directly influence the way cyberbrands are developed and marketed, and (2) the nature of participation on behalf of the consumer respondent. Why are consumers so willing to partake in online research studies? The Internet makes it easier for research companies to offer incentives for participation.

Greenfield Online (www.greenfieldonline.com) is another company that takes research to a new plateau. Greenfield Online appeals to a consumer's ego not only with messages that pinpoint the importance of consumer research guiding and directing the development of products and services, but also through an enticing incentive program. First, Greenfield Online plays up the one-on-one communication aspect with each participant to the point of stating that it's the consumer and Greenfield Online building better products and services. Then, it's the "hook, line, and sinker" approach of the program—cash, prizes, and giveaways. The process of participating is easy (nothing less is expected from the Internet), and of course, confidentiality of data is up front in Greenfield Online's privacy statement. After research candidates fill out a confidential sign-up survey, they are ready to participate in online questionnaires and focus panels. Greenfield Online uses the collected data wisely. The company matches a participant's background and interests with the nature of the survey and focus group conducted, on behalf of a brand. A portion of the Greenfield Online site, which is dedicated to informing potential research participants about the Greenfield Online process, states, "We try to match you with fun and exciting surveys that match your background and interests." A cybermarketer's translation: We want the most accurate and truthful responses from consumers who are qualified to answer specific questions. Participants are then e-mailed when a survey is available for them to review and give responses. Greenfield Online also has consumers participate in FocusChat, which is "an opportunity to discuss a variety of topics with a small group of people all with similar interests."[10] A trained moderator leads the chat, which lasts anywhere from one to two hours.

All participants are paid and are selected based upon the information given in the confidential sign-up survey. The member participants of Greenfield Online become automatically eligible for an iGain account. Talk about incentives. As in offline research, participants are looking for rewards. The free iGain account provides members with an account that accumulates "Greenfield Online incentive money," which is incentive money for participating in research studies. For every focus panel, the participant has money deposited in an iGain account. At any time, the member can elect to receive payment from the account or donate incentive dollars to a charity. With Greenfield Online, a brand benefits as more research is collected and at the same time research participants accumulate more and more Greenfield Online incentive money. The outcome—brands gain valuable and immediate research from prequalified participants who are more than willing to take part in an effort to better a brand.

As in offline research, participants are looking for rewards.

EXTENDING BEYOND OFFLINE LIMITS

Another pioneer of online research is CLT Interactive (www.cltresearch.com). According to the company's background section on its Web site, in 1993, CLT began "building, running and servicing all Internet based initiatives from the simplest of Web surveys to [its] latest online tools such as WebSim™, Reflector™, and Site Visitor @rchitecture™ (SV@)."[11] CLT is among the first of the research companies to complete an international focus group project and is also known for its development of global research industry guidelines for cyberspace. Many research companies around the world recognize CLT for its published papers and expertise in online research methods.[12] Among the many unique, trademarked methods used by CLT is its Reflector program. Reflector is longitudinal online focus groups or a new perspective that allows online focus groups to remain in session for weeks (as opposed to the normal offline or online session that lasts from one to two hours). Reflector uses proprietary e-mail technology that enables this effort and increases the amount and depth of knowledge obtained from participants.

The Reflector session is different from the normal focus group:

- The moderator e-mails a question or topic to the group of participants.
- Clients who contract the research peruse all of the responses and redirect follow-up questions, if necessary.
- Multimedia is included in all e-mails, attached as either files or hyperlinks.
- Each group member sees only questions from the moderator and not the answers of other members.
- Reflector gathers all responses from group members, at which time every respondent sees compiled answers, instead of random responses, which ultimately leads to more interactive discussion.

CLT's research technology is an example of the extent and reach of the Internet, with little geographic limitation, domestically or internationally. This type of research has the same benefit as the research used by the other companies highlighted in this chapter; however, the extended length of the session allows participants to respond at their convenience. In addition, the ability to move across borders for demographics is a tremendous advantage for global brands.

Another interesting CLT Interactive program is WebScore. Brands need to be concerned with competitors, and WebScore is a simple method that has research participants evaluating a brand and its direct competition. WebScore uses a sample of 100 to 200 research candidates (selected from a qualified database of respondents). Participants are enlisted to make a full assessment of a Web site and its competitors, evaluating the following for each: performance, content, ease of navigation, graphics, technical performance, advertising, games/contests, free downloads, etc. Again, the reach of the Internet and advanced technology make competitive intelligence easier, faster, and customized for the company contracting the research from CLT.

RESEARCH —FINDING THE MIDDLE GROUND

There are other cyber research firms that fall in the area known as the "middle ground," in between the homegrown methods and "leave it to the experts" with advanced Web technology. These companies allow brands to develop their own research tools and techniques, giving them guidance along the way. WebSurveyor (www.websurveyor.com) is an example of an online firm that allows marketers to borrow technology and obtain and calculate their own research findings. WebSurveyor is so confident about its technology to build custom online surveys that it offers a free trial account for companies to set up a test survey and calculate results (talk about an incentive for marketers). WebSurveyor provides marketers with the tools necessary to conduct a survey "without any headaches, hassles, or long-term commitments."[13] And for users who are inexperienced with research technology (WebSurveyor refers to these individuals as nontechnical managers), WebSurveyor pro-vides desktop software and an Internet service to design, construct, distribute, and tabulate research findings. According to the WebSurveyor site, the company provides "a unique hybrid approach to conducting electronic surveys [that] gives you the optimal mix of speed, control and availability while eliminating your dependence on your overworked technical support staff and webmaster." WebSurveyor leaves the design and control up to the user who can tailor a survey appropriately for a desired audience and then be involved in the distribution process (unlike the other research companies highlighted in this chapter). WebSurveyor does not provide the means to find the prequalified research participants. This is done either through a company's own database of clients or by purchasing a list from a list broker. WebSurveyor takes over the research process once the user designs the survey (by downloading desktop software and utilizing the Survey Builder Wizard) and all e-mail addresses are entered into its e-mail list manager. Then, according to WebSurveyor, it's a 1, 2, 3 step process. The built-in Publish Wizard uses customized e-mail notification to distribute the survey. Participants either receive a hyperlink to access a survey in the body of the e-mail or receive the survey as an attachment to the notification. After a participant completes the survey, a "Submit" button transfers responses to WebSurveyor.Net, where all answers are quickly tabulated and charted for a user's convenience. Companies like WebSurveyor serve as that in-between step for brands in need of timely, inexpensive research results (under $200 as priced in July 2000) that do not want to hand over the entire research process (and lose control of that process) by outsourcing the project to a research firm.

REAL-TIME CUSTOMER SERVICE: AN INTERVIEW WITH WEBSURVEYOR

The Challenge

WebSurveyor (www.websurveyor.com) faces the challenge of utilizing the Internet as a communication vehicle. "We're not out to replace traditional research methods," states Tom Lueker, market surveyor (note the clever job title to enforce branding and name recognition). Lueker, in an interview, discusses how WebSurveyor came to life on the Internet as a survey tool that requires a fraction of the time and cost of traditional survey methods. And even though traditional surveys have been around for 30+ years, WebSurveyor is confident that its online brand will become a significant survey research solution. According to Lueker, WebSurveyor is building an online business that can flourish over the next 20 years, unlike many dot-com start-ups that focus on only short-term success. WebSurveyor's long-term perspective is critical as the company puts its best foot forward. From its name selection (one that definitely states

what the company does) to its sensible spending (unlike most dot-com start-ups with first-round funding), WebSurveyor is moving forward with practical marketing strategies. Using low-cost and highly effective marketing tactics including viral marketing on surveys, customer referrals, search engine positioning, and affiliate programs, the company has grown more than 1000% within the first year of operation despite using only one paid promotional effort.

The Solution

WebSurveyor exists to provide the ultimate customer experience. At first, the company sold its survey research as "shareware." But it quickly learned that customers on the site had difficulty downloading the survey-building software. Realizing that most clients are not technical experts, WebSurveyor took away the technical frustration by giving customers access to libraries of information on survey building and a strong customer support team. WebSurveyor also made additional resources available to its clients, including newsletters on tips and techniques of survey distribution and the best types of questions to incorporate into a survey. WebSurveyor focuses on its customers' needs. Lueker stresses that when a client has an issue, it's resolved within the first e-mail or telephone call placed to the customer service department. And if that means a refund—then a refund is made. "The customer is not evil," says Lueker.

The Future

WebSurveyor's goal is to have a site that is completely self-service for individual decision makers in a company. According to Lueker, WebSurveyor puts a tremendous amount of energy into making a process that is simple to understand—one that enables customers to figure out the survey-building procedure on their own. In order to be successful, WebSurveyor has designed a clean and uncluttered site. The site design makes it easy to navigate and find information, and the free trial offer entices users to go through the survey-building process before signing up for the paid program. Most of all, WebSurveyor is proud of its customer

service and call support system. "If there's a request for sales help at 2:00 a.m., and the only person in the office is a technician, then he will respond to the inquiry," states Lueker. The fact that it's not just one person's responsibility, rather that the whole company is accountable, is an attitude that is difficult to find yet fosters success in the new economy. This attitude shows when 90% plus of WebSurveyor's customers would recommend the site and the survey tools to colleagues and friends.

It's not unusual for WebSurveyor to receive praise from its customers. As a matter of fact, the service excels just based upon the timely responses from WebSurveyor customer service representatives to clients' inquiries. Take the following response from a satisfied client after his question regarding e-mail gathering was answered thoroughly by a customer service representative:

You are incredible! You answered all my questions, and I am now able to do everything that I need to do. I am extremely impressed by the level of customer service I have received at WebSurveyor. Not only do you know your product, you answer all my questions quickly and accurately. Kudos to you and your company for developing a very user-friendly program and support system!

This enthusiastic response came from a user who received the answer to a general (uncomplicated) question. Imagine the customer's response when larger, more pressing issues are proposed and then solved immediately. Every company in the digital economy should receive praise based upon better customer service and an overall superior brand experience. This is automatic. Nothing less should be expected from a brand—quick responses with accurate answers to specific questions.

WebSurveyor has a vision, one that it has been communicating and carrying out every day since site launch. It's the quest for all decision makers in customer companies to have and utilize the WebSurveyor technology to move their businesses into the future. WebSurveyor forges ahead with the solutions that enable its customers to gather strategic business intelligence, through fast and affordable research, and build better relationships with their own clients.

(13) The System of Web Tracking Analysis

Objective:

Research has excelled to new heights—from buzzword terms and data measurements to the Web tracking software that pinpoints an online visitor's every move. Marketers are utilizing this information wisely to guide their cyberbranding campaigns. This chapter provides solid examples and expert insight into the critical online research issues including:

- The phases of surveillance and "The System"
- When too much data leads to paralysis
- How research guides the branding campaign
- Understanding the tracking measurements
- Difficulties and opportunities with professional tracking software
- Turning the tables on the trackers

THE PHASES OF SURVEILLANCE
AND "THE SYSTEM"

It's research in the year 2075—a female shopper enters her favorite brick-and-mortar department store. The moment she enters the establishment, surveillance (hereinafter referred to as "The System") identifies her as Megan Ashley Jones, consumer #000072 (hereinafter referred to as "#000072"). The System also recognizes #000072 as a female, age 37, married, mother of two children, ages four and eight, income over $175,000, professional accountant, resident of Dallas, Texas, once-a-week shopper, ... and the profile continues. After she enters the autosensor doors and steps onto the floor tram (a treadmill system that moves the customer through the facility), The System calculates and analyzes every move that #000072 makes—how much time she spends in a particular area of the store, what products she glances at or admires, the products she picks up, her facial expressions and body language. The System monitors #000072's entire shopping experience for customer profiling analysis. It knows her every move and determines what she expects to see and experience on each visit to the establishment. After spending 32.666 minutes in the department store, #000072 approaches the checkout counter, where an automated teller (humans no longer operate checkout systems) completes her transaction and sends #000072 on her way.

It's not the year 2075, and The System at the brick-and-mortar department store does not exist yet. Consumers still have names, not numbers, and humans are present at checkout counters. However, the scenario of The System sounds vaguely similiar to the technology experienced by the consumer on the Internet. With every move, click, and purchase, a consumer gives away a small piece of information. The System is similar to the customer-profiling and data-gathering methods that are rapidly evolving and implemented by cyberbrands to improve the overall customer shopping experience. The cyberbrand, like The System, gathers information on Internet audiences as they browse a Web site. Tracking software applications enable Web sites to identify online visitors in many ways including:

With every move, click, and purchase, a consumer gives away a small piece of information.

- Identification by region or general location
- Their most frequently requested pages and how often these pages are accessed (and the average time the user spends viewing a particular page)

- Detection of the visitors' least requested pages, which also uncovers which pages of a Web site are less frequently accessed

- Classification of top entry pages, showing the first page viewed when a user visits a site (most likely, this is a home page, but in some cases it may be a specific URL that the user enters to access a particular page)

- Identification of top exit pages, revealing the most common pages users abandon or their place of exit from a site

- Classification of single access pages to uncover the pages of a Web site that visitors access and exit without viewing any other pages on the site

- Identification of the countries most active in visiting a Web page

- Summary of users' activities on an hourly, daily, or weekly basis

- Classification of the most downloaded file types on a Web site

WHEN TOO MUCH DATA LEADS TO PARALYSIS

The preceding list identifies only a few of the numerous ways that Web site tracking gathers information on a visitor and how it is measured. The buzzword *clickstream data* refers to the data that is gathered by a Web site on behalf of a visitor as he or she navigates throughout a site, clicks on various pages or banner advertisements, and browses other options. Clickstream data is used to tweak or redirect the design of a Web **...collecting too much information is a common mistake.** site for optimal audience response and to guide the efforts of a cyberbranding campaign. However, a question arises. Is there a possibility that collecting an abundance of data on each site visitor will end up a mistake for the dot-com? Actually, yes, collecting too much information is a common mistake. The concept of *analysis paralysis* sums up how companies can collect too much data, not knowing what to do with the information and how to use it properly.[1] Acquiring too much information is as useless as having too little data on a Web audience.

Most companies that purchase software tracking programs are best off finding out the following specifics about visitors:[2]

- Where did the visitor enter, and what directed the visitor to the site? Was it a banner ad, a link from a partnering site, or a search engine?

- How many pages were viewed, and in what order? Establishing patterns of visitors reveals trends.

- What length of time was spent on those pages, and how many products did the visitor view on the browsed pages? If specific products are not being viewed (on less visible pages), a redesign of product positioning might be in order.

- How many products were purchased, and what was the subsequent cost of purchases?

- What total length of time did the visitor spend on the site? If visitors are abandoning the site within a small time frame, redesign of content for stickiness should be considered.

- At what point did the visitor leave? If, for example, visitors are abandoning a page frequently prior to checkout, then directions on the checkout process may need fine tuning to make them clearer and to avoid user frustration.

HOW RESEARCH GUIDES THE BRANDING CAMPAIGN

Cyberbrands are, however, quickly taking advantage of the knowledge gained from the "virtual footprints" left by Web audiences.[3] Take CVS.com and its quest to become proficient at assisting customers in navigating through an inventory of over 15,000 products. David Zook, CVS.com Strategist Alliance member, faced the challenge of studying more numbers than he might have ever imagined. With numbers upon numbers, amounting to sheets of information, the compilation of data looked to Zook more like a mixed-up jigsaw puzzle than anything else—a perfect example of how too much information often makes little sense. CVS.com needed a better understanding of its site

Cyberbrands are, however, quickly taking advantage of the knowledge gained from the "virtual footprints" left by Web audiences.[3]

to facilitate a redesign that was overdue. The purpose of the overhaul was to help CVS.com visitors move easily to desired portions of the site, without experiencing confusion or frustration. In turn, they would find the products they needed and make online purchases hassle-free. CVS.com, hopeful like every other brand, wanted to boost its bottom line.[4] CVS.com tried the basic tracking software products to learn more about its audiences' needs, and unfortunately experienced low-end results. When the company then invested a few hundred thousand dollars, the *difference* was that it got high-end results for the difference in what it paid. CVS.com used the new software and immediately gained a clear understanding of problem areas on its site that needed to be addressed. Analysis determined that customers were leaving the site at the checkout page. The procedures that CVS.com thought were clear, in fact, were confusing to online audiences. By changing checkout procedures, guiding customers with uncomplicated messages, and streamlining processes, CVS.com looks forward to lowering consumers' frustration levels so that ultimately fewer visitors will abandon the site.

UNDERSTANDING THE TRACKING MEASUREMENTS

Just for the record, number crunching and compiling statistics is not enough. It takes a thorough understanding of the Internet and Internet-specific audiences to properly analyze the information that is readily available. With all of the terms and numbers being thrown around loosely in the dot-com world, it's important to learn the differences between the terms and the basics of the measurements being recorded.

...number crunching and compiling statistics is not enough. It takes a thorough understanding of the Internet and Internet-specific audiences to properly analyze the information that is readily available.

So whether it's hits, unique visits, or page views, the numbers often vary depending on the source recording the data. Understanding the basics enables cyberbranders to weed out the unnecessary information and utilize the proper knowledge for a strategic plan of action.

Take the overused term *hits*. Many professionals still throw this term around without realizing its true meaning. First off, when it comes to Web tracking, a Web browser requests a file from a site (that's the point at which the consumer is accessing information). The log file on a site keeps a record of the "interaction" or the passing back and forth of information. The record is a single line of information that contains the following:

- The computer retrieving the file
- The date and time of the inquiry
- A numerical code (to identify a successful or unsuccessful transaction)
- The amount of data (bytes) transferred
- The location of the Web browser before the request was made to the server
- The type of Web browser and operating system making the inquiry
  (Clickz.com[5])

Why the need for this long-drawn-out explanation? Well, mostly because the long-winded process takes place for every file requested by a browser. That means that if there are five lines in a log file, then the Web page requested could contain one line for HTML code and four other lines for the graphics visible on the page. And every time a cyberbrander discusses a "hit" on a site, simply stated, that refers to each line of the log file. In other words, the term "hits" is somewhat meaningless; it describes more how a site is designed than the number of visitors on that site. In addition, when the lines in a log file are clumped together by the same browser, this is the definition of the "site visit" per user. In Net conversation, this term and *hit* are often interchanged and misused.

A question popped up on *The Standard*'s "Ask Nettie: Traffic Report," which is an online question-and-answer dialogue between *The Standard*'s Net Returns staff and its online subscribers:

Question:

We're in the middle of a site redesign. . . . Most of the decision makers are making informed choices based on traffic and clickstream data. . . . How can we use this information to find out what changes would really be useful to our customers?[6]

Answer:

Traffic data is the fastest way to read your visitors' minds. But this information often gets ignored when it comes to major revamps. The importance of spending time with your Web server's visitor log before you make any changes cannot be overstated.[7]

Nettie's answer goes on to discuss how Eppraisals.com used clickstream data to entice people to use the site's services. The company, Chicago-based, has an online presence that charges visitors $20 for appraisals of art, furniture, and memorabilia done by a panel of experts. Eppraisals.com analyzed clickstream data to find out that over 50% of its traffic came from its link on the Web site of a nationally acclaimed art and antique expert by the name of Leslie Hindman. Eppraisals realized that it could improve its integrity by placing a picture of Leslie Hindman on the site's home page. From that point on, visitors were continually clicking her image. This is an excellent example of utilizing traffic analysis to guide the branding campaign. With the newly formed partnership between Eppraisals and Leslie Hindman, both parties benefit. As a result, the site's welcome message to visitors reads:[8]

> Hi, I'm Leslie Hindman. Welcome to Eppraisals.com—a fast and affordable service for learning more about what you have and what it's worth. *Learn more.*

Analyzing clickstream data led to a powerful and credible endorsement for Eppraisals.com.

ISSUES AND OPPORTUNITIES WITH PROFESSIONAL TRACKING SOFTWARE

There are a slew of key vendors that offer Web tracking software. The companies in the news include Quadstone, WebTrends, AccrueSoftware, NetAcumen, and Personify, to name a few. The beauty of these Web tracking packages is not only the ability for marketers to compute traffic, but also to join together patterns that are revealed by the demographic information available on site visitors. Quadstone (www.quadstone.com) is recognized for its unique software tools (for the telecommunications, retail, insurance, and banking industries) to comprehend and influence the behavior of online audiences.[9] Quadstone is designed specifically for business users, who most typically are marketers. The company attracts marketers with the notion that they have the knowledge about strategies, the market, and customers and with the right tools can drive the analysis process home.[10] Not only does Quadstone provide the software tools, but it also offers recognized analytical consulting services to its clients. With its team, which has over 100 man-years of experience, Quadstone touts itself as a company that can help its clients to extend thinking beyond the traditional marketing limitations—a must for branding in the new digital economy.

WebTrends (www.webtrends.com) is another Web tracking analysis company that offers award-winning management and reporting solutions. With its WebTrends Live, for advanced real-time e-service, companies can receive up-to-the-minute information, seven days a week, about Web traffic analysis, e-commerce revenue, and ad campaign management for any size Web site.[11] WebTrends Live provides

...the amount of information from the professional tracking software product is endless.

answers to specific questions, including: How much revenue was generated by a campaign, and which products sold? How often do customers visit a site prior to a purchase and between purchases? When are peak traffic hours? What type of information do visitors look for, and which pages are the most popular?[12] The questions and answers are continuous, and the amount of information from the professional tracking software product is endless.

TURNING THE TABLES ON THE TRACKERS

But what about the customers' perspectives, knowing at any time they are being followed and that their Web site habits are stringently analyzed? How should customers feel knowing that the Internet "System" is at work, following their every move? Even if the profiling is on the "up-and-up" and respects privacy issues, consumers are still skeptical about being tracked for the sole purpose of allowing cyberbrands to get them to spend money (the negative attitude that conveys, "It's about the money and not the cyberbrand experience"). As a result, there are also companies online that specialize in "permission based personalization software that enables ebusinesses to deliver webwide profiling with built-in consumer trust."[13] For instance, Youpowered's SmartSense Consumer Trust product (www.younology.com) allows e-businesses to download software for the following purposes: to cooperate with consumer-dictated information, secure the exchange of sensitive data, build trust with

> Tracking software enables companies to tie incentive profiling into their tracking so as (1) not to irritate customers, (2) to offer relevant suggestions, and (3) to make customers feel welcome as they browse a site.

customers and turn it into loyalty and lifelong value, refine marketing strategies for each visitor, and recognize different behavioral patterns, all with technology that allows customers to maintain control over their information at all times. Tracking software enables companies to tie incentive profiling into their tracking so as (1) not to irritate customers, (2) to offer relevant suggestions, and (3) to make customers feel welcome as they browse a site—and at the same time giving the consumer the opportunity to block a communication after the visit (in the form of unsolicited e-mail).

Better yet, there are actually companies with software to combat the "Web tracking hunter" and allow the consumer to take revenge.[14] Take IDcide, Inc., a company in California and Israel that specializes in a new application known as Privacy Companion. According to IDcide, it is a one-of-a-kind product that alerts users to when and by whom they are being tracked. In addition, the program allows online audiences to disable Internet trackers. Which brings to the table the discussion of the infamous cookie, that tiny bit of digital information placed or stored on a user's computer. Cookies are standard features in browser software that assign each visitor a random, unique number. This is an anonymous user ID that rests on the visitor's computer. The cookie does not actually identify the user, just the user's computer used to access a particular Web site. Products such as IDcide's Privacy Companion intercept cookies and allow surfers to decide what level of privacy is right for them—minimal to high protection. Privacy Companion is a free download for users. It's interesting to note that IDcide does not charge online audiences for using Privacy Companion; instead, the company's cofounder, Ron Perry, states, "The goal of IDcide is to work with companies that respect a surfer's privacy, and that IDcide would be providing 'added value features' to these sites for which a fee would be charged."[15]

So here it is, The System of the year 2075 in its developmental phases—it's that of the Internet and the many ways that surveillance technology tracks on-line audiences. Just wait, The System is almost here!

Programming 101—The Language behind the Internet

Catherine Mellado is a Web programmer at PFS Marketwyse, Inc., in Totowa, New Jersey. She leads a team of programmers, and is actively involved with client projects ranging from Flash Action Scripting to complex back-end e-commerce programming. With five years of experience in her field, Catherine's expertise and devotion has led to a career that has advanced her quickly through the ranks to a senior-level position at her company.

Catherine's opinion is that there are some common misconceptions when it comes to Web terminology. The best way to clear them up is to go through the creation process from beginning to end. Catherine gives her thoughts on the process:

The first step towards making a Web site is getting a URL (universal resource locator). In simple terms, this is your Web address or domain name, for example, www.YourURL.com. This task is accomplished by registering through one of the many domain registration sites out there. Once a domain name is registered, you own it (usually for two years) and no one else can have the same name.

Once you have an address, you need a host. A hosting company usually charges you a monthly fee and in exchange provides space on its server for your Web site to reside on. A server is a computer that stays on all of the time, and is specially configured by your hosting company so that every time someone types in your URL your page will appear. The way you put files on your server is by FTP (file transfer protocol). There are programs that will help you do this; it is as easy as copying and pasting files from one computer to another.

The most basic Web sites are made up of text and pictures. These "plain" Web sites are coded in HTML (hypertext markup language). HTML is a very simple language that browsers (such as Netscape and Internet Explorer) translate; it is used for formatting purposes. You can usually see the actual file by right-clicking and selecting "view source" on any Web page. When a user goes to a Web site, the browser recognizes the file extension (.htm or .html) and then displays the contents. For example, if the browser reads this is my text, it would know that the text should be bold and it would display **this is my text.**

Images for the Web usually have extensions of .gif or .jpg. The difference is how each one is compressed, and it is important to know which one to use for each situation. A .gif is used for images that have 256 colors or less, have some transparency, or are animated. A .jpg is used for images that have more than 256 colors, such as photographs.

Of course, most Web sites have some level of interaction, some show the current date, some have pictures that change color when the mouse goes over them (commonly known as rollovers), and some even remember you when you go back. All of this interaction is usually achieved with JavaScript. This is a simple scripting language, a small version of its big brother Java. JavaScript goes right into the HTML document, and is also interpreted by the browser.

There is also another scripting language called VBScript; however, it is compatible only with Internet Explorer, so it is not very popular for front-end scripting.

Even though JavaScript can make your page do some really "cool stuff," many Web sites need to keep track of visitors, merchandise, and other statistics. It is not easy to manipulate this information using simple JavaScript; thus, back-end languages have been created to fill the void.

Until now we have discussed only front-end technology. It is important to note the difference. Front-end technology refers to Web sites coded in HTML, VBScript, or JavaScript. What actually makes them front-end is that when a user opens the page, the browser automatically translates everything for them. Back-end technology is used, but not limited to, databases, and is usually coded in languages like ASP, PHP, or Cold Fusion. The reason it is considered back-end is that when a user goes to your page, the server looks at the code first, gathers the information the page is asking for, and then spits out the HTML into the user's computer, and finally the user's browser interprets it, displaying the results.

For example, I have a database of members; I want to display all the members on my Web page. The problem is, there are many members, and my list is constantly growing. So I write a back-end script that will solve this problem. When a user goes to my Web site and clicks on the Members link, my ASP page will be called, and the server will get the page and realize that it is a back-end page. It will read through the code that tells it to "get every member name from the database!" It will gather all the information on the database, and will write the HTML for all the members. It will then give the results to your browser, which will then display all the members who are currently in the database. This comes in handy, because now, I do not have to go back and edit the page every time someone becomes a new member.

If you are planning to use back-end scripting for any of your pages, you should look into specific hosting companies for the technology that you are planning to use. Each server has specific capabilities and limitations. Many servers are Unix servers; ASP needs a Windows NT server to run on, and so a Unix server would not display your pages correctly.

You have probably also heard of Java. This is a "compiled" language. Basically, Java is coded in a special program that translates or compiles the code and creates a miniprogram called an *applet.* The applet is small enough to be downloaded easily, and will be in the user's computer memory for as long as it is needed; the moment you leave the page, the applet is discarded from your computer. Another important feature is that Java was made with specific limitations to make sure no one can code a virus with it.

Finally, other file formats that you will probably encounter on the Internet are Flash files (.swf extension). This program is used for complicated interactive animations that download fast, .avi and .mov files used primarily for short movies and videos, and .pdf (portable document format) files that make it possible to print formatted documents more reliably than simple HTML.

If you have made it this far, and understand the terminology up to this point, congratulations: you are on your way to Programming Language 102.

(14) # Ethics on the Internet

Objective:

For cyberbranders to understand that Internet ethics
encompass an enormous area, worthy of entire books. As
these ethics unfold, certain issues that pertain to
cyberbranding must be addressed. This chapter offers a
quick walkthrough of prominent ethical issues that have
surfaced on the Internet, with insight into the following
areas:

- Broadcast ethics of the past
- Ethical beginnings on the Internet
- Privacy, fraud, and other Internet issues
- Industries developing ethics
- A cyberbrand's road to ethics

BROADCAST ETHICS OF THE PAST

On the eve of Halloween 1938, the actor Orson Welles broadcast his scheduled radio program. During the live performance, a realistic announcement stated that Martians had landed on Earth (in a small town, Grovers Mills, New Jersey) armed and ready to attack. Many local residents of the town became hysterical and ran to take cover or found firearms to retaliate. The panic continued to create local street riots, as the hysteria spread to surrounding areas. Finally, the network broadcasting the program went on the air to explain that the radio listeners had been subject to an "unintended hoax" and that Orson Welles's presentation of *The War of the Worlds* belonged to the weekly series of radio programs called Mercury Theatre.[1] Although the show was preceded by an announcement stating the program was only a simulation, Orson Welles was reprimanded by "practically everybody connected with radio broadcasting."[2]

In 1964, Soupy Sales, the well-known comedian, played a practical joke on his television show that aired on WNEW-TV. "Hey kids, get those little green pieces of paper with pictures of George Washington, Benjamin Franklin, Lincoln, and Jefferson on them, send them to me, and I'll send you a postcard from Puerto Rico."[3] And that's exactly what hundreds of children did. Of course, the money was returned, and Soupy Sales' television show was suspended for seven days.

These are classic examples of how radio and television are closely monitored and regulated to assure that audiences are protected from communication that is not responsible (by intention or not), ethical, and/or suitable for audiences of all ages. Audience protection continues today in broadcast communications when warning messages on commercials state, "You must be 18 years or older to order this product," and when television and movie ratings advise audiences of nudity, adult themes, and graphic violence. Television is even equipped with channel controls for parents to monitor their children's TV viewing habits.

ETHICAL BEGINNINGS ON THE INTERNET

On the Internet, however, ethics and responsible practices are only now unfolding. The World Wide Web as a vast communication channel has saturated more homes and businesses more quickly than any other means of communication. Thus, it poses a larger challenge to regulators. In 1989, when the Internet first surfaced, the Internet Activities Board (IAB) posted a memo entitled "Ethics on the Internet." Back in 1989, it was apparent that this communication medium had the potential to cause concern. Because the Internet is largely available and accessible:

On the Internet, however, ethics and responsible practices are only now unfolding.

> The U.S. Government sponsors of this system have a fiduciary responsibility to the public to allocate government resources wisely and effectively. Justification for the support of this system suffers when highly disruptive abuse occurs. Access to and use of the Internet is a *privilege* and should be treated as such by all users of this system.[4]

To date, there are numerous instances of abuse on the Internet, illustrating how Internet users neglect to focus on the word *privilege*. When The Federal Trade Commission (FTC) instituted its Privacy Initiatives, it was clear that the initiative focused on Internet value and apprehension alike:

... there are numerous instances of abuse on the Internet, illustrating how Internet users neglect to focus on the word *privilege*.

Advances in computer technology have made it possible for detailed information about people to be compiled and shared more easily and cheaply than ever. That's good for society as a whole and individual consumers. For example, it is easier for law enforcement to track down criminals, for banks to prevent fraud, and for consumers to learn about new products and services, allowing them to make better-informed purchasing decisions. At the same time, as personal information becomes more accessible, each of us—companies, associations, government agencies, and consumers—must take precautions to protect against the misuse of that information.[5]

The FTC initiative begins with a focus on the positive communication—*the true essence of Internet communication.* However, as on any communication channel, there is the likely possibility for misuse to occur. And although the noted initiatives are clear statements, what is communicated in these documents is not necessarily representative of the WWW (World "Wild" Web). How to use technology responsibly and ethically is a question that has been asked for years. The question has moved to a more advanced technological state, and companies, associations, agencies, and consumers should no longer have to guess, Where are the ethics on the Internet? A fine line is being drawn between responsible communication and the unethical prac-

Where are the ethics on the Internet?

tices that infringe on personal safety and privacy. Privacy, especially, is a growing concern. In a study conducted by PriceWaterhouseCoopers (PWC), approximately 60% of Internet users in the United States stated they would purchase more online if they had increased confidence in an e-retailer's use of personal data.[6] In a New Zealand–based survey, conducted by SimplyQuick.com, the privacy policies of the top 100 consumer sites were evaluated. Survey results in July 2000 revealed the following:

- Over 50% of the surveyed consumer sites permitted information on customers to be shared with third parties.
- Only 11% of the sites made sharing information difficult.
- Approximately 21% have privacy policies that appear with an easy option for consumers to opt out.
- About 3% had no statement or an unclear policy statement (eMarketer 2000[7])

PRIVACY, FRAUD, AND OTHER INTERNET ISSUES

Information on the Internet is obtained on consumers who are willing to fill out user registration questions before making a purchase or viewing areas of a Web site. Most companies require consumers to give this information, and in some cases it is necessary to divulge personal information to receive a login and password before accessing a site. Companies are looking to learn more about their visitors—name, e-mail address, street address, telephone number (optional), salary, profession, etc. This *voluntary* information is utilized to respond to a consumer's requests, customize the shopping experience, and improve overall communication between the user and online brand.

Then there's the information that is gathered *without* users' awareness—the monitoring of their clicks and page views. Consumers leave numerous "footprints" behind and don't even know it. Cookies from a Web site are transferred to the consumer's hard drive, enabling a site's system to recognize the user's browser for tracking purposes. The misuse occurs when companies share

information with affiliated businesses, or sell information to third parties without the consumer's knowledge.

Every day, the news media are saturated with cases of Internet abuse. The rules of privacy are no longer a private matter, as companies are learning quickly that handling personal customer data improperly can cause serious legal complications for cyberbrands.[8] In the case of Zapme, a broadband interactive network, the company faced a "privacy meltdown" as it was accused of violating students' rights. In a deal with Yahoo!, Zapme was providing schools with the technological tools and resources necessary for learning in the new economy. Zapme was criticized early in 2000 for using the schools as a way to reach children with advertising.[9] The

> **Every day, the news media is saturated with cases of Internet abuse.**

CEO, Rick Inatome, stated that he did not collect any information that allowed Zapme to identify individual students. Zapme "only" inquires about a user's gender and age, and Inatome was adamant that the company does not sell this information to third parties or track the whereabouts of its users. The legislation introduced successfully in 1998 (and effective April 2000) known as the Children's Online Privacy Protection Act (COPPA) mandates that Web site operators targeting children under the age of 13 must post the following information to inform audiences with respect to personal data:

- Notice of the type of data the site collects and the purpose of the collection
- Requirement of parental permission prior to retrieval of such information
- Ability of parents to view and alter any information collected
- Secure maintenance of the collected data
  (*SAR*, Issue 35[10])

Take MamaMedia.com, the popular children's game Web site. This cyberbrand is an advocate of children's privacy issues. In its Web Safety Center, a parent or guardian is able to find descriptive text on how MamaMedia.com sets a good example for other children's sites, and how it prides itself on setting the highest children's safety standards. For parents, MamaMedia.com also makes available information on what COPPA means to them, Web safety tips, and the "10 Rules of the Online Road for Kids." In addition, MamaMedia.com asks children for only limited information: a screen name, password, birth date, and gender. Children must also provide a parent's e-mail address in order for parents to be informed when their child registers. MamaMedia.com is a good example of a cyberbrand that strictly adheres to the children's privacy laws and as a result gains the trust of parents.

Children's issues are among the top concerns as Internet privacy issues unfold. The case of Toysmart.com, the Walt Disney majority-owned company, was highlighted as one of the most important cases amongst privacy advocates.[11] As a part of the e-tailer's bankruptcy plan, the FTC announced a settlement to allow the company's customer

Children's issues are among the top concerns as Internet privacy issues unfold.

database to be sold.[12] This immediately raised eyebrows among legislators and privacy advocates. However, firm limitations were imposed on the proposed sale to make sure that the database would remain in a family-related retail market and would be purchased in its entirety, and that the prospective owner would have no intention of selling the database without the express consent of any persons listed.

Privacy issues are the most publicized, but other types of communication concerns are finding their way to the court systems. Moving into legal territory, *defamation cases* are high on the Internet abuse list. On an international level, there was a highly publicized case of a physicist by the name of Lawrence Godfrey who won a court battle that entitled him to receive $24,000, or the equivalent of 15,000 pounds, from Demon, the British ISP. It was a case of Internet defamation in which Godfrey accused the ISP of not

... *defamation cases* are high on the Internet abuse list.

eliminating slanderous statements from a newsgroup. According to *The Standard*, 80 suits have been filed by companies stating that their executives and management have fallen victim to derogatory comments in chat rooms and on message boards.[13] The numbers continue to grow as more policing takes place.

On the Internet, the famous saying "caveat emptor" has more meaning than ever. And not only should the buyer beware, but the seller as well. Beginning with the former, an example of Internet fraud that surfaced in the news was the cancellation of eBay's sale of an abstract painting. According to the *New York Times on the Web,* the seller of the painting artificially raised the sale price and violated eBay's auction rules.

On the Internet, the famous saying "caveat emptor" has more meaning than ever. And not only should the buyer beware, but the seller as well.

Apparently, the seller led online buyers to believe that the painting was by the famous artist Richard Diebenkorn; the misrepresentation not only inflated the bidding on the painting, but, as the article confirms, illustrated how fraud is quickly finding its way to auctions on the Internet.[14] The article further states that Internet auctions remain at the top of consumer criticism and that cases grew close to 10,700 in 1999.[15]

But that is only the *buyer* portion of the caveat. With respect to the *seller,* there is just as much at stake. Experts say that online sellers have much to worry about. They have little protection. The buyers of faulty goods through online auctions have remedies through credit card companies and insurance plans. On the other hand, there is no recourse for sellers who end up with phony money orders, stolen credit cards, or checks that do not clear.[16] The Gartner Group performed a study, released in July 2000, stating that although brick-and-mortar merchants face their fair share of stolen credit card incidence, the online sellers are 10 to 18 times more likely to be confronted with the issue.[17] According to the FTC, there are people who have the sole responsibility of reviewing all data to recognize instances of fraud on the Internet auction sites. The FTC has remained on top of the fraud cases and is responsible for providing the information to the proper local law enforcement agencies.[18]

INDUSTRIES DEVELOPING ETHICS

A simple dictionary definition of *ethics* reveals that ethical practices are the morals and customs considered normal or standard for a group or profession. Ethics on the Internet unfold as groups of professionals develop their working codes. Take health care online and the e-code of health. Professionals in health care early on saw the need to develop standards of privacy and confidentiality as scores of health care sites appeared on the Internet. In May 2000, the "eHealth Code of Ethics" was initiated. Dr. Helga E. Rippen, Ph.D., who is cochair of the eHealth Ethics Initiative's steering committee, affirms that the code focuses on ethics (more so than law) and is considered an all-inclusive and comprehensive initiative.[19] Other groups, such as online advertising networks, are in the hot seat receiving attention from privacy advocates and consumers alike. As a result, a coalition has formed that represents approximately 90% of the United States' online advertisers. The Network Advertising Initiative's (NAI) plan, which is backed by the U.S. government, identifies issues including Internet firms' using data—whether it is a person's Social Security number or medical or financial information collected on behalf of that user—for the purpose of selecting advertisements to put on users' computer screens.[20]

Ethics on the Internet unfold as groups of professionals develop their working codes.

The number of cases continues to grow as the government and industries involved in Internet communication define and enforce clear standards. Privacy law is still a budding field. As issues surface, the battles continue between proposed legislation on Capitol Hill and privacy advocates who feel the planned initiatives are too weak. The "spirit" of the Internet started with open communication and modest regulation. To start off with few guidelines and then quickly increase communication restrictions is a natural cause for controversy. As much as groups are hungry to step in and give the Internet the kind of control they feel it needs, the Internet brands continue to fight against this legislation. These brands are reacting to the ease of loose communication in the beginning and fear of a future of too much control in the end.

An optimistic answer, although not necessarily a simple one, lies in the principles of ethics. In the interest of the cyberbrand, there has to be a conscious effort on the part of professionals to enforce ethical communication standards (everything from a Web site's privacy policy to how data is handled). Following the guidelines and the continual use of ethical, responsible communication will, in the long run, help prevent overzealous laws and allow the online brands to better serve customers with the data they collect. There will always be groups that feel the need to take more control. This is not exclusive to the Internet. Taking an active stance to communicate privacy policies and the proper use of personal consumer data is the first step to minimizing the controversy.

A CYBERBRAND'S ROAD TO ETHICS

In the spirit of open communication, and as clear standards are devised, here's how companies and professional branders can take an aggressive stance on privacy issues:

- Develop a clear privacy clause that defines the collection of data on customers.
- Ask customers for permission to collect data.
- Provide up-front information about the transfer of data to third parties (if any).
- Inform customers how information is used.
- Give clients access to review and update information.
- State policies on how records are kept secure.
- Explain policies regarding accidental leaks or theft by third parties.
- Analyze the type of information the company needs to collect and what is necessary for accurate profiling— eliminate any information that is not useful.
- Allow visitors to review the information and erase information that they feel is not accurate.
- Explain how cookies operate on a Web site and make a site more responsive to the needs of a visitor.

Remember, the use of the Internet is a privilege (never forget this word). It was a privilege in 1989, and is just as much a privilege

Remember, the use of the Internet is a privilege (never forget this word). It was a privilege in 1989, and is just as much a privilege now.

now. And make sure that whatever is stated in your privacy policy is true. Otherwise, the door is open for a lawsuit!

Privacy Q&A With Blakes, Cassels & Graydon, LLP

David Fruitman is an associate of Blake, Cassels & Graydon, LLP. Blakes is a Canadian national business law firm with offices in Toronto, Ottawa, Calgary, and Vancouver, in Canada and in London, U.K., and Beijing. David practices in the Toronto office in the areas of privacy, competition, foreign investment, and e-commerce. He has provided privacy advice to a number of Canadian corporations including Canadian subsidiaries of foreign-based multinational corporations. In addition, he has a long-standing interest in Internet issues including privacy. He has been a member of various on-line communities since the late 1980s and has maintained his interest through membership in numerous Internet and privacy-related list servers. In a Q&A e-mail exchange, Fruitman gave his insight into Internet privacy issues. He was able to take a complex topic and answer questions in a user-friendly manner.

1. With respect to privacy issues and legislation, which countries are introducing stronger policies?

Largely as a result of the European Privacy Directive, a number of countries have begun reevaluating their existing privacy protection. According to a report issued in late 2000, nearly 50 jurisdictions have, or are in the process of enacting, comprehensive privacy and data protection statutes, and over a dozen countries have enacted such statutes or updated previous statutes in the past year.[1] Close to home, the first phase of Canada's federal privacy legislation comes into force January 1, 2001, and will become fully effective January 1, 2004. Various provinces are also in the process of reviewing their existing privacy policies and the province of Quebec has had privacy legislation for a number of years. Other countries, which have recently introduced or are in the process of introducing stronger privacy legislation or protection include Denmark, Germany, Spain, Italy, the Netherlands, Austria, the United Kingdom, Mexico,

[1]David Banisar, *Privacy and Human Rights 2000: An International Survey of Privacy Laws and Developments,* published by Electronic Privacy Information Center and Privacy International.

Switzerland, Argentina, and Australia.

2. **What should companies on the Internet be doing to address privacy issues? Is a privacy policy enough? What information should be included in a company's privacy policy?**

The response to this question will vary based on the jurisdiction(s) within which a company's privacy policy is intended to apply. In general terms, a privacy policy alone is not sufficient but is a necessary step in addressing privacy issues. It is also essential that a company ensure that it establish appropriate practices and implementation procedures to comply with its privacy policy and the privacy laws of the relevant jurisdiction(s).

A company intending to address privacy issues should examine its entire business model to determine what personal information is gathered and how it is gathered, stored, and used. A company should ensure it understands why it gathers, uses, or discloses personal information and determine whether it is collecting more information than is necessary, whether it is retaining the information longer than necessary, or whether it is using the information for purposes other than for which it was collected.

A company that wishes to be proactive should then attempt to model its privacy practices in accordance with the requirements of the relevant jurisdiction(s) or, as a starting point, the privacy principles established by the Organization for Economic Cooperation and Development or regional or industrial standards associations. Applicable privacy principles can generally be focused down to a few simple components:

1. *Obtain the informed consent of an individual with respect to the collection, use, and disclosure of their personal information;*
2. *Protect that information both internally and contractually when disclosing that information to third parties;*
3. *Permit individuals to access their personal information, and amend it when necessary or retract their consent; and*

4. *Ensure that the company has a representative who can be contacted by individuals or relevant regulatory authorities.*

These issues should be addressed in both a privacy policy and in implementation procedures. Privacy policies often also address issues such as cookies and information related to minors.

3. **What laws have been passed regarding privacy issues, and what laws are pending that you know of?**

In addition to the information provided in response to question 2, other European Union member nations are presently addressing the need to comply with the Privacy Directive. Japan, Thailand, and South Africa are also expected to pass privacy laws in the near future. Recent developments in the United States are discussed below.

4. **How can companies protect themselves from lawsuits resulting from privacy issues?**

A response to this question is complex and may require a company to comply with the laws in all jurisdictions in which the company is doing business or effecting transactions. However, compliance with a properly crafted privacy policy and ensuring that the company follows appropriate procedures to support that policy will go a long way in protecting the company.

5. **Please comment on the different industries (advertising, health, etc.) that are facing government regulation as a result of privacy issues.**

Many industries including advertising, health, and financial services have specific privacy guidelines through industry associations or through industry specific legislation or regulations. Traditionally, many privacy concerns were initially raised in the context of specific sectors such as the ones listed above. In Canada, the Canadian Marketing Association, Canadian Bankers Association, and the Insurance Bureau of Canada all maintain industry specific privacy guidelines. In the United States, where there is currently no general federal privacy legislation, federal privacy regulation is generally addressed on an industry specific basis such as the Gramm-Leach-Bliley Act that applies new restrictions on how financial institutions can use personal information gathered from customers.

6. **Please comment on the United States and privacy law.**

Finally, one of the most important recent developments in privacy law has been the European Commission approval of the United States safe harbor principles for purposes of compliance with the Privacy Directive. This approval has been the subject of controversy given the European Parliament's resolution to reopen negotiations and the significant criticism of the effectiveness of these principles. The safe harbor creates a voluntary code of conduct for United States companies. Despite the lack of generally applicable national privacy legislation in the United States, the European Commission decision that the safe harbor principles provide "adequate" protection for personal data transferred from the European Union permits certain exchanges of personal information between companies resident in the European Union and the United States. The European Commission has put the United States Department of Commerce on notice that it may seek improvements if the principles do not provide adequate remedies for individuals.

While recent articles have suggested that the next United States congress may pass Internet privacy legislation based around the Federal Trade Commission's privacy principles of consumer notice, access, choice, and security, these reports appear speculative. Despite extensive privacy regulation on an industry basis and media attention on this issue, it is unclear whether there will be any significant movement toward generally applicable federal privacy legislation.

4

Cybermarketing to Enhance the Brand

15 Changing Market Landscapes

Objective:

To focus on changing Internet landscapes and how the scope of competition in the dot-com world is changing as well. Cyberbranders need to grasp the major issues and understand how to outmaneuver competition by providing the best interactive experience and customer service. Topics of interest relating to changing landscapes include the following:

- Five seconds of stability and fifty-five seconds of change
- Lessons from the heavy hitters
- Straightforward examples of gaining customer share
- How cyberbrands are gaining customer share

FIVE SECONDS OF STABILITY AND FIFTY-FIVE SECONDS OF CHANGE

The changing landscape of the Internet has turned the modern world on its side. The digital revolution is characterized by long periods of change and short periods of stability. What can you count on in the new economy? Only 5 seconds of stability and 55 seconds of change that brings forth more technology than one could ever imagine. From the Internet to wireless technology, consumers have additional choices and expect more from the companies in which they invest time, money, and interest. With such rapid growth and so little stability, what can brands expect from the digital economy? A humorous scene from the movie *Meet Joe Black* sums it all up, when Anthony Hopkins and Brad Pitt are at the boardroom table and Pitt's character (Joe Black, representing death) for the first time learns that "in this world *nothing* is certain *except* death and taxes." (Of course, this is also a famous quotation from Mark Twain.) This is still true in the new economy (even though tax law on the Internet is not yet fully enforced).

The digital revolution is characterized by long periods of change and short periods of stability.

Because of shifting landscapes, brands face new challenges daily. The nature of competition has taken on a whole new meaning. It is still critical for a company venturing into cyberspace to understand its target market, consider the strengths and weaknesses of other vendors of products and services in the market, and position the brand with a USP (unique selling proposition) that differentiates it from the likes of any other brand. However, the Internet brings to life the concept of "mega superstores" or "Net-partment stores" that house everything from commerce to stock quotes to varied news content. No longer is the competition just from like products, in similar industries, within the same geographical location.

No longer is the competition just from like products, in similar industries, within the same geographical location.

For instance, with respect to Priceline.com, supermarket chain stores were forced to compete with the cyberbrand's bidding structure. However, at the present time, competition has forced Priceline.com out of the grocery and retail gasoline business. And although bidding on online tickets through Priceline.com is still available, a new competitor has entered the arena. Hotwire.com is forming an alliance with major U.S. airlines to knock Priceline.com right out of the sky. On the Internet, it's not about a single retailer selling a unique product or service. Instead it's about overgrown portals that offer everything from customized products (from A to Z) to customized content.

The rules are being made as fast as the Internet players can make them. Speed to market leads to brand recognition, but not necessarily profit margins.

The rules are being made as fast as the Internet players can make them. Speed to market leads to brand recognition, but not necessarily profit margins.

LESSONS FROM THE HEAVY HITTERS

What are the heavy hitters doing to create stronger brands and a better experience for their users, and how are they dealing with the competition? For starters, the field leaders are eliminating as many competitors as possible early on by joining forces, and in some cases, it's with the enemy. Take Toysrus.com, for instance, which realized its strengths and weaknesses as an e-tailer during the 1999 holiday season. It didn't take another season of misfortune to figure out that a strategic alliance with another powerful, forward-thinking business was necessary. By August 2000, Toys "Я" Us, Inc., announced its co-branded online venture with Amazon. Imag-

...the field leaders are eliminating as many competitors as possible early on by joining forces, and in some cases, it's with the enemy.

ine the implications of the largest toy seller and an Internet giant coming together in holy matrimony (a powerful marriage that benefits both entities). The joint venture, proposed in two phases, was to begin with Phase I, the launch of a toy and video game store in Fall 2000. Phase II was to occur approximately six months out in time with the opening of an online baby products store. The deal made a tremendous amount of sense, with each partner capitalizing on the other's strengths, and both ultimately overcoming their weaknesses together. First, Toys "Я" Us has the infrastructure to manage the inventory, and Amazon has a better grasp on the type of Web site development necessary to facilitate e-commerce, fulfillment of orders, and handling the overall online customer service experience that is friendly and familiar to loyal brand users.[1] This is an ideal example of using a partnership opportunity to increase customer satisfaction by joining two powerful entities together for a synergistic outcome—better experience for the user and e-loyalty to the brand.

Another heavy hitter, General Motors (GM), is forging ahead in the dot-com arena. The company, one of the top three automobile makers, is not taking a back seat to the Internet competition.[2] Autobytel.com has established a recognizable e-brand that allows consumers to find the cars they want at a dealer closest to their locale. However, GM takes the Internet one step further by teaming up with its dealerships to customize cars online for its loyal patrons. Stepping up to the e-commerce plate may be GM's last opportunity to reclaim glory with a position that has slipped at least 30% over the years.[3] GM will no longer be considered that big, slow company. Its e-commerce strategy will reposition the company to be known as big and fast. GM's BuyPower.com site is responsible for online vehicle orders in which customers can place an order on one day and pick up their custom vehicle within two weeks at the nearest brick-and-mortar dealership (GM includes its dealerships as key players in this Internet venture). GM has also proposed another joint venture that would provide consumers with information on other cars outside of the GM make and model. For the number 1 auto manufacturer, this is a courageous move, not to mention a strong statement to its competitors. Consumers would still be able to purchase GM vehicles online, but there would be outside links to other manufacturers' cars.[4]

The heavy hitters are strategizing in a number of ways that extend beyond the traditional principles of marketing. Moving beyond the four P's, these giants are forming strategic alliances with the enemy to capitalize on strengths and weaknesses (combining technological expertise and traditional infrastructure to create an optimum cyberbrand) and, in the case of GM, offering competitive resources to audiences as a part of a business model—a practice that would be unheard of in the bricks-and-mortar world of the twentieth century.

HOW CYBERBRANDS ARE GAINING CUSTOMER SHARE

There are e-businesses that continue to retain customers and attract new ones just by word of mouth alone—by excellent e-service. The market has changed from mass perspective to the one-on-one customer perspective. The Internet fosters customer share. And, the companies that realize that a transformation has occurred, and concentrate on share of customers, are much better off in the digital economy. These are the companies that will outmaneuver their online competitors.[5] Judith McGarry of Drugstore.com believes that cyberbrands are forced to realize early on that in order to survive on the Internet it's more than a marathon; it's a sprint to the finish line.[6] Just as for the traditional companies of years past, on the Internet it's much easier and less costly for a company to keep an existing client happy by providing superior service than it is to solicit business from a new client. There are two types of winners, the first to market, and then the best (in cyberspace, this translates into the brands that provide the best experience).

There are two types of winners, the first to market and then the best (in Cyber space, this translates into the brands that provide the best experience).

KBkids.com and eToys.com are competitors. At first glance, they both appear to be online toy sellers with little variation between

the two brands. With respect to price, they are comparable; for example, the Razor Scooter, by Razor, is priced at $99.99 on both Web sites. These brands have online stores that sell toys, video games, and software and allow users to shop by age. Now, for strengths and weaknesses and value added services. KBkids.com allows visitors to shop by price, brand, and category. KB Toy Stores positions itself as a company that takes the speed of the Internet and combines it with the convenient return policy to any of the 1300 KB Toys Store locations.[7] Then, there is eToys. The e-brand does not have a separate search component on the site to find toys by price, brand, or category, but works into the function of the site an educational component that is unique to the online seller. Discovery Toys has a segmented area of the eToys site that is focused on educational toys that are fun for children. This is a value-added service that illustrates not only the product description but also the child's learning potential when using the toy. eToys touts itself as a company that combines a commitment to excellent customer service and expertise in children's products with the convenience of Internet retailing, in order to deliver a fun and unique experience for online audiences.[8]

The following situation is a true story, and is not intended to show favoritism toward either KBkids.com or eToys.com. It does, however, illustrate a clear example of how superior service prevails and maintains e-brand loyalty.

A Toy Situation

The owner of an advertising, communications, and production firm wants to create a stress-free and fun environment for her employees who work off hours and sometimes around the clock. With the inclusion of chess and checkerboards, a pinball machine, and a box of "squishy" toys to add to the décor (the squishy toys include stress balls for squeezing and rubber frogs that stick when thrown against the wall), the agency environment is friendly, fun, and creative. The owner decides that she wants to purchase mini-basketball hoops, which would be a welcome addition to the company "fun" policy. She goes to KBkids.com with the intent of purchasing mini-basketball hoops for all of her 25 employees (a hoop per cubicle or office). On KBkids.com, a search retrieves a Spalding basketball mini-hoop set that intrigues her. With little product information on the site, the owner calls up the customer service number displayed on her computer screen. "Customer service, this is Randi speaking ..." (the names are changed to protect the innocent). The conversation continues as follows:

> Owner: Hi Randi, I'm wondering if you can help me out. I am thinking about the purchase of several mini-Spalding basketball hoops for our offices, but was unsure as to whether they hang on the wall or clip to a door.
> Randi: Well, I really don't have that information. What you see listed by the product in the site is all I really know about the product. However, you could go to the Spalding site to learn more about their products.
> Owner: Thanks anyway, Randi.

The owner's next action was a quick e-mail to the KBkids.com customer service support center, which asks, "What do you need to know?" She writes,

> "I need to know why Randi could not tell me if the Spalding Miniature Basketball Hoop sticks to a wall or gets attached to a door. She told me to visit the Spalding site to find out more about their products. This is not satisfactory. Basically, I could just order the product from Spalding. Thanks for listening."

Is there a happy ending to this potential customer service nightmare? Yes, a personal e-mail message from a higher-up at KBkids.com that addresses the frustration and concerns of the prospective customer:

> "I apologize for the lack of information you received from Randi. The information we have regarding the products on the Web site would be the same information our customers pull up when they visit our site. Our tool of product description is what information is available on our site. In regard to this product, I personally know that you can wall-mount with a screw or nail and you may also door-mount this product. Again, I apologize for the frustration and lack of information you received."

Based upon the personal response and the level of customer service that is still considered unique to many companies on the Internet, the owner decides that she will make her purchase through KBkids.com. The e-brand just illustrated what it means to win "customer share," and continuance of this type of superior service will lead to winning that Internet marathon.

Trend Micro's NeaTSuite (which includes the product AntiVirus.com) is a competitor of Symantec's Norton AntiVirus 5.0. Both antivirus products protect file servers, e-mail servers, and client PCs, and are certified by the International Computer Security Association (ICSA).[9] With similar scanning features and virus detection options, how do these brands compete? The following scenario illustrates that the winning factor is in the service aspect of the product and the quick treatment of the client. It's a story of the "good" e-brand experience with a service provider (so little is heard about a good experience).

A Computer Virus Situation

A group of authors who work together and pass material back and forth often accidentally circulate a virus through e-mail (every computer user's nightmare). One of the authors realized what had occurred when a message bounced back from his publishing house's corporate deflector shield. But for those less fortunate, the virus got through those small-town servers to wreak havoc. However, with quick thinking the author went to antivirus.com and got a free house call to sweep his PC. He then downloaded a small program and the service swept all the drives through the Internet. The service also cleaned or deleted the virus files it found. The service, which was offered by Trend Micro, Inc., frequently sends the author, by e-mail, updates of all the other viruses circulating and any warning symptoms he should be aware of. For the author, this was a helpful and easy fix that had him writing, again, in no time at all.

The competitive landscape has changed. In the bricks-and-mortar world, stores with like products would compete by location (helped by signs), adequate parking, foot traffic of a mall, traditional marketing tactics, etc. And once the customer is in the store, chances are he makes the purchase based upon the fact that he traveled to the store in the first place. That's not the case on the Internet. No matter how consumers find a Web site, they do not have to stay there. It took only a few seconds to locate the URL or to click there from another Web site. The challenge is keeping customers on the site and providing the experience and value-added service that makes the brand worth using again. In the case of Trend Micro, the timely updates and warning symptom notification are how this brand competes in cyberspace and wins.

STANDING APART FROM THE DOT-COM CROWD

The previous situations are examples of customer service marathon winners, with brands focusing specifically on the individual experience. This just might be the differentiating factor in e-loyalty. Superior service stands out above all of the dot-com noise, and weeds out the winners from the losers and the boys from the men, so to speak. Excellent service is the key to customer share even when the competition is stiff and varied and the marketing noise is thick with dot-com clutter. Service will always be remembered as a crucial part of the brand experience. Unfortunately, according to the Internet consulting firm Digital Idea, only 10 to 15% of online users would remain loyal to a Web site, feeling a significant bond with a brand with the intention of recommending it to a friend.[10] The results of a Gartner Group study revealed that a great deal of customer relationship management (CRM) is just "lip service" on the Internet. By examining the top 50 e-retail sites, Gartner Group discovered in its eService Functionality Study that the scores of the top sites were less than promising, with none of them receiving an excellent or good rating. There's a lot of room for e-service improvement in cyberspace.[11] In fact, Jupiter Communications revealed that there is a discrepancy between expectations and actual satisfaction and that "72 percent of Net surfers say good customer service is important, but only 41 percent of the customer service they received online is sufficient."[12] The

Superior service stands out above all of the dot-com noise, and weeds out the winners from the losers and the boys from the men, so to speak.

The winners of the Internet marathon are the sites that have loyal audiences because they not only fulfill expectations but exceed them.

winners of the Internet marathon are the sites that have loyal audiences because they not only fulfill expectations but exceed them. The old days of pushing products and services to mass audiences are over. The Internet has become the user's stage for experience. Internet users demand that their "stages" be built upon excellent customer service, which leads to cyberbrand loyalty.

So, it's true then, everything is changing. The Internet is changing competition, and competition is changing the Internet, and ultimately, the consumer is in control of who will be the true Internet marathon winners. The cyberbrands that focus on good, consistent, value-added service will prosper. Now, with respect to cyberbrands, competition, and the new economy, maybe the only thing you should count on is good service, taxes, and death.

16 Banner Ad Sustenance in Cyberspace

Objective:

To prove the inherent branding value of banner advertisements, and how despite controversy, banner ads have survived as one of the most popular techniques to drive audience traffic to a Web site. The marketer will be guided by tips and suggestions on the following topics:

- Banner ad survival
- Banner ads serve a purpose
- Banner ad basics
- Elements of design
- Questions to ask in banner ad placement
- Banner ad campaign results

BANNER AD SURVIVAL

News Flash: *According to Nielsen NetRatings, clickthrough rates are down from 2.5% in 1995 to 0.34% in March 2000.* [1]
Headline News: *In July 2000, Jupiter Communications predicts that online advertisers will face challenges in "taking advantage of the Internet as a global advertising medium."* [2]
News at the Top of the Hour: eMarketer *concludes that U.S. banner ad spending will decrease from 83% to 71% by the year 2002.* [3]

These are the banner advertising issues in the news every day illustrating a decline in online advertising revenue. Did someone neglect to tell the vice president of Internet marketing at Accenture (formerly Andersen Consulting) and the CEO of Ernst & Young that banner advertisements are a waste of time and money? After all, both companies post banner ads, as a part of their advertising strategy, in familiar places, such as the *New York Times on the Web*. And did the vice president of marketing at Gateway Computers forget to check the clickthrough statistics from the latest Internet advertising re-

Even though banner ads are the target of controversy, use of the banner is frequent by companies (from the Fortune 500s to the small Internet start-ups).

ports published by the Gartner Group and Nielsen NetRatings? Gateway also spends advertising campaign dollars on the Internet placing banner ads on CNET.com. It's unlikely that Andersen Consulting, Ernst & Young, and Gateway did not do their homework—there's a method to the madness. Even though banner ads are the target of controversy, use of the banner is frequent by companies (from the *Fortune* 500 to the small Internet start-ups). It's been said that banner ads, from any perspective other than branding, are questionable.

Lesson Number 1:

It's the immeasurable branding (the impression registered in a consumer's mind) that provides the banner with life and sustenance. When banners first appeared on the cyberscene, they were a novelty. Indeed, companies were quickly buying high-profile, high-visibility banner ad placements for large advertising campaign dollars. Eventually, the dust began to settle and the banner ad faced the ROI challenge. Marketing professionals had to answer to higher-ups who wanted to know, Just how do clickthrough rates turn into dollars? Banner ads will continue to face that frequently asked ROI question. It's the same question that has been asked by management about space ads for years. However, professionals are learning that the answer lies in the banner as a powerful branding tactic.

Lesson Number 2 *(a word to the wise):*

A banner ad campaign should not constitute a company's entire online branding strategy, just as the Internet is only one communication channel (a powerful one at that) utilized simultaneously with other communication channels for a well-rounded marketing campaign. Banners may not constitute an entire campaign strategy, but they certainly deserve recognition for the space they occupy. *Banners appear where consumers spend time.* However, amid the negative news stories and statistics, the banner ad lives on for a reason. In fact, it thrives with click-and-mortars and e-brands that continue to spend more and more dollars on banner ad campaigns. The negative press will continue to surface, but simultaneously so will the increasing statistics of Web advertising revenues. Thus, the news flash reads: Jupiter sees sharp growth in Web ad revenues from 1999 to 2000, when they

A banner ad campaign should not constitute a company's entire online branding strategy.

will reach over $7 billion. In successive years, growth will remain steady.[4]

BANNER ADS SERVE A PURPOSE

Banner ads serve a specific purpose. Cyberbranders realize that the average consumer recognizes the banner ad—it's that flashing box (sometimes annoying and always a glance away), usually rectangular, or possibly square, that varies in size and price. These highly recognizable banners are extremely visible on a Web page, and in most cases eye-catching by design (regardless of flashing, movement, or interactive media). Banners are registered by the eye and the brain at a mere glance and, whether the consumer realizes it or not, leave a lasting impression. Banners, to the benefit of the brand, automatically appear on a Web page. They are an integral part of the content of a page, unlike television or radio ads, which are not a part of a scheduled pro-

Banners are registered by the eye and the brain at a mere glance and, whether the consumer realizes it or not, leave a lasting impression.

gram. Thus, the consumer runs to the kitchen for a snack as a commercial interrupts a scheduled show or selects a new radio station when an irritating jingle comes on for the fourth time. On the contrary, the banner is there for the viewing until the user clicks on it or navigates to another area of a Web site. In some cases, it's been said that banner ads are annoying for consumers who travel to sites for a specific purpose. Yet the distraction may actually be a useful tactic—consumers tend to remember distractions. On the other hand, the banner ad often intrigues a consumer's curiosity with a question, a discount, or a contest offering. In either case, the fact that the brand is displayed in the banner ad and it sits prominently on a page (one that research identifies as a targeted page that will reach the demographics of the desired audience) reinforces awareness of the brand—its look, feel, and overall message. Via the banner, the brand has increased visibility and has the opportunity to restate a consistent message. In this respect, cyberbranders need to evaluate both the online audiences who click on ads and those who choose not to.[5] Measurement of brand awareness via the banner is not easy, and it is tough for anyone at this point to negatively judge or discredit the value of the banner. Not enough time or analysis has been conducted on the banner ad as an awareness tool.

It is critical for advertisers, especially in cyberspace, who fight tooth and nail for awareness to realize that the banner is an immediate opportunity to receive attention from consumers. The memory of the "impression" is valuable. The consumer may or may not have an interest in clicking on the ad, but at the same time a targeted ad on a Web site is one way to display a repetitive brand message that will eventually lead a consumer to interact with a company. At some point it just may come down to a choice between products, and the banner might be the final factor that leads the consumer to make a decision between Barnes & Noble and Amazon.com, Coca-Cola and Pepsi, or the choice of Tommy Hilfiger over Guess jeans.

> **...the banner is an immediate opportunity to receive attention from consumers.**

The memory of the impression is so valuable that breaking through the banner ad controversy is the fact that in June 2000, TheStandard.com rated banner ad popularity among click-and-mortars and e-brands at 89%. This is the highest percentage rating of all the techniques utilized to drive visitors to a Web site.

BANNER AD BASICS

To look at banner ads in terms of branding makes the most sense. It is imperative to understand everything about the banner—

> **It's the nature of the Internet to impose speed upon the brand, and in the rush to cyberspace, banner ad basics are overlooked.**

from the meaning of the banner buzzwords to where and how ads are placed to achieve an effective cyberbranding campaign. It's the nature of the Internet to impose speed upon the brand, and in the rush to cyberspace, banner ad basics are overlooked. Taking the time to understand the components and measurements of banners proves beneficial in the long run.

Test your knowledge and rate your expertise before moving forward in the development of the banner ad campaign by answering these banner ad basics (Answers in Appendix B):

1. Name the term(s) that describe the number of times a Web page is requested by the server.
2. What is considered the standard file size for the banner ad?
3. The measurement 468×60 pixels represents what size banner?
4. What does CTR stand for?
5. What is the measurement that refers to cost per thousand?
6. The number of responses to a banner ad by the user is the number of times the user does what on the banner?
7. With respect to advertising rates, what is the difference between CTR and CPM?
8. What is a banner ad conversion rate?
9. How do you calculate cost per visitor on a Web site?
10. What is considered average for banner ad rates?

These are the fundamentals of banner ads, the rudiments that deserve careful attention. Success at answering these questions leads to the next step, which is to consider the phases of the banner ad campaign: design, placement, and measurement.

ELEMENTS OF DESIGN

It doesn't matter if the banner ad campaign is developed within the brand's in-house marketing department or if an outside agency prepares the ads and the online media buying. **Design is crucial to the life of the banner ad. The wrong design will leave a lasting negative impression.** It's still necessary to have an understanding of every basic component of the phases of the campaign. Design is crucial to the life of the banner ad. The wrong design will leave a lasting negative impression. Taking the time to leave a favorable impression is as easy as becoming familiarized with these quick tips of banner ad design:

- The banner ad design should be consistent with the brand message.
- The brand's logo must be visible on the banner.
- Animation or movement piques audience interest.
- Banners should contain as little text as possible.
- Web audiences should always be guessing what the ad is all about. Give audiences only enough information for them to "chew on," prompting them to pursue learning more about the brand.
- Bright colors should be used. If the colors of the site of potential placement are known, the banner ad colors should offset the site colors.
- Easy-to-read fonts work best when audiences are glancing quickly. Fancy scripts and letters that run close together are not an advantage to the brand. Font size is also a valuable consideration as text is flashing or only appears momentarily.

...the average banner impression is three or six seconds.

- It is necessary to reveal the text of the banner just long enough for the user to read it before changing ad script to continue with the banner message. Keep in mind that the average banner impression is three or six seconds.
- Steer clear of jumbled designs with too much clutter and activity. A clean banner is the most pleasing to the eye.

QUESTIONS TO ASK IN BANNER AD PLACEMENT

Following the foregoing tips, the banner ad campaign will attract and intrigue audiences to learn more about the brand—the ultimate branding goal. However, in the effort to brand, never underestimate the value of the clickthrough rate (CTR). CTR as a measurement does count, yet may not always lead to the sale of a product or service. CTR is definitely a desired behavior in the progression of the banner ad campaign and moves the user in the right direction—one step closer to interaction with the brand. Companies are struggling with banner ad placements and measurements, CTR versus CPM (Cost Per Measurement), and are not always asking the appropriate questions regarding these rates on a Web site. First, before even considering the actual media buys, it is in the brand's best interest to thoroughly research potential sites to house the banner ad campaign. Then, upon requesting banner ad rates from these sites (for comparative pricing), it is necessary to raise the following questions:

- *What are the page views on the site?* Page views determine the amount of traffic and, in turn, let the advertiser know the possible number of views the banner ad will receive in a specified time period.

- *What is the audience breakdown on the site?* This makes a difference with the CTR. For instance, CTR is higher when the banner is placed on a targeted site, such as a female pharmaceutical product on Women.com. The reverse is also true: lower CTR for the same product ad on a more general site on CNET.com.

- *What is the user return rate on the site?* The more a visitor returns to the site and views an ad additional times, the more likely will the brand capture that visitor's awareness.

- *How many advertisers are on the site?* It is important to find out the number of advertisers to determine the exact positioning and opportunities available on a Web site.

- *Does the banner ad rotate with other ads, or will it capture the ad space alone?* Knowing the scheduled rotation (e.g., six advertisers rotating on the top banner ad of the home page) tied into the page views on the site gives the advertiser an indication of the number of impressions available and how often the banner will be viewed. Having 20 banners rotating on the top banner ad of the home page of a Web site offers less of a chance to be seen than six advertisers rotating on the same space.

- *Is there any reporting software available on the site to track an advertiser's CTR?* The Web site where the ad is placed is responsible for keeping track of its advertiser's clickthrough rate by providing banner ad documentation including how many times the banner ad was "hit" by visitors.

- *Where is banner ad space available on the site?* Is banner advertising available on the home page? Although more expensive, this is the optimal spot and is the gateway to all the other pages. It is also important to inquire which other pages on the site receive heavy user traffic. Run of site (ROS) is less expensive, but often not as visible as other popular pages.

- *Is the banner method on refresh, or does it rotate for the visitor?* If the banner is on a rotating scheduling, then several advertisers will rotate in one ad while one viewer remains on a Web page. Refresh mode is a single banner impression per Web page.

- *Are banner ads on a three-second rotation or six-second?* This is extremely important in the design of the ad, to know if a series of textual messages will be visible long enough for the user to read and understand.

Answering these questions thoroughly will lead the brand to an easier decision regarding banner ad placements in order to receive desired campaign results. More important, *remember that it's a buyer's market and CPM and CTR are negotiable.* The rates on the online rate card are only a starting point. Depending on the Web site and the brand's relevance to that site, there's quite a bit of flexibility. Web sites are still hungry for advertisers, and smaller sites with growing page views will practically give the space away.

BANNER AD CAMPAIGN RESULTS

The banner ad campaign designs are complete. The questions regarding online banner advertising are answered. The media buys are placed. The ads are live and the expectations are high. Now, what about the measurement of the results of the banner ad campaign? As mentioned earlier, it's practically impossible to measure the branding element without going directly to Web site audiences.

> ...it's practically impossible to measure the branding element without going directly to Web site audiences.

Ways to measure the effectiveness of branding for online ad campaigns would be through surveys of viewers to find out their responsiveness to designs and campaign messages, or to ask consumers and/or clients which means of advertising led to the purchase of a product or service. However, to date most of the campaign measurement falls with CTR and cost per sale (CPS). Unfortunately, the likes of the positive banner campaign results often take the backseat to the negative press. For instance, no one was shouting from the rooftops that the women's site iVillage.com received spectacular clickthrough rates, up to 52%, with a banner ad campaign that reached out to women interested in entertainment topics. iVillage.com was able to run a campaign that utilized online advertising to add a "Celebrity Horoscope" on Hollywood.com's "Women in Film" section. The banner ads placed in this section of Hollywood.com allowed its audience to visit iVillage.com and share audience traffic. A combined effort of banner ads throughout the Hollywood.com site along with promotion in weekly member e-mails led to stellar banner ad clickthrough rates for iVillage.com.[6] Another banner ad success story involves the launch of iWin.com, with results that would have heads turning—approximately 3.2 million female visitors on the site. According to Mark Stroman, senior vice president of sales and marketing at iWin.com, the company did its homework. All of the advertising was online, with banner ads tested on over 1000 sites and then placed on 100 sites on a regular basis. As a result of smart online banner ad buys, the results of the campaign included site traffic jumping 30% and a top 40 ranking in MediaMetrix's Web properties.[7]

Measuring banner ad effectiveness can also be calculated from the CPS perspective. In fact, the number of clicks on a banner is not representative of the number of purchases of a product or service. CPS is still heavily relied upon in cyberspace, because in the final review of the clickthrough report, *CTR does not provide ROI*. The only way to differentiate the clickthrough audience and the actual buyers is through sophisticated tracking software. Cookies on a site will make this differentiation for the brand, determining ultimately the best results from ads placed on the winning sites that resulted in sales for the brand.

Of course, CPS is affected by the amount of clicking on the banner by the audience as well as the actual CPM price. Higher CTR and lower CPM rates on a Web site will result in lower CPS (a desired outcome). However, all too often advertisers are quick to place on-line media buys at a CPM rate without negotiating price. In addition, they often do not consider an alternative banner ad pricing structure—the pay per banner ad click method. The pay per click method enables an advertiser to pay only when the ad is clicked on by the user. This method, known as cost per click (CPC), facilitates ad buys that are strictly pay-for-performance. These CPC buys usually fluctuate between $.25 and $.50. At times the CPC method is combined with the CPM model.[8]

Regardless of the model, CPM or CPC, or whether or not evaluation is based on CTR, CPS, or branding, the banner ad is not going to fade away anytime soon. Yes, it's been difficult to prove the correlation between banner ads and branding in the past. However, as new technology surfaces and banner ad strategies advance, more companies will take the time to analyze banner ads as a branding tool. As these companies probe audiences directly, they will find out that impressions do in fact lead to interaction with a brand. The future is bright for banner ads as they change shape, advance with rich, interactive media, and eventually take the form of entertainment as well as an awareness tool for users. The power of banners as a branding tactic also increases as online audiences continue to recognize these flashing boxes. This is not to say that the banner ad controversy will cease. The disbelievers will always have their say. Yet, with respect to branding, no one has concrete evidence to dispute that banner ads are as noticeable

The future is bright for banner ads as they change shape, advance with rich, interactive media, and eventually take the form of entertainment as well as an awareness tool for users.

as other online and offline advertising strategies. As such, and to their benefit, banner ads cannot be turned off or thrown out. The value of direct mail, for example, with a 2% return rate on a campaign, is constantly questioned over the years. With the realization that most direct mail pieces are filed in the "circular file," most professionals still utilize direct mail as a part of the marketing mix. The threat of the circular file does not stop the company from using the direct mail strategy. This is proof that each marketing method faces its own set of trials and tribulations, and in every case there is a method to the madness. The development of the banner ad simply follows suit, and in the long run, it will prevail.

17

Affiliate Marketing for the Future

Objective:

To clarify how affiliate programs extend beyond the standard clickthrough commission program and provide brands with an opportunity to increase exposure, awareness, and sales of a product or service. The affiliate program has suffered from lack of attention in the cyberbranding arena, and now it's time to revisit the strategy and jazz up the program options by considering the following:

- Moving beyond the "traditional" model
- Setting up a winning program
- Implementing a program that attracts affiliates
- Working with affiliates to maximize results
- Jazzing up programs for the future

MOVING BEYOND THE TRADITIONAL MODEL

The advantage of the affiliate model is that it allows for multiple possibilities. There is much to offer both the merchants who initiate affiliate programs and the member affiliate sites that want to become involved in the program. Cyberbrands are just learning to move beyond the basics. As a

Cyberbrands are just learning to move beyond the basics.

result, the following scenario is all too familiar. When the owners of a click-and-mortar enter their advertising agency's office for a strategy meeting, the affiliate program is thrown on the table for open discussion. The agency stands by the affiliate program, pointing out the success of the Amazon model for the following reasons: (1) it's the industry standard, (2) it gives affiliate members anywhere from a 5% commission on up to a 15% commission, and (3) Amazon boasts over 400,000 affiliates in its program. The company's executive team hems and haws over the value of this strategy with questions like, How much business could we possibly obtain from continuing this program, and how many more resources will have to be directed toward program maintenance? The bottom line—is it really worth the effort? The agency does not have any hardcore, convincing, jazzy stories to persuade the executive team about the real value of affiliates, only the basic facts. As a result, the group does not reach a definitive answer. It moves to the next item on the agenda.

When Joel Gehman, the author of the article "What Is Affiliate Marketing," attended International Institute of Research's (IIR) Online Affiliate Conference, he was somewhat surprised. Conference participants asked panel members to discuss "the basics" of affiliate programs.[1] It's the new economy, the twenty-first century, and the hype is still centered on the basics. The premise behind the conference—to bring forth cutting-edge strategy; to listen intently to industry experts discuss their views on the direction and future of affiliate marketing. Instead of futuristic tactics and enthusiasm, there was nothing more than simple, straightforward, rudimentary elements. Why? A simple answer—because cyberbrands are still grasping the basics, and rightly so. It's understandable that professionals grasp technology at varying speeds. Of course, learning the basics is a must, and will elicit the program's true potential.

SETTING UP A WINNING PROGRAM

Moving beyond the basics does not mean sidestepping the basics. The first set of affiliate programs, as demonstrated by the early contenders (do they have to be named?), focused on the basic

Moving beyond the basics does not mean sidestepping the basics.

elements and received consideration from two perspectives: the merchant side and the affiliate side. The essential considerations for *merchants* developing a program included:

- Having a secure domain name (although this is very obvious), one that is uncomplicated and has brand recognition.

- Possession of a valuable and reputable product or service that will attract audiences from an affiliate's site.

- A thorough clickthrough tracking system that allows merchant to calculate commission payments and run reports for affiliate members.

- The desire to share the wealth, which must be a fair portion of a sale. Five percent is a bit on the low side (without any other incentives), and with all of the many programs surfacing on the Net, affiliates are looking for the most attractive package.

- Designation of an affiliate manager or team (depending upon the scope of the program) to work with affiliate members and to analyze results for smoother operation of the program.

(www.webtechniques.com, June 2000[2])

The necessary considerations for *affiliates* interested in joining a program are the following:

- The very obvious: a functional Web site to link to a merchant site.

- Belief in the value of the product or service being offered by a merchant site. Whatever you put on your company's Web site is an automatic reflection of the brand.

- A feel for the navigational system and functionality of the shopping cart process (from the number of steps to get to the checkout, all the way to the responsiveness of customer service for inquiries) on the merchant's site to make sure that your audience does not get lost, annoyed, or perplexed when trying to make a purchase.

- Making sure that the merchant's offering appears on the appropriate pages of the Web site. The merchant kiosk should be relevant to the content on a page.

- Being choosy about the number and type of programs. The last thing a cyberbrand needs is clutter on a clean and easy-to-read site.

- Being sure that the program links from the affiliate site directly to the merchant product pages. Sending your audi-

ence to the merchant's front door might be frustrating and confusing. Avoid sending consumers on a wild goose chase.

- Whether the merchant requires a fee from an affiliate to participate in the program. If so, don't bother with the affiliate registration—most programs are free!
(Ibid[3])

IMPLEMENTING A PROGRAM THAT ATTRACTS AFFILIATES

There are four key elements to the success of an affiliate program (this holds true for the traditional models as well as the jazzed-up, futuristic ones):

1. No one benefits from a skimpy program—neither the merchant nor the affiliate members. The decision to move forward and take on affiliates is the decision to build a program utilizing the proper resources. The merchant site must have a team of professionals who are able to guide the program and work side by side with affiliate members. The days of tossing the program to an IT employee who is juggling other responsibilities are over. The team's ultimate goal is to increase the traffic to the Web site and the number of purchases on that site. *Affiliate programs do not function successfully without supervision and proper attention from dedicated managers.* Forrester Research reported in its "New Affiliate Marketing Models" study that most companies, up to 50%, dedicate two or more employees to manage an affiliate program.

No one benefits from a skimpy program—neither the merchant nor the affiliate members.

2. The merchant site must invest in a reliable tracking program, of which there are several. These affiliate management packages usually include software to set up a shopping cart, a third-party processing system, e-mail list management, IP address and cookie tracking, as well as tiered commission rates. A few of the well-known affiliate management packages can be researched and located at the following Web addresses:[4]

www.theaffiliateprogram.com
www.myaffiliateprogram.com
www.cybertrakker.com
www.affiliatetrackingsoftware.com
www.groundbreak.com.

There are a number of software options. A word to the wise: Prices range from a couple of hundred dollars to thousands of dollars as a base price, and then there is an additional monthly charge. Research your options carefully and pay the higher price for management software only if your program warrants it. If an e-brand answers to investors, advertisers, affiliates, and an in-house marketing team, you will need to know all of the profile, demographic, and tracking information. Thus, the larger end management system is required.

3. It is necessary to distinguish affiliate member program levels. Perhaps that means a rating system of 1 to 4 stars, similar to that of a movie or hotel rating system. Or you might use the gold, silver, and bronze Olympic hierarchy that will differentiate the top affiliates (the members of the program that drive the most traffic and whose audience makes the most purchases) from the lower-tier group (unfortunately, they may comprise a larger percentage of your affiliate members). A first objective is to set up a system that rewards top affiliates with bonuses, higher commission, and

> ...set up a system that rewards top affiliates with bonuses, higher commission, and other attractive incentives. Keep these affiliates happy by rewarding their efforts as they drive traffic to your site.

other attractive incentives. Keep these affiliates happy by rewarding their efforts as they drive traffic to your site. The next objective is to move every lower-rated affiliate member to a higher plateau. Constant communication with affiliates is achieved through newsletters and e-mail programs. This type of ongoing communication provides them with the tips and suggestions that allow the affiliate to earn more from the program. As of March 2000, sites including Reel.com and Lending Tree Brand Network were giving new banners on a weekly basis and $12 per lead, respectively.[5]

4. Launch the affiliate program and make some noise. If potential affiliates don't know that the program exists, there is little need to allocate the resources to have a program in the first place. Of course, start with your existing customers. Setting up links, for starters, in the many program directories is crucial for attracting members.[6] Listings can be submitted manually in these directories or an outsourced company, e.g., Affiliate Announce can submit listings. There are a number of helpful directory sites: (1) PlugInGo Affiliate Network has a two-tier affiliate program directory. (2) Associatecash.com lists, rates, and reviews associate and affiliate programs. (3) Affiliate Options allows the prospective affiliate member to search for programs that are either one- to two-tier, multiple-tier, or by category of product. (4) ClicksLink.com has an extensive program directory including apparel, electronics, sports, and software to name a few. ClicksLink.com allows interested parties to register for the affiliate program through the search directory.

WORKING WITH AFFILIATES TO MAXIMIZE RESULTS

Put yourself in the shoes of the affiliate you would like to attract. Reverse roles if you must. Start thinking of what you would want to get out of a program. Is it a higher commission? What about a bonus check per referral? Would you like a free banner ad in a prime location on the merchant's site? Is an e-mail sponsorship opportunity on the merchant's newsletter appealing? Perhaps it might be a matter of sending your affiliates a small token of your appreciation (mugs, T-shirts, hats, or other promotional items) as another way to say thank you for a job well done. It might be one or all of these incentives. The affiliate manager plays a key role in determining the likes and dislikes of an attractive program, and understanding the preferences of the members is critical. The key to a successful program is to understand what affiliates are looking for and to really push these positive relationship-building tactics. Strategies that are not creating better relationships with affiliates should be reevaluated and redirected to promote better program performance. Listening to the affiliates, and what their thoughts are about a program, makes the difference. The affiliate manager is not only a professional responsible for smooth strategic operations to maximize results, but is also the primary customer care representative who takes the time to listen and respond to any member inquires. Shawn Collins, author of "Communication 101 for Affiliate Managers," gives some good tips about communication. Collins, as an affiliate manager for ClubMom, Inc., and the founder of the New York Affiliate Manager's Coalition, makes it a point to respond to affiliates within a 24-hour time period, every day of the week.[7] Collins also started an e-group, which is basically a focus group using affiliate–members. Treat the affiliates as if they were the members of your sales team. Affiliates need to be guided by a sales manager, must understand the company's offerings, must be constantly updated with company information and promotions, and should be treated as an outside entity that has an extremely important function—a communicator of the cyberbrand. Would you hire a sales team and not train them? Absolutely not!

The key to a successful program is to understand what affiliates are looking for and to really push these positive relationship-building tactics.

Another tactic to get the program "stirring" is publicity. Take off your marketing hat for a moment and think public relations (free promotion from a third party). Let the media know that you have a success story to tell about an affiliate program. Case studies are an excellent tool to getting noticed. Select the top affiliates in the program. Ask them to participate in a public relations campaign that highlights the affiliate–merchant relationship and how the affiliate has reached a top level. Information of this type should be forwarded to editors of advertising, marketing, and Internet publications, to start. These publications are interested in sharing with their readers the ways to jumpstart a successful program. In addition, generating news releases on a monthly basis naming new affiliates (especially relationships with well-known e-brands or click-and-mortar brands), and any interesting reward system that is devised for revealing program growth, is another tactic for getting the program and the cyberbrand in print. Public relations is a win–win situation for both the merchant and the affiliate member. Gathering information for success stories or news releases is not particularly time-consuming and ultimately leads to reliable third-party endorsements and greater awareness for a well-executed affiliate program.

JAZZING UP PROGRAMS FOR THE FUTURE

Affiliate programs usually start with a commission program. But there are many cyberbrands developing jazzier programs to attract and keep their affiliate members satisfied (because they extend beyond the traditional model). Take Commission Junction, otherwise known as the CJ Network (www.cj.com), which allows affiliate members to benefit in a number of ways. Of course, CJ Network has the successful click-through lead program that enables affiliate members to receive a commission on each lead generated through the affiliate's site. However, CJ Network also provides an affiliate the opportunity to place targeted advertising banners its Web site to drive e-commerce revenues. CJ Network

> ... there are many cyberbrands developing jazzier programs to attract and keep their affiliate members satisfied (because they extend beyond the traditional model).

works with over 1,000 merchants from which the affiliate member can select banners suitable to site content. For every banner ad placed, the affiliate has the chance to receive $2.00 for each new lead transaction and then a continuous 5% commission for the length of the affiliate partnership. CJ Network is listed among the top affiliate programs according to the affiliate program directory, top10affiliates.com. CJ Network is cited for its two-tier program as well as opportunities to engage in sweepstakes, "free-stuff," and Lotto.[8]

At Cruel World (www.cruelworld.com), a Web site that is revolutionizing the online job search, the affiliate program is not even based upon a commission of sales. Cruel World has experienced recruiting specialists who use cutting-edge technology to match mid- to senior-level opportunities with interested and qualified professionals.[9] Cruel World's mission is to help professionals "work happily ever after." In its quest to fill job positions, it looks to its affiliate members for potential recruits. Cruel World specifically targets cyberbrands that attract a business professional audience of software developers—a select audience. The premise behind the program is to make money—$2.00 per user from an affiliate site that clicks through and fills out a career profile, which is confidential and free, as explained on the site. No mess, no fuss, just an easy way to make money with no purchase necessary.

Vstore.com has an interesting affiliate program. Vstore.com invites small businesses and individuals to open up their own store, stating, "You've got a great idea. We've got the products, the services, and the e-commerce savvy to make it more profitable...."[10] Vstore.com shows would-be merchants (who in reality are affiliates) comparisons between its affiliate program and those of Amazon, CDnow, Barnes & Noble, and FogDog. One notable comparison: Vstore.com gives commissions ranging from 5% to 25% on sporting goods (for the first sale and every sale) as compared with other affiliate programs that give higher commissions based upon a sales amount. At Vstore.com, there is a set commission for each product the "merchant" chooses to sell. There is also a 7% to 15% commission on return visitors who purchase as well. Another benefit is the program's payout system, which is awarded quarterly as long as the merchant has a $10 minimum commission (most quarterly payouts have to exceed $100).

Last, Lobster Net in Maine (www.lobsternet.com) has an appealing program. The Web site, which offers a Down East lobster feast, provides its affiliates with a 5% commission on gross sales (not net, but gross). And the lobster gift basket commissions are way above the $.50 commission (average orders at ProActive sites are $250). As Lobster Net puts it, "We're talking real money."[11]

Affiliate programs have come a long way, but still have a long way to go. Merchant sites are concentrating on what would make a better program and how to satisfy affiliates. They are realizing that an affiliate program, in and of itself, is an extension of the sales team. The communication, information, and attention paid to the affiliate member are to the benefit of the cyberbrand. At the same time, affiliates are realizing that they have options including commissions and then some. The most attractive programs have the higher-tier payout scale, promotions, sweepstakes, bounties, referral programs, public relations, and set dollar amounts for just directing a visitor in the right direction. Affiliate programs will move into the future with stronger affiliate management teams, better tracking systems, and better reporting options to analyze program successes. There will be more information available than ever before (this comes naturally with the progression of the Internet and the cyberbrand). That means that the next time the click-and-mortar meets with

Affiliate programs have come a long way, but still have a long way to go.

the agency and the affiliate program is thrown out on the table for open discussion, there will be a celebration of the affiliate program as the jazzier programs surface and are recognized by more cyberbrands.

18 Driving Traffic on the Cyberhighway

Objective:

To reinforce the necessity of well-rounded marketing strategies both online and offline to support the cyberbrand. Although the Internet has tremendous reach as a communication channel, it is one medium in an entire branding campaign. Cyberbranders fare best by understanding the following:

- Communicating to suit the new-economy lifestyle
- Using more vehicles for more reach and greater impact
- Getting cyberattention the "traditional" way
- Moving out of the box

COMMUNICATING TO SUIT THE NEW-ECONOMY LIFESTYLE

Reaching the customer is the number one priority. Even the most Internet-savvy individual does not lead an existence chained to a desk viewing a computer screen or strapped to a wireless device. A Worldcom advertisement that appeared in the September 11, 2000, issue of *Business Week* states, "The siren's song of the Internet gets more alluring everyday. And as a member of the chorus, we're not about to tell you the Internet isn't a tool your business needs. It's just not the only tool your business needs."[1] Although this quote comes from a different context (more from a technological perspective than a marketing one), it's thought-provoking and draws attention to the reality that many communication tools are available.

Reaching the customer is the number one priority.

The following two scenarios are a representation of life on the go in the digital economy and the filtering of messages via many communication vehicles:

Scenario I:

Picture this—A calorically charged man with more scalp than hair, in his mid-40s. They call him Joe. He is an average type of guy who stumbles out the door each morning with a cup of coffee in one hand and a briefcase in the other. Joe's tie is usually undone because he can fix it by the time he reaches his office. With a piece of toast in his pocket, Joe runs to the bus stop. While waiting for the number 194 to arrive, he buys a daily newspaper, eats his toast, and then reads for the 45-minute ride to work. Joe arrives, just on time, and is bombarded by the stimuli of the big city—lights, billboards, and posters. Once at work, Joe turns on his computer and his radio (for sanity) and conducts his normal daily 9-to-5 schedule. He returns home on the same number 194 bus that he took in the a.m. The minute Joe gets home he turns on the television and settles into his nightly routine.

> Question: Where does Joe go to find the next "big" thing that will impact his life?
> Answer: Joe needs more than a flash piece and a banner ad (and he needs a life).

Scenario II:

Picture this—Mary grabs her two-year-old in one arm and her five-year-old by the hand, and checks to make sure a milk bottle is in her pocket as she scurries out the door. Once in the car, she turns on the radio, looks in the rearview mirror at both her children, then tilts the mirror her way and attempts to fix her hair and put on lipstick. On the way to school, Mary passes other buses, bus stops, and local merchant signs. She gets to school and kisses her child goodbye. On the way home, she stops at a coffee shop and watches a cable television program as she waits for her order. On the way out she also grabs Self magazine. And once she is finally at home, Mary plops her toddler in front of the television and turns on the computer to check out Self magazine's Web site. By lunchtime, the routine repeats itself when she picks up her kindergartner from school.

Question: Mary, Mary, quite too busy, is it fair that you have no time to download?

Answer: Mary needs more than an online opportunity to be reached during the course of her very busy day.

(PFS Marketwyse[2])

USING MORE VEHICLES FOR MORE REACH AND GREATER IMPACT

For each scenario, there are at least 10 missed opportunities for a cyberbrand to reach either Joe or Mary. And in all seriousness, cyberbrands need to grasp the urgency of utilizing offline

> ... cyberbrands need to grasp the urgency of utilizing offline marketing strategies to increase brand awareness and drive traffic to a Web site.

marketing strategies to increase brand awareness and drive traffic to a Web site. There is every indication from the two scenarios of Joe and Mary that the following factors come into play:

1. Work and play patterns of the average consumer in the new economy are fast-paced.

2. Joe and Mary contribute to the rising statistics and research findings from consumer reports on daily media intake.

3. Joe and Mary represent audience fragmentation, based upon the number of communication vehicles they encounter in the course of their busy days and on the division of their attention spans, given the media choices in the digital economy.
(ICONOCAST, June 2000[3])

First, to address the way audiences deal with the busy new-millennium lifestyle. Consumers are proficient at multitasking. Examples of multitasking are present when Joe eats a piece of toast and runs to the bus stop and when he reads a newspaper as he waits for the bus. Signs of multitasking are present in Mary's hectic schedule when she puts on her lipstick, fixes her hair, and drives the car all at the same time. Yes, this is the true essence of multitasking, so familiar to professionals, nonprofessionals, and just about every human creature known to mankind. On a higher plateau is the concept of "multimedia tasking,"[4] which takes multitasking to a new level and is a phenomenon of an ambidextrous and technologically advanced society. Multimedia tasking is the ability for Joe to turn on his computer and complete his work while he listens to the radio. It also occurs when Mary has the television on in the room where she reads her *Self* magazine. There are many communication vehicles from which the consumer receives valuable messages. And, when

There are many communication vehicles from which the consumer receives valuable messages.

it comes down juggling the requirements of a busy lifestyle, multimedia tasking is becoming a preferred method of operation.

Now for the multimedia tasking facts. According to Erdos & Morgan's 2000 study, 73% of the study participants watch television and read a magazine simultaneously. Also according to the study, 40% of the respondents use a computer and listen to the radio, and only 27% use the computer and watch television at the same time.[5]

No longer can a brand rely on just one mass medium to spread a message to an audience (as in the historical days of television networks capturing over 90% of consumer reach). The same principle holds true of the cyberbrand. Cyberbrands cannot solely focus on the Internet as a main source of communication to reach audiences. According to the 1999 *eAdvertising Report,* Volume II, "While the Internet is growing rapidly, it will never totally supplant advertising in traditional vehicles."[6] Cyberbrands are struggling to rise above the clutter and combat a diffused attention span. They just want to be heard and must do so by relying on clever online and offline strategies that add to a diverse line of attack.

What is the most powerful mode of attack to deal with a diffused attention span and be able to drive traffic to a Web site? Although television, radio, and print advertising are proven strategies because they are visual and engaging (and can incorporate a URL address into a message), even these vehicles are saturated with dot-com noise. The cyberstrategies are popular too (although it's not recommended to use a cyber-only campaign), and a natural part of the dot-com existence. E-mail, viral marketing, search engine registration and keywords, banner ads, etc., are all naturally associated with the online brand. But what makes a campaign interesting, different, and, above all, something that makes the brand stick in the consumer's mind? A unique combination of cyber and offline strategies, and that means, of course, not necessarily focusing on the obvious. The real difference lies (1) in the many interesting ways messages are communicated and (2) how the strategies of today have a heavier emphasis on out-of-the-box thinking, event and guerrilla marketing tactics, and strong public relations efforts (which take root

Cyberbrands are using the popular, proven strategies with a bit of zest, even if these tactics might be considered somewhat risqué or off the wall or were even unheard of in the twentieth century.

from the good, old-fashioned, traditional methods that really create some noise). Cyberbrands are using the popular, proven strategies with a bit of zest, even if these tactics might be considered somewhat risqué or off the wall or were even unheard of in the twentieth century. This is the subtle but important difference between being heard (and possibly diffused) and being noticed (and absorbed subconsciously) above and beyond the clutter.

GETTING CYBERATTENTION THE "TRADITIONAL" WAY

Getting cyberattention the "traditional" way means a unique mixture of communication vehicles, even if the brand's existence is completely online. Letstalk.com launched its campaign with a focus on guerrilla marketing, which is the term coined by Jay Conrad Levinson describing marketing events that are more theatrical, shrewder, and less expensive than the conventional communication strategies.[7] As an online retailer of wireless phones, Letstalk.com created a national buzz with what its agency referred to as an "alternative" plan. As a part of a guerrilla marketing effort, the company created a pseudopolitical campaign, with a fictional character by the name of "Uncle Cell," for the purpose of reaching consumers on an intimate level. Professional actors dressed as Uncle Cell visited cities across the United States wearing purple-and-yellow striped outfits, with white wigs and long white beards. A motorcade ran the streets of Washington, D.C., with a yellow Cadillac and yellow-and-purple motorcycles. The purpose of the event was for Uncle Cell to stop pedestrians, have them answer survey questions, and reward consumers with Letstalk.com promotional items including mobile telephones, accessories, and coupons. The guerrilla marketing campaign turned into numerous public relations opportunities on 40 television and radio stations to discuss Letstalk.com.[8] That's the way to rise above the clutter.

> Getting cyberattention the "traditional" way means a unique mixture of communication vehicles, even if the brand's existence is completely online.

The director of marketing of AssociationCentral.com needed a clever strategy to enlist the many American associations (there are over 135,000) in its directory for a small fee of $19.95 to receive a general site listing. If the executives who head these associations are not at the stage of surfing the Web to gather information, what is the best way to reach them and sign them up for the program? With the knowledge that a great number of the country's associations are headquartered in the nation's capital, the director decided to launch a campaign that would have association heads clicking to register. The campaign was a twofold effort. The first effort focused on positioning visible posters around the five local subway stations in Washington, D.C. (executives use Washington's Metro public transportation). The other part of the campaign centered on the radio and reaching executives during early morning and evening drive times. The radio spots appeared on National Public Radio affiliate stations and local radio stations. The director was extremely pleased with the results of the campaign when at various conferences she was approached about AssociationCentral.com by interested executives who remembered the posters and were familiar with the radio commercials. There's nothing terribly glitzy about the strategy, but certainly a good example of a simple and cost-effective campaign to draw attention to a cyberbrand.[9]

Reflect.com is an online retailer of lotions and potions and beauty wonders for women. Executives working on the marketing campaign of this dot-com wanted to "…distinguish the newcomer [Reflect.com] from its rivals by stressing the customized products sold at the site…."[10] As a result, the advertising campaign is somewhat "quirky," with print illustrations that use humor and are whimsical. The ads assert that it's not about being a supermodel (because supermodels are under contract and have to wear specific products dictated by their contracts). Instead, it's about being women, "real-looking" women (also reflected in the illustrations of the ads), making choices because they are free to create what they like and not what is dictated. The ads appear for the "beauty-involved" in notable magazines including *Vogue, Allure, Self,* and *Elle,* to name a few. Reflect.com's campaign is an example of effective advertising, a bit on the quirky side, all to benefit the cyberbrand and drive traffic to its Web site.

MOVING OUT OF THE BOX

It's not difficult at all to think of a handful of commercials, print ads, or radio advertisements that pinpoint thought-provoking issues and use visuals that would have shocked twentieth-century branders and consumers. Some of the out-of-the-box cyberbrands are making noise. Bluefly.com's print **Some of the out-of-the-box cyberbrands are making noise.** advertisement is clever, with a young man wrapped in a towel (it appears as if he has just showered) and a young woman sitting on a chair in her underwear mesmerized by her laptop screen (she's relaxed and logged onto Bluefly.com). The ad leads the consumer to believe that visiting Bluefly.com is just as satisfying as smoking a cigarette, let's say, after being intimate with that special someone. Then, there's the UPS commercial, which aired in September 2000, with an older woman pulling skimpy women's underwear out of a box (this is definitely not your usual UPS commercial) that was shipped to her by UPS. The commercial announcer says, "You ordered online...." Last, is the truth.com television commercial that shows beautiful people enjoying the sun and the surf when people start dragging body bags onto the beach, trampling the sunbathers. The "nonsmoking youth of today" are pulling the bags over the sand and lining them up. The last scene shows a graveyard of body bags with one living youth left asking, "Does any body need lotion?" A person sitting in the lifeguard chair is holding up a piece of driftwood with the message, "What if cigarette ads told the truth?"

And it's not difficult at all to find those cyberbrands that are *way* out of the box. Safesense.com is the perfect example. Safesense.com is an online retailer of condoms and related products, home tests, books, and videos. The Web site aims to inform visitors about safe sex and allows them to purchase items in a manner that is private, convenient, and much less embarrassing than trips to the drugstore.

...it's not difficult at all to find those cyberbrands that are *way* out of the box.

With cyberpartners that include Durex and Dr. Drew, the online sex therapist and the well-known doctor who appears on CBS's hit show "Big Brother," Safesense.com is on its way to becoming the preferred condom e-retailer. From the onset Safesense.com wanted a marketing campaign that was purely event-driven. Its guerrilla marketing events were to include "waking up a sleepy American town" with the highest per capita pregnancy or AIDS statistics by donating over 1500 condoms to its residents. And what's even more eye-opening is the manner in which they wanted the condoms presented: with a helicopter that drops the condom packages from midair, with a news tip-off to the local television stations and press. There were other way out-of-the-box guerrilla marketing plans. Safesense wanted to drive across America in a Volkswagen Bug with the Safesense.com Girls (who all practice safe sex). The Bug would travel across the country informing students at colleges and universities about the Safesense.com "Don't Catch the Bug" campaign. And better yet, the Volkswagen would have Velcroed condoms attached for any interested parties to grab as a free sample.

Safesense.com uses "shock" for a reason—the sake of education. With every promotional effort, the cyberbrand enforces education about sex in a professional as opposed to an offensive manner. Even the cyberbrand's media kit rises above the clutter—not only are business cards included, but each recipient receives a free condom that comes with the kit. For Safesense.com, out-of-the-box is the only way to cut through the clutter (even though they say that sex sells).

The important points to remember are that cyberbrands need to extend branding beyond the Internet and that online/offline strategies drive traffic to a Web site. Whether the strategy is a simple or a quirky one or that way out-of-the-box thinking by the new breed

> ...cyberbrands need to extend branding beyond the Internet and that online/offline strategies drive traffic to a Web site.

of branders, the patterns for branding in the twenty-first century are established. Consumers will get busier, the clutter will get thicker, and attention spans will be more diffused. This is only the beginning for the cyberbrand, so choose those communication vehicles carefully and rack your brains for clever, out-of-the-box thinking, because there's a long road of noise ahead.

Expert Viewpoint

Interactive Technology Still Needs Offline Methodology: An Interview with WILL Interactive

Sharon Sloane and Lyn McCall founded WILL Interactive, Inc., in 1994. Under their guidance and direction the company forged ahead quickly from a training, consulting, and instructional technology business to a high-tech product–based business with the development of CD-ROMs and other interactive programs. These programs provide users with virtual-experience interactive movies where personal lifestyle choices determine the outcomes. The interactive movies are a cross between a feature film and a video game. Players make decisions that alter the storyline every 30 to 40 seconds. WILL launched its Web site, www.willinteractive.com, in 1996 to attract cyberaudiences interested in the use of its educational and consumer software programs online. For WILL, the Internet was an excellent vehicle to promote its brand, yet the company still relied on offline communication to drive traffic to its Web site.

In an interview, Sloane discussed how the virtual-experience movies focus on educating users and altering high-risk behaviors. WILL Interactive software products run the high-risk behavior gamut and include everything from binge drinking and unplanned pregnancy, to substance abuse and violence. "These unique educational products reach the youth population in order to prevent them from getting involved in these types of problematic behaviors," states Sloane. "And, they have been shown to work in independent studies by Boston University and Walter Reed Institute of Research," she adds. WILL patented an interactive behavior modification system that corners the market on the use of virtual-experience movies to reduce high-risk behavior. Although www.willinteractive. com is an effective forum, the interactive movies are also delivered on CD-ROMs, PCs, and other technological formats. The virtual experience software known as VEILS (Virtual Experi-

ence Interactive Learning Software) is a methodology that provides viewers with lifestyle choices in which a simple yes or no response could lead to their happiness or their demise (will the user make the choice to drink another beer, and if so, what will occur?). This technique of decision-making training is tracked, and choices are analyzed for educational purposes.

WILL's Web site is one of the main communication vehicles, and with the use of Webisodes (Web episodes), audiences are engaged in interactive learning tools. However, the Web site alone is not enough to reach WILL's professional and consumer audiences. WILL, faced with several challenges, devised a marketing campaign with the underlying premise that, "Wherever they [an audience] are, that's where we need to be," explained Sloane. "And, whatever kind of technology they need, we must have it," she added. Knowing fully that the Internet and the use of Webisodes for a cyberaudience to watch is not enough, WILL focuses on several communication strategies to reach new-economy audiences, including the following:

■ Kiosks installed in youth centers (this was a testing ground for one of

WILL's first products, Interactive Nights Out 1)

- Shopping mall and movie theater kiosks to replace the use of video games for young adults
- Pilot studies and market research programs at various organizations, such as Walter Reed Army Institute of Research
- Trade show and convention exhibits to display CD-ROM products
- Infomercials that advertise WILL's product line on cable television
- Public relations strategies to attract media attention (which resulted in coverage by local television network affiliate stations)

As a result of WILL's offline marketing effort, along with its strong cyberpresence and the licensing of Webisodes to its partner organizations, the company has secured several high-profile working relationships with the FBI and the United States Army to produce training software products.

Sloane's final thoughts focused on WILL's initiative to accommodate customers regardless of where they are on the technology continuum. According to Sloane, "This is the type of visual media that needs to be viewed in order to be truly understood and appreciated—talking about an interactive movie or trying to describe it is not enough. We find any way that we can at WILL [offline or cyber] to get the virtual training programs into the hands of our users. Once they experience the programs personally, they get 'addicted' to them."

JOBS.COM: THE SUCCESS OF BANNERS

Jobs.com is claiming its stake in the online recruitment arena. The company, based in Dallas, Texas, is a cyberbrand that leverages the power of technology and the use of banner advertisements to drive job seekers and employers to its Web site. According to Dave O'Neill, Vice President of Marketing, Jobs.com enables Web visitors to search for new opportunities to create professional resumes and "manage their careers." The company is attracting large corporate entities through the use of banner ads and offline marketing activities that drive traffic to these banners. O'Neill, with a background in computers and working with *Fortune* 500 companies, joined the Jobs.com team with the belief that cyberbranding is an effective method. "I remember viewing a CNBC program and agreeing that cyberbranding is the most effective method; it's the only branding that has eye-and-hand coordination," stated O'Neill. He discussed at length how cyberbranding the Jobs.com site has its challenges and rewards based upon entrance into a competitive marketplace, the nature of the online audiences, and technological advances that continue to add dimension to the digital realm.

The Power of the Banner

Believing in the power of the banner advertisement, Jobs.com offers banner advertising on its site (tied to other promotional packages) for corporations and businesses looking to attract interested job candidates. "Jobs.com is particularly successful with its clickthrough rates—as high as 45%," stated O'Neill. He further explained that for Jobs.com, the power of the banner for maximum effectiveness depends upon the following:

- Placing banners in the top right-hand corner.

- Recognizing that there should be an obvious tie-in between banner content and branding.

- Creating color schemes so banner advertisements stand out on a page.

- Being careful not to over-advertise and clutter a Web page.

- Avoiding the least effective spot for a banner advertisement, which is the bottom left-hand corner of a Web page.

Banner Ad Benefits

For Jobs.com, banner advertising is a serious business, and the company is treating it as such. Jobs.com has developed a 15-page manual on how to treat its own logo in the scope of banner advertising. "After all, being a guest on someone's site, you are recognized by your logo," said O'Neill. "And, although people may say that they generally do not like banners, they are actually helpful in the job-hunting process," he further explained.

Jobs.com sells banners to companies, and then ties the advertising, with a click of the mouse, to an area of the Jobs.com site that has testimonials for various corporate sponsors. Jobs.com is very much into utilizing rich media and finds that this interactivity provides a new way for the job-seeker to participate on the site. Through Jobs.com, a company, such as Honeywell, with a fixed budget, can retain a three-month contract and have a banner ad to lead a user to both a video and audio testimonial on Jobs.com. "The benefit of the on-line testimonial is to reduce misconceptions between employers offering jobs and prospective employees," stated O'Neill. He added that a company places a great deal of effort into the hiring and training of an employee and then to lose that employee is extremely costly to the company. The Jobs.com online

testimonials set better expectations between employers and employees. For instance, Jobs.com has Cruise West as a testimonial advertiser with the following campaign: first is the banner ad, "Be a part of the Love Boat Cruise"; second is the area of the site with the testimonial, which includes a 30-second video clip with footage of real people working on the ship to reflect the job being offered by Cruise West. The video and personal testimony show the job criteria and set better expectations. Clearly, the banner advertisements on the Jobs.com site have proven to be the driving factor that gets jobs seekers to review company testimonials.

Other Marketing Strategies Tie into Banner Advertisements

With the many banner advertisement offerings on Jobs.com (including run of site banners all the way to specialized placement), the company uses its affiliation with CBS and six different radio stations on the West Coast to enhance its cyberbranding effort. When these radio spots run on CBS affiliate stations, announcements include, "For these exciting jobs, check out Honeywell at Jobs.com." As a part of an advertiser's package with Jobs.com, the advertiser receives

(continued...)

(...continued)

radio coverage with cumulative reach of 2.5 million people a week. The use of radio in the marketing campaign has a two-fold strategy: it drives interested parties to the Jobs.com site, and it directs them right to advertisers with engaging testimonials. Jobs.com makes sure that their advertisers are highly visible to immediately capture the attention of a potential job candidate. In addition to radio, Jobs.com believes in the use of other integrated marketing strategies that have resulted in more banner ad clicks on its site. These strategies include placing ad panels on the backs of buses, including the Metro Line in downtown New York, and plastering Penn Station with Jobs.com billboards.

Challenges:

- Every method of advertising is difficult to track, except for the banner ads.

- For the ad panels on buses and billboards, the tracking numbers are not confirmed.

- There is the option to ask the online visitor how they heard about Jobs.com, but there is the risk of "probing too far."

- External mediums, on the whole, have much less control.

Successes:

Final thoughts from Dave O'Neill on the successes of Jobs.com, based upon its cyberbranding efforts, include:

- Technology allows Jobs.com to find out minute details that continue to aid in the development of its marketing strategies; everything from information regarding the time of day a user is on the site and their navigation control, as well as which audio/video profile is the most popular with job candidates.

- Jobs.com's strongest marketing push has been the heavy reliance on banner ads to lead visitors to testimonials, along with a blend of radio promotions and moving and stationary billboards.

- Jobs.com has found its success as a major player in the online recruitment industry by concentrating on driving traffic to banners to benefit its corporate advertising audience.

- Most of Jobs.com's competitors drive traffic through heavy advertising campaigns that include television, and Jobs.com does not have to spend exorbitant amounts on mainstream media.

5

Cyber Public Relations—The Credible Online Endorsement

(19) Public Relations—Is There Room for Tradition in Cyberspace?

Objective:

To confirm that the public relations tactics of the past are quite present and effective in cyberspace. This chapter focuses on Internet PR and angles to reach the media for publicity and brand awareness. Cyberbrands will find value and appreciation for the practice of public relations online, and need to consider the following:

- PR of the past updates in the twenty-first century
- Proven PR techniques are still apparent
- From static to interactive
- Know the media in cyberspace
- PR comes full circle

PR OF THE PAST UPDATES IN THE TWENTY-FIRST CENTURY

In 1985, Company No Tech introduced its first widget into the marketplace with a campaign that kicked off with a news conference dazzling the local media. The company invited business editors of newspapers and widget journals and radio and television personnel to the star-studded, gala event to catch a live speech from the president, Iam Widget. Company No Tech's public relations agency, My People Will Talk to Your People, Inc., was on hand to direct the sequence of events, to take photographs of Iam Widget holding the new product for post-PR measures, and to field media questions. The PR representatives worked diligently from the time of the initial decision to host the conference right down to calculating and securing all of the fine details. The PR representatives' days were filled with meetings: pinpointing the location, deciding upon menu choices, choosing the design of the invitation, compiling lists of potential guests, agenda and speech writing, and, of course, the measures to publicize the event (mailings, telephone calling, and faxing to the media). It seems as if the telephone calls to the media were endless, right up until the night before the occasion.

What is it about PR in this instance that is so valuable?

- It's the PR of the past that has evolved with successful strategies.
- It's PR that evokes interest from credible third parties.
- It's the intangible PR, so hard to grasp and often forgotten, that has the power and strength for changing behavior, relationship building, and increased awareness of a brand.

What happens to public relations when it goes cyber, and how does this affect the public relations practitioner? Cyber PR, when implemented correctly (as any public relations strategy must be), can be the practitioner's dream—with increased speed of communication, broadness of scope to reach audiences,

> **Cyber PR, when implemented correctly (as any public relations strategy must be), can be the practitioner's dream—with increased speed of communication, broadness of scope to reach audiences, and quicker tangible publicity results.**

and quicker tangible publicity results.

Here's another hypothetical example, updated to reflect the twenty-first century. Whatagreat.com is launching its new "dotbox" video system for game-playing audiences. Whatagreat.com hires Peppy PR Associates, Inc., to handle the product launch and the public relations campaign. Their job is to make as much noise as possible with print, broadcast, and Internet media that will (1) attend the event, (2) watch the scheduled Webcast, and/or (3) write a story based upon post-PR efforts. To gear up for the launch event at a San Francisco hotel, Peppy PR has to accomplish the following: design of the invitations, compilation of the lists of potential guests, agenda and speech writing, coordinating the production crew to film the Webcast, updating Web site content to inform visitors and the media of the event, and, of course, the measures used to contact the media (broadcast e-mails, the World Wide Web wire services PR Newswire and Business Wire, and telephone calls). Right up until the night before the event, Peppy PR Associates is planning and staging the Webcast and contacting the media via e-mail and telephone to beef up attendance. Peppy PR will be on hand for the festivities to direct activities, field questions, and take photographs of the president's speech (does this sound familiar?). When all is said and done, Whatagreatdot.com will have live Internet and television coverage of its product's entrance into the marketplace; several newspaper and magazine articles written by reporters discussing the event and the product, both in print and online; cyberaudiences logged on to the Internet for the Webcast; and, for those who are not able to participate, the ability to view the video-on-demand version on the company's Web site.

What's happening in this hypothetical instance is a familiar scenario. PR of the past meets cyber PR strategies of the digital economy, and the potential for brand awareness

Public relations is profoundly impacted by the Internet and the PR person's use of the computer.

is tremendous. The difference between the two scenarios and the benefit to the brand is the ability to communicate faster and in a broader fashion. Public relations is profoundly impacted by the Internet and the PR person's use of the computer.

PROVEN PR TECHNIQUES ARE STILL APPARENT

PR has evolved through and is continually affected by technology. Take the traditional definition of PR from *Encyclopaedia Britannica*, which states that PR involves actions intended to communicate information on and improve the public's attitude toward any individual or group, whether it's a government agency or a corporation.[1] Public relations efforts still focus on responsible communication to enhance a positive image and raise awareness of various groups. The core PR strategies, visible throughout PR history, have maintained their presence in the modern day—from the public relations tactics to lobby for a political cause, to the need of large industries to implement public relations as a means to help relations between the government and the private sector. As public relations became apparent as a growing field, there was a realization that technology was the driving force.

In the fifteenth century it was the invention of the printing press by Johann Gutenberg that enabled a communication vehicle to persuade large groups of people. In the twenty-first century, it's the technological

In the twenty-first Century, it's the technological advances of the Internet and wireless devices that carry powerful messages to an individual, corporation, government agency or organization.

advances of the Internet and wireless devices that carry powerful messages to an individual, corporation, government agency, or organization.

The difference between public relations of the past and the public relations of today is more in the advent of technology than in the nature of the practice, objectives, and goals of the public relations practitioner. After all, the types of campaigns have not changed. Public relations is widely known for investor relations, media relations, crisis management, publicizing new product and service launches, community affairs, and planning and publicizing events and exhibitions, to name just a few. Formulating the messages and targeting the audiences have not changed either. Messages need to be clear, concise, consistent, and tied to the campaign objectives. That might translate into more hits to a Web site, a change in behavior of the target audience, a more favorable attitude with regard to a brand, etc. And the same types of research are still utilized to identify groups that would benefit from a particular type of campaign based upon demographics, pychographics, and behavioral characteristics. A great deal of tradition and foundation from the twentieth century is present in public relations campaigns today. However, the

...the most significant change is the technology—how it changes static PR to interactive PR and less tangible to more concrete results.

most significant change is the technology—how it changes static PR to interactive PR and less tangible to more concrete results. Cyber public relations is effective and reaches large groups or publics when approached in the appropriate fashion.

FROM STATIC TO INTERACTIVE

Public relations on the Internet is user-friendly. With the same premise that a Web site audience is always one click away from the next-best product or service, content providers—i.e., the media—need to offer targeted, interactive information for audiences. *Note:* Public relations is *not* exclusive to just contacting media for online placements (i.e., magazines and newspapers with Web formats); many Web sites are seeking interesting content to interest users and to promote cyberbrands.

...many Web sites are seeking interesting content to interest users and to promote cyberbrands.

users and to promote cyberbrands. As a result, Web sites are offering interactive material, such as Webcasts, chat sessions, "Ask the Expert" sections, and Q&A forums. In any one of these instances, there is an opportunity for a cyberbrand (or a representative of the cyberbrand) to take part in an interactive forum for the sake of promotion. Having the CEO of Whatagreatdot.com on a game-playing site (as the featured guest of a chat session) or video-on-demand clips from an interview (that covered the product launch event) on a San Francisco radio station's Web site is excellent PR. It's not static, because the user is involved in a hands-on display of sound bytes, or a direct back-and-forth discussion between participants of a chat session. Cyberbrands benefit from the fact that content providers need useful targeted content. That also means on the part of the cyberbrand knowing what a Web site is looking for to entertain its audiences and interest an audience. This, too, is a proven public relations tactic of the past. A public relations professional would *never* pitch the editor of a magazine or producer of a radio or television station without understanding the following:

- Who is the audience?
- What are the demographics?
- What are the reporters writing about or reporting on?
- What stories or features are in upcoming issues (check the editorial calendar)?
- Do you really understand what that media representative needs to inform an audience?

KNOW THE MEDIA IN CYBERSPACE

It's the same story on the Internet: *don't bother with the pitch if you haven't done your homework.* Take the following scenario to heart.

It's the same story on the Internet: *don't bother with the pitch if you haven't done your homework.*

An overzealous company representative of a new dot-com decided to try his hand at cyber PR. Being somewhat unfamiliar with the nature of public relations (both online and offline), he forwarded a news release and a simple cover letter to ZDTV without fully understanding the nature of the Web site, ZDTV's programs, or its audience. The producer received the information and was kind enough to let the young man know that this was not the best way to proceed with a pitch. The entire scenario takes place via e-mail between the young man and the producer, beginning with the producer's response to the first pitch e-mail (names are concealed to protect the innocent):

> *Producer:* First, let me say that we appreciate your thinking of ZDTV for your pitch. As one of the head producers in this department, I wanted to also pass along some advice on pitching to ZDTV. I do not know if you had a chance to see our programming yet, but a trip to ZDTV.com will certainly give you access to streaming video, audio, as well as show overviews that highlight content. This information will greatly help you in developing a more targeted and direct pitch that will get the attention of the booking department and show producers. I alone receive over 200 pitches coming into my e-mail box every week. If a pitch reflects no understanding of ZDTV's content, and also shows that the person pitching has not made an attempt to find the specific contact for the pitch, well, those pitches are discarded. I will go ahead and pass this information to the right contacts for you, but would strongly recommend for the next time around that you take a look at ZDTV.com and clearly target your pitch based upon the kind of material we cover. Here is some information you should consider in your future efforts:

> - What trends or issues does this company [the one you are pitching] address?
> - What makes their technology better than any solutions that might already exist?
> - Is this something that has never been done before?
> - Who's running the company?

> This type of valuable information will go a long way toward a story getting attention by ZDTV, and it might have a stronger chance of making it onto the show. I hope this information is useful, and if you have other questions please let me know.

The ZDTV producer's comments are passed to the company's PR/marketing department and handled from a "marketing" perspective:

> *Marketer/PR representative:* Thank you for your response to our inquiry. I appreciate your input and realize that my colleague e-mailed to you a standard cover letter accompanied by a news release.

Producer: So, some people still do send form pitches? It's surprising to hear that in this day and age.

Overall, the ZDTV producer was helpful to the marketer/PR representative, providing constructive criticism. However, this is not always the case when there is a media contact/PR representative confrontation. On the contrary, there are times when an inappropriate pitch automatically leads to a lost opportunity for the cyberbrand.[2]

PR COMES FULL CIRCLE

Based upon the incident between the dot-com and the producer of ZDTV, it is apparent that whether public relations is practiced online or offline, professionals need to practice the basics. They must pay attention to what would interest a media representative and a respective audience to produce better public relations results. The days of "mass anything" are over. Technology should enable cyberbrands to become more efficient and targeted in public relations practices. There is no reason for industry professionals to use standard letters or to con-

The days of "mass anything" are over. Technology should enable cyberbrands to become more efficient and targeted in public relations practices.

struct media lists that are not directed to an exact media contact that specializes in a particular subject. However, that does not necessarily mean sending a pitch letter to an e-commerce reporter if he just wrote a story on e-commerce. There has to be more to the pitch: an interesting angle and a reason why his audience would benefit. In the article "Eyeball Wranglers,"[3] which appeared in the *Silicon Alley Reporter,* Sabine Heller, UGO Network's PR manager, commented on a growing problem with public relations agencies. She discussed how lower-level executives, the "underlings," are called upon to contact the media representatives who appear on a company's "A" list. Heller also noted that these high-caliber media contacts were not receiving customized pitches because the underlings are not familiar enough with a particular media outlet to truly understand what type of pitch would be appropriate. A procedure such as this needs to be reworked for any type of tangible results for the brand. It's the same predicament as the ZDTV situation. The point of contention is that professionals are not using the proven public relations tactics of the past. *Knowing the media before a pitch is not a new development.* In fact, the rules about pitching are *more* stringent with the newer technology. Practitioners should be able to find targeted information quickly and conveniently on Web sites, including online editorial calendars, e-mail address lists of editors and/or producers, and their areas of expertise.

With technology advancing, every aspect of communication and branding, in all likelihood, will result in cyberbrands' looking toward cyber PR to benefit from the speed of the pitch and the tangible results it produces (if, and only if, the targeted approach is pursued). Public relations has been around for a long time and has survived technological advances with benefit to the brands that are aiming to raise awareness, change behavior, and/or inform the public. Technology allows professionals to have better tools and resources to complement each and every public relations tactic—now just let the proven tactics guide you in a new interactive forum.

Technology allows professionals to have better tools and resources to compliment each and every public relations tactic—now just let the proven tactics guide you in a new interactive forum.

Interview: Public Relations and Internet Technology

At the Public Relations Society of America (PRSA) Professional Day event, the president of the organization approached the podium to introduce the keynote speaker. She stated, "Our honored guest needs little introduction as he is well known and well respected in the field of public relations . . . Fraser Seitel." The 25-year veteran of public relations counseling, and author of *The Practice of Public Relations,* was greeted warmly by a crowd familiar with his work. Seitel, a charming and charismatic speaker, took the podium and dazzled an attentive audience with his discussion of the digital economy and the Golden Age of PR. Following the conference, Seitel discussed in a candid interview the role of the PR practitioner in the new economy and how technology has a profound influence on the field of public relations. "The Internet has impacted every level of society," stated Seitel. "The primary way is the speed in which people communicate." He further commented that the ability to communicate has expanded rapidly as has the volume of communication available. "In this economy, everyone knows and values the importance of communication; an organization constantly needs to talk to its public, and at the same time that organization is constantly talked about. Public relations becomes more important, and as a consequence, the field has expanded with professionals who are hired to be Internet monitors, and specialize in Web site design." Seitel stressed how in this day and age, PR counselors need to be tech-oriented, not only in terms of the role they play for tech companies, but also in the promotion of any company that is Internet-savvy.

The role of the PR practitioner has grown tremendously with the Internet and the computer. Thus, the awakening of the Golden Age of public relations is manifested in the number of public relations positions available and in the increased salaries for professionals in the field. In addition, public relations companies are merging into larger, more established organizations, and a field once unknown to society is becoming well known. Yet, according to Seitel, public relations continues to face an identity crisis; the field is not easily defined. And

with the advent of Internet communication, there is, unfortunately, the danger of losing the traditional elements of the counselor's role. "Public relations is not an 'old' field; it is less than 100 years old. The first PR surfaced in the day of Ivy Lee and John D. Rockefeller around 1910. In the past, public relations was strategic, less a commodity," explained Seitel.

Traditionally, public relations was identified as crisis management, relying on practitioners for advice relating to strategic matters and the most effective manner to communicate to the public. However, the computer compounds the identity crisis. The question becomes, Is public relations still a means to advise companies and to be of counsel, or is it the tech function simply to promote and publicize? As the computer overwhelms the traditional function, the counseling aspect of the field risks being submerged. With the many public relations agencies that are tech-based, the strategic importance becomes vulnerable and the PR professional is viewed as the person who monitors the Internet and the person who takes on the responsibility of print, broadcast, and Internet publicity. Seitel describes this function as a lower level of public relations. There is a correlation between the loss of the counseling element and the heavy emphasis on the tech function, which has led to PR's being considered more of a commodity. However, one would think that with all of the advanced technology and the ability to communicate broadly that organizations would grasp the counselor aspect of PR. For instance, Seitel discussed the Bridgestone/Firestone faulty tire incident and how some folks in management still downplay the importance of strategic PR. The "head in the sand" approach will only lead to further public bashing of the brand. And with the case of Bridgestone, at long last, the company fired its president and hired PR counsel. Another newsworthy case is Oracle's admittance to "snooping through the trash of consultants to archrival Microsoft." CEO Larry Ellison admitted that he was aware of the snooping practice and was unapologetic—an unfortunate scenario that warrants PR counsel. Overall, Seitel feels that even though there is a tremendous need for strategic counseling, there are not all that many strategic counselors; this is unfortunate and diminishes the importance of the field.

However, there is a positive side. The computer is a direct way to reach every public quickly, whether it's investors, the media, or customers. The Internet allows companies to move at warp speed. Seitel discussed the positive aspects of the Internet on the profession. "The media over the last few years have really taken to e-mail. Although you have the same mechanisms at work, with junk news releases by fax or mail, now there is junk e-mail," he stated. PR professionals have the ability to reach the media not only directly, but frequently as well. However, with every positive, there is the potential for a negative. Thus, the Internet allows "any yahoo" to communicate on Yahoo! This could be an organization's greatest threat to its reputation and viability. With unmonitored chat rooms and message boards, companies are bombarded by comments that directly affect stock performance and brand reputation. It all boils down to the PR profession, and in this day and age, the ability for the brand to be online is also a call to action to have a professional monitoring the Internet at all times. PR is fortunate in the respect that in good times, and in times of crisis, the field prospers and there is work for the practitioner.

Seitel's final thoughts are to inspire young professionals and individuals not familiar with the field of PR: the knowledge of the Internet is obligatory. Young professionals have this knowledge, and definitely have a leg up in the digital economy. Yet, what they also need is the philosophy behind what they are doing and why they are doing it. A word of advice would be to avoid being pulled into the Internet, and not to believe that the knowledge of the Internet is enough in the digital economy. Understanding what you are doing, and why, will lead to an attitude toward counseling that is actually the "juice of the field."

(20) PR Cybertools for Cyberspeed

Objective:

To illustrate how PR techniques, advanced technology, and cyber resources enhance a public relations effort and produce light-speed results. This chapter focuses on the cybertools that facilitate faster and stronger media relations and how targeted public relations campaigns are a direct result of the following:

- Retiring outdated PR resources
- Updating PR tools cyberstyle
- Using basic cybertools—media guides move online
- More Cybertools—editorial calendars; clipping and monitoring services

RETIRING OUTDATED PR RESOURCES

For decades, public relations practitioners have used the trusted PR resources (media guides, editorial calendars, clipping and syndicated news services, etc.) to guide campaign efforts. Take the simple task of compiling a broadcast media list. More than 10 years ago

For decades, public relations practitioners have used the trusted PR resources (media guides, editorial calendars, clipping and syndicated news services, etc.) to guide campaign efforts.

in a small agency in New York, an assistant account executive was given this project. Back in 1988, this was not as easy as it appears to be. The directive given by the vice president of the company was clear: "We have a new client. He is a financial analyst, who just completed his first book on future market trends. Our public relations campaign will focus on a broadcast media tour that concentrates on the major hubs in the United States—New York, Atlanta, Chicago, Houston, Los Angeles, and San Francisco. We need to book radio and television interviews for the author as he tours each city. We are looking to interest radio and television stations that have talk show interview formats, with topics that include business and the economy." With that said, the assistant account executive knew she had a great deal of work ahead. First she needed to compile the list of radio and television programs and the producers who would accept the information on behalf of the agency's client. This process was completely manual and extremely time-consuming.

Unfortunately, this was the day and age of large books of media contacts (updated with stick-um labels over previous outdated entries). Looking through the large media books, pulling out the names, titles, telephone numbers, addresses, and fax numbers, and placing them into a cohesive format was only the beginning of the process. The next phase was the verification phase—to make sure that every piece of information on the list was accurate, especially the contact person listed to receive the information. This is among the top rules of public relations and building media relationships: make sure the package ends up in the appropriate media contact's hands, or it will surely find the circular file. The assistant account executive used the bulk of her days to verify each and every piece of information to accurately compile a national media tour list. The process took at least one week to complete.

UPDATING PR TOOLS CYBERSTYLE

Ten years later, the same young woman, now a public relations manager for an agency just outside of New York, is working on a project to publicize a fashion show for a well-known charity, the Juvenile Diabetes Foundation. She is working with her team of account executives and assistants as well as other PR and marketing staffers. She gives the directive to the assistant account executive to compile a list of print and broadcast media in the New York metropolitan area to invite to the fashion extravaganza. The assistant account executive knows that she will have to use the company's media contact database (CD-ROM format) to compile her lists. This will take approximately two-plus hours of formatting, and then she will have another few hours of telephone verification (the CD-ROM is usually accurate, especially if she takes the time to keep the database current by updating it with the quarterly revisions sent to her on disk by the company that produces the database). Total time to implement the process is, at the most, three days. This very same woman years ago would also expend countless hours making calls for media kits, spend time on the telephone inquiring about subscription information from PR industry newsletters, and attempt to access industry information through colleagues or through her organization, the Public Relations Society of America.

The examples illustrate a transition over time; they reveal in one particular instance (over the course of a young woman's career) how technology changed the resources available to public relations professionals between the 1980s and the 1990s. And now, in the twenty-first-century economy, another drastic change has occurred, one that facilitates retiring the outdated methods of the past and celebrates the new technological processes. There are tremendous differences between the resources of prior decades and the offerings on the Internet today for public

Cyber PR resources are surfacing in abundance—from the companies that have been around for years that update their services and retire outdated material, to the new e-brands that are stepping into the PR arena with significant impact.

relations practices and brands seeking public recognition. Cyber PR resources are surfacing in abundance—from the companies that have been around for years that update their services and retire outdated material, to the new e-brands that are stepping into the PR arena with significant impact.

USING BASIC CYBERTOOLS—MEDIA GUIDES MOVE ONLINE

Take a look at Bacon's Media (a PRIMEDIA Company). This is a company that in the past has provided various media guides with updated labels to stick on existing pages of its books. In 1988, that poor assistant account executive dreaded the day that she opened the mail and the Bacon's stickers were in the envelope. Years later, she has the experience behind her and the knowledge to recognize the need to have an extremely targeted media list. That "once willing to stick labels on a page of a media book" assistant account executive now owns her own company and makes the decision to sign up for a yearly contract for an online directory of print, broadcast, and Internet media contacts. Through Bacon's online, the process is amazingly simple with thousands of media updates performed by the vendor daily. The process is effortless, and, better yet, quick and accurate—just what is expected of an Internet service. Bacon's, as well as other media guide software companies, is taking its resources online in response to the PR professional's needs for advanced technology to facilitate a targeted campaign with faster results. When the woman reflects on the years of countless hours spent compiling lists by hand, typing them into the computer, and verifying each and every entry, she sighs with relief knowing that her employees will have a quick cybertool that provides five times as much detail as ever before.

Standard information is only the beginning with these online directories. The newspaper and magazine directories (print and online formats) provide specifics: editorial lead times, wire services used, editorial profiles, special feature sections, types of publicity accepted, and, more significantly, editor pitching information (building the relationship still exists and works extremely well in this day and age).

. . . building the relationship still exists and works extremely well in this day and age . . .

For broadcast media, the directory provides targeted research regarding shows by topic, show profile, format, descriptions, air time, and what type of publicity is accepted (video news release, public service announcement, news release, etc.)

If only the good "stuff" came cheap. Prices for an online media guide, including print, broadcast, and Internet media contacts, can range from $2000 to $3000. That sounds like a heavy price tag for a year's contracted service. But from the perspective of saving time and human resources (the salary paid to an assistant account executive who religiously uses the directories), the online service pays for itself. The assistant account executive or even an intern could pine away for a week compiling lists. A service that is Internet-enabled and updated daily allows lists to be compiled more efficiently than a hard copy manual version or even the use of a CD-ROM version. What is paid up front in cash will result in proficient service, accuracy, and better campaign results (which translates into more publicity mentions, bigger-ticket items in the news, interviews with the media, hits to the Web site, and overall increased recognition).

MORE CYBER TOOLS—EDITORIAL CALENDARS; CLIPPING AND MONITORING SERVICES

Another significant advancement for the practice of public relations is the ability to view online editorial calendars. The ability to review an editorial calendar of a print publication is a key to targeting "the pitch" for an editor or a reporter. An editorial calendar is an up-front calendar of what a magazine will be focusing on in each issue. These calendars are planned yearly and guide the PR professional to pitching a particular story for a particular issue of a publication. Again, the online calendar is one more way to have targeted ammunition that will gain the attention of a media contact and not waste his time with an angle that does not even fit the format, interest, or scope of the magazine. Going back to that same woman in the late 1980s and the early 1990s, editorial calendars were not the easiest to access. Telephone call after telephone call was made to editorial departments of magazines and trade journals, which would then send out packages via mail or facsimile transmission. Although the average practitioner survived this painstaking manual task, there is *no* survival of this kind in the twenty-first century.

The digital economy is all about knowledge at your fingertips, and the Internet is a wonderful medium when it comes to retrieving quick research and information. There are services available, such as www.edcals.com, that enable public relations professionals to access over 130,000 story opportunities in consumer, business, and trade publications as well as the leading daily newspapers.

The digital economy is all about knowledge at your fingertips, and the Internet is a wonderful medium when it comes to retrieving quick research and information.

Similar to online directories, this type of service updates calendars weekly for "accurate media intelligence." However, for smaller PR budgets, the online services are not necessarily a consideration. Professionals will still benefit from the readily available information from online publications. For instance, *Business Week* online (www.businessweek.com) makes it a straightforward process to access its online editorial calendar. There is no subscription fee to preview the information. With easy admittance into the site from the navigation bar (with a click of the mouse on the Media Kit button), a new section appears: "Editorial & Planning Calendars." Under this category, there are a few options, including an editorial and planning calendar for the current year and the next year's issues.

Most Internet-savvy publications are making these resources readily available, complete with special editorial features and issue dates. The media, too, realize the need for PR people to be extremely targeted in their efforts. The use of the online directories to access information, and the ability to target a particular media contact and view an online editorial calendar to pitch appropriately (considering angles and lead times), is an asset to the PR person who wants to interest a media contact and build a relationship. When it comes to the media, knowing their business and the audience they reach is key to getting "ink." The Internet facilitates this process quicker, more than any other technology of years past.

Directories and editorial calendars are only the beginning; clipping services and Internet monitoring for public relations (and competitive analysis) are available. Companies such as eWatch (www.ewatch.com) and CyberAlert (www.cyberalert.com) act as clipping services to track articles and mentions of brands on the Internet, but also go a step further as a cyberintelligence unit. Although there is a fee involved, these services also act as Internet monitors to provide companies with not only a clipping portfolio but also a review of how their products and services are discussed on message boards and in usenet groups.[1] Clipping services have been around for over a hundred years, but the ability to use an e-brand for online competitive intelligence is just one more way that the digital economy aids in brand development and awareness. CyberAlert, for instance, searches the Internet daily as a part of its "Brand Reputation" program. The Internet has a track record for abuse—misinformation and rumors are no stranger to the medium. In 2000, the incidents of the infamous 15-year-old Cedar Grove, New Jersey high school student who posted misleading information on a message board to raise the value of shares of stock and the college student indicted in the dissemination of a false news release on behalf of Emulex are perfect examples of Internet misinformation, rumors, and abuse punishable by law. Apart from countering such *illegal* activities, however, CyberAlert provides brands with newer and broader PR tactics that are an "early warning system to identify malicious commentary in 'attack' Web sites. . . ."[2] With the ability to clearly identify Web surfers who are practicing their First Amendment right to speech on message boards and in chat rooms, this type of commentary is handed over to the brand's PR team for early action to coun-

> ...the ability to use an e-brand for online competitive intelligence is just one more way that the digital economy aids in brand development and awareness.

teract negative opinion, if it is not too late to change that opinion. Of course, with this type of intelligence there is controversy. eWatch says that working through the cleansing of information, "We can neutralize the information online, identifying the perpetrators behind the uncomplimentary postings and rogue Web sites."[3] However, that is not to say that the idea of "information cleansing" is not unsettling to privacy advocates and could actually end up in more of a PR mishap than intended.[4]

Public relations is successful when it is knowledge-based, i.e., when it comes from knowing the industry, the media, and how other PR professionals are con-

Public relations is successful when it is knowledge-based, i.e., when it comes from knowing the industry, the media, and how other PR professionals are conducting business and handling industry issues.

ducting business and handling industry issues. One of the best tools and most well known PR newsletters is *Jack O'Dwyer's Newsletter.* Years ago, this newsletter, which by industry standards is the "inside news" of public relations, was available only via subscription. In 2000, a subscription to *Jack O'Dwyer's Newsletter* was $275.00 for 50 issues in a year. However, the newsletter can also be found online at www.jackodwyers.com. At least 75% of the newsletter is available online with archived issues to peruse. Having easy access to relevant PR industry news is key to understanding how to handle PR practices for brands in the digital economy.

There are also new e-brand PR newsletters. For instance, WebPR@mediamap.com is a weekly PR newsletter that highlights relevant and current public relations issues in the news with a helpful letter from the editor, feature stories, and information regarding the media. For those who cannot afford the online databases, MediaMap.com provides information on media contacts from promotions to resignations, making it easier for the PR person to reach out to a contact and build a relationship on behalf of a brand. Although MediaMap.com does not have the same reputation as *Jack O'Dwyer's*, it is still a useful and free service that aids in better understanding the nature of PR and gives helpful PR do's and don'ts practices.

Last, adding to the changing nature of PR tools is the way in which the news wire services are branching out on the Internet to offer other useful PR tools. Aside from the ability to send out news releases over the wire, PR News Wire (www.prnewswire.com), for instance, offers *Virtual IQ* or *Investor Relations* Web pages to cyberbrands. These Web pages are hosted and maintained by PR News Wire with the sole purpose of convenience to deliver the investor relations message for the

The possibilities are endless for the cyberbrand to increase awareness based upon the updated PR tools that aid in the recognition-building process.

company. The pages of *Virtual IQ* are designed to look like the brand's corporate pages. And with the same look and feel, they are delivered to investors and various publics in a concise, straightforward fashion for them to retrieve information on behalf of the brand.[5]

The possibilities are endless for the cyberbrand to increase awareness based upon the updated PR tools that aid in the recognition-building process. Becoming familiar with the cybertools is a process in and of itself, and the following should always be kept in mind:

- Retiring old tools does not mean abandoning the relationship-building strategies necessary to attract an audience. Rather, it means better cybertools to foster stronger relationships with the media, which, in turn, will get the word out to the public.

- New tools are surfacing on the Internet from both the companies that have been around for generations of PR professionals and the new e-brands with their cybertools. The PR budget will determine the vendors and the tools used.

- The Internet has the means to facilitate quick, efficient, and targeted information gathering that in the past was performed manually and took five times more manpower to perform. With more resources becoming readily available in cyberspace, careful researching of tools, prices, procedures, and benefits is always in order before signing a contract with an online service or data provider.

- The practice of utilizing public relations organizations to guide the cyberefforts, such as the Public Relations Society of America (PRSA), will continue. Except now, it's not necessarily a telephone call to access information, but rather the ability to log onto www.prsa.com for information on conferences and seminars for local chapters that touch upon cyber issues, tools, and tactics.

21   Relationship-Building Tactics with the Media

To learn to use the Internet to enhance a relationship with the media and increase PR campaign results. When it comes to public relations, the audience that needs to be addressed, first and foremost, even before the client, is the media.

When it comes to public relations, the audience that needs to be addressed, first and foremost, even before the client, is the media.

It's the media that will spread the third-party endorsement on behalf of the brand. PR relationship-building tactics and other topics of interest include:

- A quick PR relationship-building test
- Don't let yourself be labeled as the non-PR professional
- First things first—nail down the relationship-building basics
- Technology to enhance relationships

A QUICK PR RELATIONSHIP-BUILDING TEST

Here's a quick PR quiz called, "Who am I? Guess my nickname." Test your PR knowledge with 10 simple statements that should enable you to reveal the character's identity by the tenth statement. Good luck.

1. I call myself a PR person.

2. I want to get "ink" for my company, and I am trying to make as much noise as possible.

3. I send out at least six news releases a week (sometimes more) that alert the media to anything and everything that happens in my company—even when I receive editorial publicity from another outlet, I let other media contacts know where they can read the story.

4. I follow up with the media to see if they receive my press releases. Sometimes I call every day and leave messages until I get them on the telephone.

5. I believe that advertising in a publication gives me an automatic right to publicity in that venue.

6. I insist on seeing any articles a reporter writes on behalf of my company prior to publication—it is my duty and right to do so.

7. I send out at least four news releases to each editorial department just to make sure that all of the different reporters and/or editors know what's happening in my company.

8. When dealing with the media, I find it easier to attach fact sheets, news releases, and contact information as an attachment to e-mail. Then, of course, I follow up to see if they received the e-mail.

9. I send information to the same editorial contacts every time, even if they do not necessarily cover a topic. It's easier for them to pass it on to a colleague than it is for me to look up another contact.

10. I like to create news releases that are as comprehensive as possible—sometimes three pages is not even enough information to convey.

Who Am I? *Hint:* There is a new Web site named after me! Here are some choices:

- I am a marketing person who is stuck with some PR person's job, of which I know nothing.
- I am a CEO of a dot-com who needs to get his hands into everything.
- I am the eight-year-old child referred to in the article "Fire Your PR Consultants and Replace Them with Eight-Year-Olds from the Neighborhood."
- I am a public relations professional with 15+ years of PR experience.
- I am a temp hired to help out with the PR while the real PR person is on vacation.

The answer: None of the above. Although the marketer, CEO, eight-year-old, and temp definitely fit the bill to implement all the PR blunders listed, the true identity, well known to many reporters, editors, producers, program directors, and PR professionals, is the stereotypical *PR flack.* Unfortunately, there must be quite a few PR folks out there annoying quite a few media representatives

Unfortunately, there must be quite a few PR folks out there annoying quite a few media representatives...

(although there are always three sides to the story: his side, her side, and then the truth), for a Web site to be developed in the PR person's honor. Whackaflack.com is a site that actually allows all of those annoyed media representatives to release some stress and get back at those "pushy" PR professionals. The site has a message that is loud and clear:

> Tired of those pushy PR flacks and overzealous young account execs huffing breathlessly over the virtues of the next useless.com? Feeling bombarded by inane hype? Here's your chance to give them a taste of their own . . . media kit.[1]

Does this sound like a group of people who have gained the respect of the media? At whackaflack.com, the user can choose a PR agency of his choice that was the most irritating (there is a long list

of choices). The game gives the user a perfect opportunity to "fling," with the click of the mouse, paper airplane news releases at various PR personalities who pop up and down during the game. After all, the site goes as far as saying that it's practically impossible for the true PR person to lay low and stay out of the picture for any significant amount of time.[2] For users, it could be that there's tremendous pleasure in hitting the fictitious characters, such as Prentice Newman who just graduated from college, ambitious and overly conscientious—he's the one who sends out multiple e-mails a day. Or perhaps there's a bit of bliss in whacking Hardy Knox, the old-time PR guy who was in the business pre-fax machines and overnight courier service. The hypothetical characters, the nature of the game, and the humor in mocking the flack (because it really is meant to be humorous and not offensive) offers PR professionals a taste of reality.

Another well-known Web site that is receiving attention in the media realm is Jim Romenesko's *MediaNews* at www.poynter.org/medianews, a site that he developed for the not-for-profit journalism school, The Poynter Institute. "PR Beefs" is an area of the site that allows both journalists and PR representatives to post their differences. *MediaMap* editorial newsletter discusses Jim Romenesko's site in its October *WebPR* issue and states, "This may not win MediaNews a Nobel Peace Prize, but it can be said that he's getting people talking."[3] And according to the article, Jim Romenesko realizes the intense emotions that brew on both sides, those of the media contact and the PR person, knowing that each group has a grievance. Romenesko states, "PR people see many reporters as being arrogant, and reporters see PR people as being annoyances when they send materials that are 'off topic.'"[4] Some of the postings on "PR Beef" include an opinion from a media contact at the Boston Herald who is denouncing the practice of sending the media person a gift because it's viewed as a form of bribery.[5]

A senior writer from *Philadelphia City Paper* posts his thoughts on how PR agencies should do themselves a favor and hire experienced journalists as PR account executives. He even goes as far as saying that individuals right out of college who majored in PR (which, in his opinion, does not mean a great deal) are clueless. In fact, making these people the "front line" is of no benefit to the company.[6] The comments about PR people go on and on, ranging from their not knowing the publication being pitched and acting like telemarketers making cold calls, to not answering questions in a timely fashion and attempting to get ink in a competitor's publication the day after a story runs. There is far more bashing of PR people going on than there is negative commentary *from* PR people directed toward the media.

Let's clarify the record. It certainly is not a sin to be zealous and conscientious. And there is nothing wrong with graduating with a bachelor of arts degree in communications concentrating in public relations. Most of all, in this business, it is not a sin to want to make some noise about a brand that has a novel, instructive, or provocative story to tell. It's the way of going about the process that has given PR people the bad rap. Technology enables professionals to make contact quicker, easier, and more frequently. Unfortunately, the very same technology can work to the practitioner's disadvantage. Technology is an advantage only when it enhances the relationship

> ...it is not a sin to want to make some noise about a brand that has a novel, instructive, or provocative story to tell.

(sparking the relationship with relevant news and information that, in the past, would take longer to uncover); otherwise it's a case of non-PR performance by the professional. *Non-PR will not build media relationships, non-PR will not get the "ink," and non-PR does not enhance awareness of the brand.*

Finally, non-PR has been going on for a long time, and, as a result, affects ROI. PR people are held accountable when it comes to results of the PR campaign and ROI, especially in the digital economy with the fierce and changing nature of competition and the speed of changing technology.

FIRST THINGS FIRST—NAIL DOWN THE RELATIONSHIP-BUILDING BASICS

There are simple steps to address even before considering the way that technology plays a part in the PR effort. These simple PR tactics will combat the negative PR flack stigma:

1. Do your homework and know exactly which medium you are pitching and what type of story is of interest to a particular contact.

2. Do not bombard the media with excess news releases that have no bearing or relevance. Stick to the facts and keep it concise.

3. Do not overestimate the reality of the company and have "egomaniac expectations."[7] Keep in mind the types of companies that get coverage in publications such as the *Wall Street Journal* and the *New York Times.* If the company or the cyberbrand is not a forerunner in the industry, then don't pitch the company that way to the publication.[8]

4. Do not send multiple copies of news releases or materials to reporters and editors of the same editorial department. With busy schedules that often do not concur, it is humiliating to have two contacts working on the same story.

5. Do not ignore the media and avoid questioning. If they do not hear it right from the PR people, they can always seek outside sources that may not pose a situation in a favorable light.

6. Do not interrupt a reporter or editor who is on deadline. It's best to ask if he or she has a moment to talk, or when it

would be a better time to discuss the information that you want to pitch.

With the basics intact, the PR person quickly discovers the capabilities of the Internet in one of two ways. First, there is the likelihood that he or she gets caught up in the frenzy of a fast-paced industry, and uses the Internet inappropriately; and second, there is the distinct possibility that the Internet becomes a medium that informs, educates, connects, and assists the PR person to better communicate with a contact. Will the Internet continue to add fuel to the PR flack fire? Absolutely not, if the PR person considers the following:

1. Do not ever assume that a media contact wants to be "spammed" by anyone, not a PR person, another colleague, or even a relative. As a matter of fact, Len Stein, a 20-year veteran who founded Visibility PR, discusses in his article "SPam, SPAm, SPAM…Fire Your PR Agency" how he hopes that PR professionals are developing targeted lists and managing them properly. With hundreds of e-mails to sort through daily, media contacts begin to resent seeing the same person or people clogging up their inboxes with unsolicited e-mails.

Do not ever assume that a media contact wants to be "spammed" by anyone, not a PR person, another colleague, or even a relative.

2. Technology is the PR person's dream—it's so easy to shoot out numerous e-mails and attach documents of interest to the many media contacts. Wrong. Few journalists of print and cyber publications prefer to receive attachments. In fact, with the high incidence of computer viruses, more media representatives are setting their browsers to pass over attached documents.[9] Besides, when you are building a relationship with any business contact, it is a normal business practice to inquire as to how the person wants to receive information. Then, of course, respect the method your contact prefers. If the method of choice is not e-mail, but, rather, the U.S. Postal Service or messenger service, then that's the way to go (any other method would result in the PR person's losing face and maintaining flack status for not listening).

3. Use the Internet to provide further information on a brand and any developments in a company. Too many cyberbrands in their hurry to send out news releases over the wire, and forward packages to broadcast and print media, are not fully set up on their Web sites for an unexpected visit from the media.

Too many cyberbrands in their hurry to send out news releases over the wire, and forward packages to broadcast and print media, are not fully set up on their Web sites for an unexpected visit from the media.

Before any material goes out the door, it's in a brand's best interest to have an area of the site devoted to media and/or investor relations. The area should be easy to locate and contain the company's fact sheet, news releases, mission statement, updated product information, investment information, etc. In addition, this section of the site must be updated frequently to reflect time-sensitive information and issues (updating Web pages goes without saying for Internet audiences). However, cyberbrands should avoid imposing registration and password entry for the media—this practice slows their efforts and sends them off to another site's online pressroom for information (possibly a competitor's).

4. The Internet is a great tool to research information to become fully knowledgeable about industry occurrences. The PR folks at Grayrun Group (www.grayrun.com) feed into media relations by keeping an eye out for tips and stories to provide to reporters whom they have worked with in the past.[10] Watching for stories that cover a reporter's beat is particularly helpful. The Internet is as global or as local as you want it to be, and finding information to provide to a contact further aids in the two-way street media/PR relationship.

The Internet is as global or as local as you want it to be, and finding information to provide to a contact further aids in the two-way street media/PR relationship.

Having relevant information available helps the media person who suffers from time constraints and, in some cases, is assigned a story that might not necessarily be in his or her area of expertise. Imagine being assigned several of these types of stories in a short time frame. The PR person looks like the knight in shining armor when valuable information is exchanged. Flack? Flack, who?

Granted, the digital economy stirs up industries, and there is the incessant need to rush, rush, and rush some more! However, keeping the rush factor in mind, it's worth taking a little extra time to access Internet information and know exactly who, what, why, when, and where you are going with a PR push. Squashing the flack issue is not easy. It's psychologically embedded in the minds of both parties. But for the new generation of PR people in the digital economy, if you want to make some noise on behalf of your cyberbrand, then take the time to understand the media's needs in order to gain their trust and mutual respect. Relationships take time and effort. The best business partnerships were not built in a day, any more than the best marriages and unions. *The PR/media relationship is like any other relationship that requires two-way communication and, of course, is a two-way street.*

To recap, the cyberbrand will build better and stronger relationships when the PR team adheres to the following tactics:

- Don't waste the media's time. Remember, egomaniac syndrome gets the cyberbrand nowhere.
- Pitch a good story, one that is appropriate for the contact.
- Be responsive to the media (avoid evasiveness), and they will not only take your explanation, but will come back to ask for more expert opinions and comments.
- Make the media's job a little easier. Listen to how they need information, and get the information to them appropriately.
- Don't treat PR like a sales call. Telephone call upon telephone call, or endless spamming, will not benefit the cyberbrand.
- Take the time to understand the different types of stories the media find newsworthy: timely disclosures, company progress, human interest, novelty, trends, and stories of prominent figures. Then, use technology to provide this information as quickly as possible.

Building Media Relationships: An Editor's Point of View

Thomas J. DeLoughry, executive editor of *Internet World,* has received thousands of pitch letters and news releases over the course of his 13 years in the field of journalism. As executive editor of the ever popular and quickly growing Internet publication, DeLoughry relied on technology every day to make his job easier. In an interview, he touched upon how technology fosters a relationship between the media and public relations professionals and how to use technology properly when dealing with editors.

Beginning with the use of the Internet, "Lots of times I want to make a telephone call or need more contact information about a company, which might even include directions to their offices for an interview," stated DeLoughry. "Now most companies have Web sites and make this type of information readily available." According to DeLoughry, the "About Us" section of a Web site is tremendously helpful to provide detail on lesser-known facts about an organization (regarding venture capital funding and where it originated). "The more information—the better," he explained. These sections are valuable for a company to profile its executives and its business plan. In fact, DeLoughry mentioned that one of the most difficult aspects of understanding the many companies that cross his desk is to figure out just what is their vision and business model.

Unfortunately, in the digital economy, many companies are moving too quickly and hiding behind jargon in their correspondence with the media. This, ultimately, makes an editor's job more difficult; straightforward information is best, and high-tech, intricate verbiage usually does not impress a media contact. DeLoughry offered a list of surefire ways that would induce him, as an editor, to give a company an editorial placement in *Internet World:*

- Make the story accessible—leave out the jargon and stick to the facts that *Internet World*'s audience would understand and appreciate.
- Watch the hype—beware of discussing unknown companies that are "the leading forces" yet have no customers and have only just launched a product or service.
- Confirm that the information being pitched ac-

tually fits the format of *Internet World*. Spamming an editor or reporter about ideas that are not covered in the magazine is useless.

- Work with any executives of a company to understand the message to be communicated—then, the pitch to the editor is more concrete and pertains to the company's overall branding strategy.

- Do not let the "rush to the Internet at 80 miles per hour from the get-go" be the driving force. Getting useless information out quickly does not impress anyone, and it only wastes valuable time. DeLoughry poses the question, "Venture capitalists look for companies that are full throttle, yet, consider the recent dot-com Super Bowl commercials. Does anyone remember the name of the actual company?" His point is to beware of the five-times-the-normal-pace mentality when it comes to PR and building media relationships—even if the client or ven-

ture capitalists push too hard.

- Do not call an editor to find out if he received your e-mail. "Put it this way," said DeLoughry, "send it when you have time and it will be read when the editor has time."

- Avoid mentioning the fact that you are an advertiser in a publication. This may work in lower-end magazines, but it is insulting to the media representative who takes pride in every story written.

- For *Internet World,* faxes are a waste of time, and snail mail is a thing of the past. E-mail is the best way to go, as it can be forwarded to members of the *Internet World* staff in various parts of the country. "However, this is not to say that every editor wants e-mail," stated DeLoughry. "There is a tremendous difference between an Internet publication and a daily newspaper. Newspapers still house large editorial departments where a fax can go a long way. But, for *Internet World* faxes are antiquated."

- Know the company you are pitching. Do not waste an editor's time with uneducated pitches. The steps to get to the right person for accurate information are time-consuming—it's best that the PR person know the company inside and out.
- Never send a blind pitch—understanding the publication is crucial, and it lets the editor know that you have done your homework. It also shows the editor that the company is well positioned for the publication. Editors give credit to those professionals who take the time to read the publication being pitched—it's worth the effort.
- Refrain from calling every media contact on the masthead of a publication. For every editor and reporter, at a small editorial department, to hear the same pitch and bounce around the idea is a waste of valuable time. It's much more effective to target a contact. DeLoughry

discussed how the *Internet World* Web site gives the information on who covers what (he even says this in his telephone message to PR folks).

- *Major pet peeve:* When PR folks send information to Tom DeLoughry at *Interactive Week* or *The Industry Standard*. Whether that's a typo or just a funny thing that happened in your e-mail program, it's a sure way not to get any attention.

DeLoughry's final thoughts focused on solidifying good, long-standing relationships. His best relationships are with PR professionals who are totally plugged into a client. They can understand the clients so well that answering questions is second nature. "These are also the practitioners who know the client's industry and can let us know when something is going to happen that is newsworthy," said DeLoughry. For DeLoughry, these are the companies that get noticed based upon the PR person being considered a partner. "Let's face it, the best PR comes from professionals that offer insight and information that is valuable to our readers— it's these folks that make our jobs a bit easier."

(22) Best PR Practices

Objective:

To appreciate the value of public relations and provide insight into public relations campaigns and the professionals who run the programs. Cyberbranders who wish to do well should know the following:

- Telltale signs of PR fluff that raises the red flag
- PR accountability demonstrated by professionals
- Best-case scenarios to generate interest
- Helpful PR hints for successful campaigns

TELLTALE SIGNS OF PR FLUFF

Superstoredotcom is among the many e-tailers to enter the on-line marketplace to sell women's, men's, and children's clothing. PRdotcom is the company that wants the $10 million PR account. In a large, comfy meeting room in Silicon Valley, PRdotcom is anxious to start its presentation. The senior vice president of PRdotcom dims the lights in preparation for the PR pitch. The projection screen lowers from the ceiling and the festivities begin. There's energy in the air, and PRdotcom puts on the performance of a lifetime: audiovisuals, stimulating interaction, and lots of heavy media name-dropping to further entice Superstoredotcom into a contract. When the dog-and-pony show ends, the group is ready for questioning.

VP of marketing, Superstoredotcom: Thank you for an exciting presentation. Did you happen to mention what types of PR placements (offline and cyber) we can expect if we hire PRdotcom?

Director of PR, PRdotcom: We have numerous contacts with major newspapers, consumer and business publications, and television stations across the country. We envision Superstoredotcom to be picked up by these media if we get involved with the account.

VP of marketing: What benchmarks can we count on with this type of large national effort?

Director of PR: We just completed a campaign for a dot-com in the high-tech sector and were picked up by several publications with circulations over 200,000. However, for proprietary reasons I am not able to discuss the account in detail.

VP of marketing: Can we see a bio of each member of the PR team assigned to this type of account?

Director of PR: Accounts are so specialized that I do not have the information at hand. However, I would be happy to put something together for you.

Has the red flag been raised yet? What's wrong with this scenario? Besides the fact that the PR company did not partake in the cardinal rule of selling, that of INPC (introduction, needs, presentation, close), the presenters engaged in the following tactics:

- Evasiveness—no straight answers or concrete facts
- No clear-cut benchmarks and no numbers or percentages to back up information
- A sense of a lack of accountability
- Name-dropping but no substance or physical placements to present
- The distinct chance that upper management puts on a dog-and-pony show but the account executives work the campaign

It's tough to find the right agency to outsource a public relations campaign. And a company that shows the telltale signs of "fluff" from the get-go just might be the same agency that does not feel accountable for the outcome of the campaign. PR, like any other type of marketing

PR, like any other type of marketing communication, is accountable for ROI, and so are the professionals who run the effort.

communication, is accountable for ROI, and so are the professionals who run the effort. PR fluff begins with the company that talks a good game (but has no substantive proof), and $30,000 a month later with no increase in traffic or commerce on the Web site, the cyberbrand's executive team wonders: Where's the ROI?

PR ACCOUNTABILITY DEMONSTRATED
BY PROFESSIONALS

Alas, the ever-familiar scene in the cash-burning dot-com community. Even, the click-and-mortars have found their share of lack of PR accountability. There has to be a *clear set of standards* to consider before signing on for PR services. According

There has to be *a clear set of standards* to consider before signing on for PR services.

to Jack O'Dwyer (a long-time veteran of public relations practices), there are several standards to consider before making the commitment. Companies should be on the lookout for the following:

- PR agencies that discuss "grandiose future plans and strategies described in glowing terms."[1]

- PR agencies that constantly bash the media.

- PR agencies that are evasive with respect to any key players on the PR team (signaling that the handoff might be a lower tier of expertise).

- PR agencies that do not provide a lengthy client list. If they don't offer the information, by all means, just ask.

- PR agencies that do not discuss full PR campaigns and just mention random placements.

- Most of all, watch out for the hype, the fluff, or the stuff that only sounds good in a presentation but never surfaces otherwise.[2]

...watch out for the hype, the fluff, or the stuff that only sounds good in a presentation but never surfaces otherwise.[2]

Looking for the foregoing characteristics will help to weed out the "all talk" agencies from the successful PR professionals who perform with a sense of urgency and accountability. Employing the right professionals to handle communication on behalf of the cyberbrand will result in better campaign results. But there are still challenges to be faced by brands in the digital economy. With the speed of technology and timely news, the saying goes, "News occurs every half hour." With that said, what types of campaigns could possibly capture the attention of the media who communicate the messages to the public? At a PRSA Professional Day conference in October 2000, different speakers discussed what it takes to gain the attention of the media and how to rise above the clutter. The tactics ranged from shock PR and "a coat of varnish" to pure newsworthy facts and steering away from the "spin" mentality. However, in all cases, the professionals who believe in PR accountability are the professionals who communicate the very essence of the brand to audiences.

BEST-CASE SCENARIOS TO GENERATE INTEREST

Take a look at three brief PR campaigns, each one different (from conservative to risqué, and to "out-of-the-box" thinking). The campaigns possess unique strategies (utilizing the Internet) and result in greater brand awareness.

General Mills

Background:

General Mills wanted to roll out with a new promotion to enhance its position as a pioneer in the "world of premiums."[3] How could the company stay current with the needs of consumers in the new millennium?

Objectives:

- To develop a campaign that gains the interest of the media in order to inform consumers about General Mills' latest cyberpromotion

- To step into the digital realm with a one-of-a-kind promotion and special added value for audiences with "high-tech interests"[4]

- To boost the campaign by fostering a relationship with a software company to give away free software and Internet access to consumers

- To gain the interest of the media with a clever media kit that symbolized a company that moves with technology

Strategies:

General Mills formed an association with Microsoft to give away MSN software and free Internet access to consumers. General Mills also designed a unique press package to resemble a laptop computer (which was actually made of cardboard) that, when opened, displayed the "Cyber Savings" campaign (with both the General Mills and MSN logos) on the screen. Underneath each "keyboard" were the press materials, which included news releases and samples of software, as well as video news releases (VNRs).

Results:

With distinct media tools and a promotional idea that moved the company into the twenty-first century, the campaign resulted in approximately 13 million page views for Cyber Savings based upon the numerous print, radio, and television placements.[5]

Pharmaton Natural Health Products' Venastat

Background:

The Venastat Great American Cross-Out is an event that asks women to participate in a one-day healthy legs awareness program. Pharmaton, the developer of the dietary supplement Venastat, runs the program annually to promote the product by educating women about healthy legs and proper vein circulation.

Objective:

- To raise the level of national awareness among women that Venastat is a natural way to promote healthy legs
- To develop a campaign that makes women think about healthy legs and how the habit of frequently crossing legs can lead to improper circulation and varicose veins
- To employ both traditional and cyber PR strategies to promote the annual program

Strategies:

Pharmaton developed a survey that questioned women about leg crossing, which was a somewhat quirky way to gain interest about the popular habit.[6] Survey results were then released to the media for publication. Pharmaton also contacted producers of national talk shows. The hosts of programs were happy to discuss the "Venastat American Cross-Out" and started a buzz by talking about leg health awareness, the scope of the national program, and the dangers of habitual leg crossing. Finally, along with working with high-profile women's Web sites to keep the buzz going, Pharmaton made sure to register Venastat in key word searches for consumers to find easy access to Venastat Web pages. By typing in leg crossing, leg health, and varicose veins, consumers could access links to Venastat for research and information. The specifics on leg health week reached the media via VNRs, Cross-Out news releases, press kit distribution, and distribution of releases over the wire.

Results:

The goals of a well-rounded campaign proved successful and beyond expectations. The PR campaign behind the "Great American Cross-Out" generated over 100 million media impressions. There were several big-ticket publicity items, including coverage on Today, CBS This Morning, and more than 200 local TV stations. The buzz was also present in print as seen in Redbook, Better Homes & Gardens, USA Today, and the New York Daily News, to name a few.

DeskDemon.com

Background:

DeskDemon.com is a service for office managers, free of charge, that provides all of the resources and tools necessary for professionals on any given workday. The cyberbrand needed a clever campaign that would attract the interest of the media and working professionals in an effort to promote brand awareness. The company knew that with a name like DeskDemon.com the campaign approach would have to be somewhat lighthearted and could definitely get away with being a bit risqué.

Objectives:

- To interest the media with some out-of-the-box thinking that is representative of the company's name
- To interest professionals in a cyberbrand that assists them with their daily functions

Strategy:

DeskDemon.com hired two male models, scantily clad in red shorts (and nothing else), to visit several publishing houses in London. Because the objective of the campaign was to raise a few eyebrows and entertain female audiences, the bare-chested boys were a powerful tactic. Referred to as the DeskDemon Break Boys, these models personally delivered energy drinks and press releases to female audiences (in the online and offline arena). DeskDemon.com even went as far as branding the Boys across their bare chests.

Results:

- Lots of smiles and raised eyebrows—one editor could not resist and stroked the chest of a DeskDemon Break Boy.

- Press coverage included broadcast media nationwide and a number of editorial pieces from the publishing houses that were graced with the presence of the DeskDemon Boys. *New Woman* and *Ms. London* were among the publications to pick up on the story.

- Ann Roberts of Bard & Brown Communication felt that the event captured the audience's attention and was relatively low-cost to the cyberbrand. As a result, further activities with the DeskDemon Break Boys will be pursued in the future from the company's Web site, including a contest to win a visit from the Boys or even send them to a friend. (That's viral marketing in every sense of the word!)[7]

HELPFUL PR HINTS FOR SUCCESSFUL CAMPAIGNS

In each case, the use of public relations in the cyber and offline effort led to positive results on behalf of the brand. Through credible third-party endorsement (by the hand, the pen, or the keystroke of the media), cyberbrands are using PR to drive people to Web sites to research information, change opinions, and purchase products and services. Public relations is used more now as an integral part of the marketing promotional mix as other marketing strategies lose their ability to rise above the clutter. However, even the most out-of-the-box thinking requires PR tactics that always communicate the essence of the brand. Making noise for the sake of making noise is not good enough in the digital economy. Making noise for the sake of making noise does not benefit a cyberbrand. In this day and age, both the media and the public are well aware of the difference between noise and newsworthiness.

> **Through credible third-party endorsement (by the hand, the pen, or the keystroke of the media), cyberbrands are using PR to drive people to Web sites to research information, change opinions, and purchase products and services.**

Here are some helpful PR hints that get the cyberbrand and the agency off in the right direction; an agency that strays from these hints is not the right agency to run a campaign for maximum results:[8]

- PR should be used to create a positive image and goodwill and to humanize a cyberbrand.

- PR is not straight persuasion or manipulation (you can first spot this type of communication with the "all talk agency"), although it may skillfully integrate elements of persuasion into a journalistic writing style.

- PR is the practice of using the media and leaving the interpretation of the message up to the media and the public.

- PR is seen as newsworthy as opposed to a commercial advertising message.

- PR uses mass media, as well as other venues that are considered more personal to a cyberbrand—for instance, speaking forums, or community involvement.

- PR is not advertising, direct marketing, or any form of personal selling and should never be considered as such or approached in the same fashion.

Agencies that demonstrate the PR ideals and educate a company on the differences between PR and other marketing strategies are the agencies that stand out from the crowd. Agencies that "talk the talk" and "walk the walk" have concrete examples of campaigns and a lengthy list of satisfied clients and should be the companies of choice. These are the agencies to join forces with in the cyberbranding arena. These companies know the PR arena, they definitely know the media

Agencies that demonstrate the PR ideals and educate a company on the differences between PR and other marketing strategies are the agencies that stand out from the crowd.

building strategies, and they do their homework about the clients they represent and the markets in which they compete in the digital economy. These companies have learned from experience how to use technology properly and the importance of accountability when it comes to producing campaign results.

ATLANTIS GROUP, INC: PREPARING FOR PUBLIC RELATIONS

"Our sole existence is to transform the mind's creation into an innovative world of sound design and vision."

John Chominsky, CEO Atlantis Group, Inc.

John Chominsky is CEO of Atlantis Group, Inc., a sound design studio that opened in the heart of Santa Monica, California, not only with fierce competition less than a block away, but also during the AFTRA (American Federation of Television and Radio Artists) strike. "These factors did not stop us from pursuing our dream," stated Chominsky. Despite the obstacles, Chominsky, a self-starter with over 15 years of experience in the recording industry, set his sights on Los Angeles, where he immediately fast-forwarded himself to a sound design engineer at one of Hollywood's leading production and recording studios. For Chominsky, the first step was to hire a public relations firm to increase awareness of Atlantis Group in the LA area, and also on a national level as he and his studio had the capability of digital sound patch recording (this enables sound recordings from any point in the country).

Chominsky realized that Atlantis Group faced several challenges. These are presented in the following case study on how the company achieved its goals in a short time-frame.

Background:

Atlantis Group is an all-inclusive audio recording and post-production studio in Santa Monica, California. Atlantis Group is equipped to provide a multitude of services for clients ranging from musicians to independent motion picture studios to advertising agencies. Services include:

- Recording, editing and mixing audio.
- Conducting ISDN patches.
- Designing sound.
- Recording voiceover talent.
- Providing 5.1 surround sound.
- Providing a lounge area with amenities.

Objectives:

- To inform potential clients of Atlantis Group's products and services, and convince clients that Atlantis Group is the key to their business.
- Create/increase awareness among clients and media outlets in the recording/post-production and advertising/communications market(s).

Target Audiences:

- VP or Director of Marketing for agencies outsourcing client production needs.
- Sound engineers, voiceover talent and other production companies.
- Media representatives, both print and broadcast.

Challenges:

- Position Atlantis Group as "the" answer to fulfill all audio recording needs.
- Demonstrate that Atlantis Group has national capabilities through its digital sound patch.
- Creative material must stand out among dense competition in the Santa Monica area—Atlantis Group must break through the clutter.
- To prepare the company's Web site for public relations by developing an area on the site for media representatives to access company information.
- To present the media to a company that is on the cutting edge of sound design technology, one that produces better end-results for its clients.
- To discover new methods to reach and interest media contacts who are bombarded with news releases and pitch letters on a daily basis.

Atlantis Group, Inc. needed to move quickly. However, deciding to move forward with public relations meant having the required programs in place to entertain media inquiries. Questions to ask before moving out of the gate included:

1. What type of PR program is in place? Are the objectives and goals clear?
2. Will the company partially utilize an in-house team or will PR be outsourced entirely to an agency?
3. Who in the company is trained for media relations?
4. Does Atlantis Group have its public relations materials updated to reflect the CEO's vision?
5. Is Atlantis Group's Web site ready for media/investor relations?

Strategies:

Atlantis Group answered these questions by implementing the following procedures prior to rolling out with its PR efforts:

- Hiring a PR agency to set up the strategies and plans to communicate with the media.

(continued...)

- Designating John Chominsky as the key contact person to deal specifically with media inquiries and for interviews, as well as providing Chominsky with the coaching necessary to facilitate media relations.

- Setting up news wire services (BusinessWire) to distribute releases relating to any major announcements, i.e., the Alien Voices project with Leonard Nimoy and John Delancie (of the original Star Trek episodes and the Next Generation).

- Developing a print PR program that would utilize traditional news release mailings or even fax mailings (depending on the media outlet), announcing company growth, new hires and Atlantis Group events.

- Developing an Atlantis Group media kit with inserts to compile the necessary company facts, executive profiles and publicity tearsheets.

- Developing a digital version of the media kit to reach media contacts who are tech-savvy and appreciate materials in an easy and timely fashion.

- Building media relationships with key media contacts, including editors and reporters of newspapers, business, communications, advertising/marketing and sound engineer trade journals. Broadcast interview programs will be explored in a second-phase effort to move Atlantis Group on to a higher PR plateau. Media-building strategies include keeping editors up-to-date with sound design industry occurrences and trends and making Chominsky available to provide expert quotes on a technologically advancing industry.

- Hiring a clipping service to track all of the offline and online placements on a national level.

- Preparing the Web site to become media-friendly, with an area specifically designated to Atlantis Group corporate facts, the executive team, news releases and contact information for media inquiries.

Atlantis Group Successes:

"Prior to any public relations, Atlantis Group has done well for itself," stated Chominsky. "The company has attracted the attention of large advertising agencies, including BBDO, Dailey & Associates and J. Walter Thompson." According to Chominsky, Atlantis Group prides itself on remaining on the cutting edge of sound design as reflected in the state-of-the-art systems found on-site. "As far as the PR goes, the first news release distributed in the LA and New York regions generated several news items. We look forward to rolling out with a constant effort to inform the media about our studio. Of course, the true success of the program is in the proper planning and implementation of the PR strategies, and the continual steps to build relationships with the media."

(23) Cyberbranding—Beyond Trial and Tribulation

Conclusion

The best brands have stood the test of time. They are the brands, in our history, that have been nurtured, supported, and communicated effectively and have adapted over time to societal and technological changes. One hundred years from now, Coke, Pepsi, Heinz, Campbell's, Nike, and many other well-known brands will still capture a remembered feeling or positive experience (whatever the brand means to the user). These brands are more than monikers. They have a place and a stronghold in the consumer's mind and heart. They have climbed mountains and faced head-on challenges. And, if Yahoo!, Amazon, MSN, AOL, and eBay continue to brand with the constant speed and strategy that has been exhibited so far, 100 years from now they too will maintain their powerful brand presences. Cyberbrands are forging ahead in the new economy. The

Cyberbrands are forging ahead in the new economy.

power of a well-known brand combined with a medium that enables it to reach audiences instantaneously, enhance user experience with engaging interaction (prior to any purchase of a product or service), and increase overall awareness allows the brand to reach new heights.

However, past cyberbrand performance warrants that we ask several qualifying questions: What happens to the brand promise in cyberspace? Where do the new cyberbrands find their biggest challenges? Is it in the rush to the Internet, in the cash-burning mentality, or in the fervor to succeed at the speed of light, without the careful planning or infrastructure necessary to carry out any business venture? We have learned from the recent flurry of cyberbrand quick success and tumbling failure rates that launching a brand does not mean rushing its presence, forgetting to honor its promise or neglecting its 24 hours a day, 7 days a week interaction with online audiences. This past stretch of dot-com death tolls (approximately 130 Internet companies from January through November 2000) is trivial in the Internet "scheme" of things to be considered. In other words, it's just the market's way of weeding out the weaklings in order to make room for the real performers. As a matter of fact, the prediction is in: cyberbrands will continue to launch, but with more business strategy and branding behind the venture—learning from the past will facilitate new successes.

Moving beyond trial and tribulation means learning from past trial and tribulation. Another prediction: Because there is much more territory to conquer, a frontier so vast, this is only the beginning of years of cyberbrands to come. The highs and lows and ups and downs of the Internet are simply history in the making. As for the cyberbranders, the professionals handling the branding decisions, they are being educated by a digital society that teaches new rules with each passing day and with each passing cyberbrand success and/or failure story.

The past 10 years have been an eye-opening experience, to say the least. The use of the Internet has spread globally as an immense network that continues to take new direction. Changes occur daily, from the technology that is readily available to the brand and the way competitors are at each other throats (or better yet, joining forces for better brand experiences), to the way in which consumers are shopping one minute and then online sales are plummeting drastically. Opinions change as well, as audiences and the brands that serve them perceive the horror stories of companies that rise and fall—enough to make anyone pause and reflect on the inevitable Internet leap. It's the Internet that evokes that love/hate relationship with all who come in contact. Consumers praise the Internet when they can access information quickly and yet simultaneously blast its ability to infringe upon privacy. Business owners are thrilled at the concept and capability of e-commerce, but raise their hands in disgust when ROI appears to be as far away as the next solar system. Wall Street invests in the potential of a powerful medium, yet pundits are quick to report and comment on the dot-com death toll. And among all of the back-and-forth swaying of emotion, the Internet continues to grow as more people universally are logging on to gain a personal or business edge. At the same time, new cyberbrands continue to launch in a seemingly endless cycle.

True brand builders in the digital economy are figuring out the core concepts. They are understanding that the Internet as a communication channel must be used properly to provide the brand

...the Internet as a communication channel must be used properly to provide the brand with the maximum exposure and enhanced user experience it seeks.

with the maximum exposure and enhanced user experience it seeks. The Internet has become a stage for the user's experience, not like the communication channels of the past with mass messages for mass audiences. With this new avenue for persuasive tactics, the brand is able to call an audience to action in ways that did not happen as quickly pre-Internet—to spend more time learning about a product or service, to make a specific purchase, to inquire for more information, to participate in a brand-sponsored event or contest, and to embrace everything the brand has to offer on a new interactive level. Branding professionals have also learned through all of the trials and tribulations that the newer cyberstrategies fare well with a blend of traditional marketing practices that are fundamental to a brand's life. After the "first to market" crowd surfaced, herds of competitors came running on the open plains. Many of these cyberbrands did not realize that in order to stand out they would have to be deemed the "best" in terms of user experience by their audiences. Reaching this status would gain repeat traffic and customer loyalty.

Yet, even if they could provide a steady flow of traffic to a Web site, that didn't always spell out ROI. Many companies in the year 2000 faced a harsh reality. The shakeout of the cyberbrand losers from the winners was fast and furious, and even shocking in some cases (Priceline.com for gas and groceries, Furniture.com, and

Pets.com, to name a few). However, with every downfall, there is newfound knowledge to educate the successors. There is a great deal to learn from the companies that have downsized drastically and/or have recently closed their doors. A few of the key issues plaguing many (the less than sound cyberdecisions), with respect to branding on the Internet, are the following:

...with every downfall, there is newfound knowledge to educate the successors.

- Many cyberbrand visions fall short from the onset, and the success of the brand relies upon living up to what is promised in terms of the technology offered, as well as the time frame set forth.

- Cyberbrand visions that are not backed by organizations and do not have strong upper management support every step of the way do not meet cyberbrand goals.

- Cyberbrands that have no more than just a static presence will not be the brands that keep an audience interested and stand the test of time. In fact, a brand's existence online focuses mainly on heightened experience, everything and more that's expected from the brand in a much quicker time frame.

- From the short history of cyberbrands presented, the audience is an instrumental part in deciding a brand's fate. Even if an audience grants permission for the cyberpresence, if that audience is not satisfied with experiencing the brand online, the brand (as an e-brand or click-and-mortar) is marred.

...the audience is an instrumental part in deciding a brand's fate.

- Unrealistic goals for the cyberbrand lead to cash-burning strategies and, ultimately, do not address the here-and-now issues of technology and how to meet and exceed audience expectations.

- A promise in cyberspace, like any other promise, must be fulfilled. If a cyberbrand says it will deliver products, services, entertainment, etc., then it had better do so. Too many cyberbrands make the promise and then fall short in the delivery department, disappointing audiences that will never return to that Web site again.

A promise in cyberspace, like any other promise, must be fulfilled.

- Neglecting to put a continued emphasis on research, planning, strategizing, and troubleshooting from the onset will surely get the cyberbrand off to a less than desirable start (from both a branding and a business perspective).

- Technology and tradition need to come together—brick-and-mortar brands must step up to the technology of the times, and e-brands with Internet savvy need better infrastructure or roots that stem beyond the Internet (a good, solid traditional leg to stand on).

As stated, the strength of the brand together with technology has the potential to produce the "optimum brand." Brand builders in the digital economy must strive for two types of optimum brands. The first optimum brand is the one that recognizes its traditional roots and can change with technology to develop a strong cyber counterpart—one that enhances overall brand value. The second type of optimum brand relates to the new dot-com start-up that quickly incorporates several traditional, offline branding strategies (and builds infrastructure) along with cyberstrategies to have an existence that extends beyond the Internet.

Moving forward on the Internet means focusing on targeted issues that concern cyberbrands. Many of the success stories that will be discussed in years to come will be from the cyberbrands that realize the following:

- Online audiences will not be forced to do anything on the Internet—they are in control of the territory they roam. Trying to spam customers will not get their attention or cause them to act favorably—only to react unfavorably toward the brand.

- Viral marketing has proved to be a valuable strategy. Word of mouth is one of the oldest traditional strategies: consumers trust the word of a friend, relative, or colleague over any other type of endorsement.

- Attractive design, relevant content, and ease of navigation all play a part in the

The cyberbrand has one opportunity to provide the user with an engaging experience.

cyberbranding equation. The cyberbrand has one opportunity to provide the user with an engaging experience. These elements enhance the experience and make users want to return to a site again and again.

- Audiences are not impressed with a site that spurs them off in too many directions or takes them too long to find what they need. Online audiences are easily frustrated by too many clicks in the online process. In addition, long download time (from heavy graphics or even poor Internet connections) will send the user scurrying to a competitor's site.

- Personalization matters, as branders learn that the Internet is not a mass "anything." As a matter of fact, the Internet is customer-oriented and branders need to fixate their strategies on how to build better relationships with customers through the use of Internet technology. Technology allows the cyberbrand to know more than customers names when they return to a site—the cyberbrand has the ability to know their preferences and is able to make recommendations. In essence, personalization builds the relationship and thanks the audience for its loyalty.

- The Web also spells out instant communication and rewards. Thus, audiences expect instantaneous service and results—anything less is substandard and is not acceptable in "Internet" time.

- Privacy issues are a growing concern, and cyberbrands that collect marketing data must also respect an audience's concerns about the use of that data. Confidence, trust, and earned respect on the part of the audience are tremendous considerations—a relationship the brand works diligently to create.

Yes, the past dictates the future, but that is *not* to say that, from this brief historical period in the twenty-first century, every cyberbrand will crash and burn. Each new invention has its casualties for whom the bell tolls and its success stories to shout from the rooftops. This is only the beginning of the Internet. A crystal ball prediction reveals that the Internet has the ability to be present in every space occupied by an audience—in their homes and work environments, when they are traveling by car, plane, or train, or simply when they are at play. It's exciting to know that companies such as Microsoft are currently developing technologies for computing and Internet capabilities from anywhere in and around a person's home. The ability to connect to the Internet from a telephone, entertainment appliance, or kitchen appliance, for that matter, will be just as common as reaching the Internet from a PC. However, as the frontier gets wider, the size of the frontier is proportional to the extent of the growing challenges, which need to be addressed continually to secure the long and healthy life of the brand online.

Someday, an Internet museum of the future will proudly display the best online products and services that the world has to offer. Who do you think will be displayed, and what will be attributed to their success? The Cyber Hall of Famers will be the brands that (1) harness the power of the Internet, (2) address and tackle the branding issues that exist in cyberspace, and (3) combine the proper management of technology with a keen sense of how to take a brand message to new interactive levels to fulfill a brand promise. The Internet, hands down and without question, has the capability to impact an audience that not only enjoys its convenience, but also

Users are thrilled at the ability to see, feel, and experience their favorite brands at any given time, at the speed of light.

looks to it on a daily basis to quickly fulfill needs. Users are thrilled at the ability to see, feel, and experience their favorite brands at any given time, at the speed of light. As a result, there is an even greater need to address branding issues on the World Wide Web. The careful consideration of the cyberbrand and the presentation of strategies to tackle branding issues in this book are meant to provide a realistic framework and understanding of what makes a brand thrive and/or what leads to its demise on the Internet. By now, we know that all of the hopeful cyberbrands face similar risks and challenges. This will not change. There will always be that rushed feeling with respect to speed to market, tackling the changing competitive landscapes, overcoming technological issues, and meeting the new demands of online audiences. But

...the overwhelming pressure will always be that of the need to maintain a strong cyberpresence.

the overwhelming pressure will always be the need to maintain a strong cyberpresence, because that's where the masses are investing a great deal of their time.

Good luck in all of your branding efforts in the digital economy. To discuss any areas illustrated in this book or any strategies that you have encountered that facilitate better branding on the Internet, please e-mail dbreakenridge@pfsmarketwyse.com. Your feedback is always welcome and appreciated. Of all the ideas to remember, the most important is that the life of the cyberbrand rests upon its careful treatment and constant development on the Internet. Thankfully, there are many years ahead to practice and perfect the principles of cyberbranding, especially as the Internet continues to increase in size and scope and brands continue to capture our "digital" lives.

Appendix A

1. Good to the last drop—Maxwell House

2. We bring good things to life—GE

3. That heavenly coffee that only a millionaire can buy—Chock Full of Nuts

4. Smooth sippin' Tennessee whiskey—Jack Daniels

5. When it rains, it pours—Morton Salt

6. Say it with flowers—The American Flower Association

7. The quicker picker-upper—Bounty

8. Mmmm mmmm good—Campbell's soup

9. 99 44/100% pure—Ivory soap

10. The pause that refreshes—Coca-Cola

11. Put a tiger in your tank —Exxon

12. The skin you love to touch—Woodbury's facial soap

13. Even your best friend won't tell you—Listerine

14. 57 varieties—Heinz

15. This Bud's for you—Budweiser

16. Breakfast of Champions—Wheaties

17. Don't leave home without it—American Express

18. The beer that made Milwaukee famous—Schlitz

19. Snap crackle pop—Kellogg's Rice Krispies

20. The foot doctor—Dr. Scholl's

Appendix B

1. **Name the term(s) that describes the number of times a Web page is requested by the server.** This is referred to as page views.

2. **What is considered the limit for banner ad file size?** In most cases, 16K is the maximum.

3. **The measurement 468x60 pixels are what size banner?** A full-size banner ad.

4. **What does CTR stand for?** CTR stands for Click Through Rate, which is a basic measure of banner ad effectiveness.

5. **What is the measurement that refers to cost per thousand?** This measurement is CPM.

6. **The number of responses to a banner ad by the user is the number of times the user does what on the banner?** Clicks on the banner.

7. **With respect to advertising rates, what is the difference between CPC and CPM models?** The CPC model refers to Cost Per Click, which allows the advertiser to pay based upon performance. CPM is a measurement of impressions, where the advertiser agrees to pay a set dollar amount per 1,000 impressions on a Web site.

8. **What is a banner ad conversion rate?** This is the percentage of shoppers on a Web site that actually makes a purchase.

9. **How do you calculate the cost per visitor on a Web site?** Cost Per Visitor = CPM/1000*CTR

10. **What is considered an average price for banner ad rates?** According to *AdKnowledge's 1999 Advertising Report*, the average CPM is slightly above $33.

Notes

Part I: What the Marketer Needs to Know

Chapter 1: The Power of Branding

1. "To Yahoo! With Love," *Silicon Alley Reporter,* Issue 32, p. 28.
2. "What Is Yahoo! Really?" *Fortune,* June 22, 1998.
3. Ibid.
4. "Yahoo! Pepsi Forge Online-Offline Marketing Pact," *Internet News,* March 22, 2000.
5. www.amazon.com, About Amazon.com, April 2000.
6. Ibid.
7. Amazon.com
8. www.levis.com, History, April 2000.
9. Bill Bryson, *Made in America,* Morrow, New York, 1994.
10. Holding Associates, February 2000.
11. www.buildingbrands.com, March 2000.
12. Bryson, *Made in America.*
13. "Who Am I? Assessing Brand Equity," *Brand Report,* Vol. VIII, fall 1998.
14. Bryson, *Made in America.*

15. Terri Lonier, CEO, Working Solo, Inc., from *Smart Strategies for Growing Your Business,* Wiley, New York, 1999.

16. Cooper Hewitt National Design Museum brochure.

17. "E-Branding Is More Important Than E-Commerce. Here's Why," ZDNet.com, December 2, 1998.

18. Holding Associates, February 2000.

19. www.urbanlegends.com.

20. "Branding in Asia-Pacific," *Brand Report,* Vol. IX, winter 1999.

21. Ibid.

22. *Advertising Age,* 1995.

23. "International Naming," *Brand Report,* Vol. VI, summer 1996.

24. "Law of Borders," www.ries.com, Chapter 18, 1998.

25. www.geocities.com, March 2000.

26. www.buildingbrands.com, March 2000.

27. "Successful Branding—From Main Street to Wall Street," *Brand Report,* Vol. VIII, fall 1998.

28. Ibid.

Chapter 2: Making the Transition to the Internet

1. "E-Branding Is More Important Than E-Commerce. Here's Why," ZDNet.com, December 2, 1998.

2. *E-retailing World,* March 2000.

3. Brand Consultancy, Turning Your Brand into a Cyberbrand Seminar, 1999.

4. Brand Consultancy, Turning Your Brand into a Cyberbrand Seminar, 1999.

5. Forrester Research, 1999.

6. "Now for the Really World Wide Web," *Silicon Alley Report,* Issue 31.

7. ACNielsen Net Ratings, March 2000.

8. ACNielsen Net Ratings, April 2000.

9. Ibid.

10. "Half.com Launches National Branding Campaign," *Internet News,* March 1, 2000.

11. *CEO Conference Magazine,* February 2000.

Chapter 3: The Impact of the Internet on the Brand

1. www.benjaminmoore.com, March 2000.
2. www.geocities.com, March 2000.
3. *ICONOCAST,* January 2000, www.iconocast.com.
4. Interview with Alan Bergstrom, president, Brand Consultancy, March 2000.

Chapter 4: The Emergence of the Cyberbrand

1. *Screaming Media* survey, May 2000.
2. Ibid.
3. Turning Your Brand into a Cyberbrand, The Brand Consultancy, 1999.
4. www.geocities.com, March 2000.
5. Ibid.
6. "Boo.com Online Fashion Retailer Goes Out of Business," *New York Times on the Web,* May 19, 2000.
7. *Electronic Advertising & Marketplace Report,* March 2000, Simba Information.
8. "Secrets of the New Brand Builders," *Fortune,* June 22, 1998.
9. Ibid.

Chapter 5: Using Technology Properly to Cyberbrand

1. www.discoveryhealth.com, Ask the Doc, Q&A, May 2000.
2. ClickZ.com, May 2000.
3. CNET.com, Builder.com—Authoring: 10 Questions about Meta Data, May 2000.

Chapter 6: Web Site Design to Enhance the Cyberbrand

1. ClickZ.com, May 2000.
2. Ibid.
3. www.apple.com, 1-Click program, May 2000.
4. "To Yahoo! with Love," *Silicon Alley Reporter,* Issue 32, p. 28.
5. Ibid.
6. *Silicon Alley Reporter,* Verdict section, discussion of iVillage.com by Jennifer Eno, Issue 31.

7. *Silicon Alley Reporter,* Verdict section, discussion of Women.com by Ted Werth, Issue 31.

Part II: Impacting Audiences with the Cybervision

Chapter 7: Start with the Organization and the Cyberbrand Vision

1. "Show Me the Money," *Silicon Alley Reporter,* Issue 32.
2. "APBnews.com Runs Out of Money," *New York Times on the Web,* June 6, 2000.
3. "Show Me the Money."
4. "Greed, IPOs for Everyone," *Silicon Alley Reporter,* Issue 31.
5. "Punky IPOs," *Silicon Alley Reporter,* Issue 31, Backspace.
6. "Spinning Out of Control," *Silicon Alley Reporter,* Issue 31.
7. Carol Holding, *Brand Vision,* Holding Associates, February 2000.
8. Reprinted by permission of Harvard Business School Press. From *Leading Change,* by John P. Kotter, Boston, MA 1996, p. 68. Copyright ©1996 by John P. Kotter.
9. Ibid.
10. Ibid.
11. "Through the Looking Glass," *Chief Executive* magazine, February 2000, p. 36. Reprinted by permission of the Chief Executive Group. Copyright 2001.
12. Allison Kopichi, "Old-Line Firms with High Tech Vision," Bloomberg Personal Finance, March 2000.
13. Bloomberg.com, Marketwise, February 10, 2000.
14. Brooke Hilliard, *CEO's Web Review,* July 1999.
15. *Internet Week,* December 20, 1999.
16. *Internet Week,* January 17, 1999.
17. Telephone Interview with Alice Uniman, president, Phoenix Brand Strategies.

Chapter 8: Empowered Online Audiences

1. Greg Sherwin and Emily Avila, "Attack of the 50 Ft. Empowered Consumer," ClickZ.com, June 2, 2000
2. www.alloy.com, Stylewise, June 16, 2000.

3. www.Nike.com, June 2000.

4. www.landsend.com, Anxiety Zone, June 2000.

5. "Treating Customers Like . . . Customers," ClickZ.com, June 9, 2000.

6. www.ClickReward.com, June 18, 2000.

7. "AltaVista Shopping.com Launches Web-Wide Rewards Program," press release, www.altavista.com, May 18, 2000.

8. Ibid.

9. "Secret Shopper: One Size Fits None," *The Standard,* June 5, 2000.

Chapter 9: Cyberstrategies to Optimize Audience Response

1. "What to Look for in a Search Engine Optimization Specialist," Clickz.com, April 13, 2000.

2. Ibid.

3. Karen J. Bannan, "It's Catching," *Adweek,* June 5, 2000, IQ20.

4. www.hotmail.com.

5. www.Etour.com, Send to Friend.

6. "Spreading the Word," *Adweek,* June 5, 2000.

7. Ibid.

8. "Opt-In Marketing's Popularity," www.eMarketer.com, June 19, 2000.

9. Claudia Kuehl, "Spam's Good Twin," *Internet World,* May 1, 2000.

10. www.netdomination.com, June 2000.

11. Ibid.

12. www.homegain.com, Newsletter, June 21, 2000.

13. "The Elements of a Good Pitch," *Internet World.* Reprinted with permission of *Internet World.* May 1, 2000. Copyright 2000. All Rights Reserved.

14. "Gauging Attitudes about the Internet," *New York Times on the Web,* June 12, 2000.

15. "Targeting the Privacy Issue," Clickz.com, April 27, 2000.

16. "Another Industry Group Tackles Online Privacy Problem," *New York Times on the Web,* June 2000.

Chapter 10: Persuasion in Cyberspace

1. "Hollywood's New Status Symbol: A Web Site," *New York Times on the Web,* January 27, 1999.
2. "Dot-Com to the Stars," *New York Times on the Web,* June 6, 2000.
3. Ibid.
4. Jennifer Aniston's interview with Hilary Atkin, Voxxy.com.
5. "Talk to Me Like I'm a Person," Clickz.com, May 8, 2000.
6. www.pncbank.com.
7. "Women Rule Online Shopping," daily_stat@emarketer, July 3, 2000.
8. WCBS Radio, 880 AM, Marketwatch, June 2000.

Part III: Market Research for Effective Cyberbranding

Chapter 11: Traditional Research Aids in Cyberspace

1. www.jupitercommunications.com, July 2000.
2. Jeffrey Graham, "Building a Research Mosaic," Clickz.com, August 1999.
3. "Marketing to Girls on the Net," www.usatoday.com, July 6, 2000. Copyright 2000 *USA Today.* Reprinted with permission.
4. Ibid.
5. "Focus Groups Go Online" to Measure the Appeal of Web Sites," *New York Times on the Web,* July 6, 2000.
6. TheStandard.com, July 5, 2000.
7. Ibid.
8. "Focus Groups Go Online," *New York Times on the Web.*

Chapter 12: Online Research – Leave It up to the Technology Experts

1. "Are You Being Served?" Business 2.0, Numbers, August 8, 2000.
2. "Ask Nettie: Focus Online," TheStandard.com, July 3, 2000.
3. www.vividence.com, July 2000.
4. Ibid.
5. "Ask Nettie," TheStandard.com.

6. Mavis Scanlon, Internet World, "Company to Watch" section, May 1, 2000. Reprinted with permission.

7. www.intersurvey.com, July 2000.

8. Ibid.

9. "InterSurvey Difference," www.intersurvey.com, July 2000.

10. www.greenfieldonline.com, July 2000.

11. www.cltresearch.com, July 2000. CLT e-terpretations.

12. Ibid.

13. www.websurveyor.com, July 2000.

Chapter 13: The System of Web Tracking Analysis

1. Mubarak Dahir, "How Much Is Too Much?" TheStandard.com, May 8, 2000.

2. Ibid.

3. Mubarak Dahir, "Just for Clicks," The Standard.com, May 8, 2000.

4. Ibid.

5. Richard Hoy, "Traffic Analysis Solutions for Small Business: Part 1," www.Clickz.com, June 9, 2000.

6. "Ask Nettie: Traffic Report," TheStandard.com, June 5, 2000.

7. Ibid.

8. www.eppraisals.com, June 2000.

9. www.quadstone.com, July 2000.

10. Ibid.

11. www.webtrends.com, July 2000.

12. Ibid.

13. www.younology.com, July 2000.

14. "E-Consumers Now Can Track the Trackers," eMarketer, March 15, 2000.

15. Ibid.

Chapter 14: Ethics on the Internet

1. Michael Benedikt, "Of Orson Welles' Remarkable 1938 Radio Program 'The War of the Worlds'," http://members.aol.com/benedit2, August 2000.

2. Ibid.

3. "The Soupy Sales Show," Yesterland.com, August 2000.

4. Internet Activities Board (IAB), January 1989.

5. Federal Trade Commission Privacy Initiatives, August 2000.

6. "Guarding Their Privates, See?" *eMarketer,* November 29, 2000.

7. daily_stat@emarketer.com, July 2000.

8. Neuburger and Monkarsh, "Well-Known Laws Hit the Net," *Silicon Alley Reporter,* Issue 35.

9. Pamela Mendels, "Criticism for Company Offering Free Computers to Schools," *New York Times on the Web,* February 2, 2000

10. Neuburger and Monkarsh, "Well-Known Laws Hit the Net.

11. Matt Richtel, "Toysmart.com in Settlement with F.T.C," *New York Times on the Web,* July 22, 2000.

12. Ibid.

13. Neuburger and Monkarsh, "Well-Known Laws Hit the Net."

14. Saul Hansell and Judith Dobrzynski, "eBay Cancels Sale in Auction of Abstract Painting," *New York Times on the Web,* May 11, 2000.

15. Ibid.

16. Lisa Guernsey, "A New Caveat for eBay Users: Seller Beware," *New York Times on the Web,* August 2000.

17. Ibid.

18. www.cbsnews.com, July 2000.

19. "E-Code of Health," *Silicon Alley Reporter,* Issue 35, Bedside.

20. "Internet Privacy Safeguards Approved," BBC News, July 27, 2000.

Part IV: Cybermarketing to Enhance the Brand

Chapter 15: Changing Market Landscapes

1. "Amazon, Toys R Us Plan Online Toy Stores," TheStandard.com, August 10, 2000.

2. "Five Get It, Five Don't," *Business 2.0,* June 13, 2000.

3. Ibid.

4. Ronna Abramson, "How about a '73 Gremlin in Harvest Gold?" TheStandard.com, August 14, 2000.

5. Jeremy Rifkin, "The Age of Access," TheStandard.com, March 13, 2000.

6. Sam Howe Verhovek, "Dot-Com Leaders Await a Shakeout of Losers," *New York Times on the Web,* April 23, 2000.

7. www.kbkids.com, September 2000.

8. www.etoys.com, September 2000.

9. Steve Rigney, "Network Antivirus: Defend Your Network," *ZDNet PC* magazine, April 14, 2000.

10. David Lake, "Wanted: Loyal E-Shoppers," TheStandard.com, August 7, 2000.

11. "Flunking Customer Service 101," *eMarketer,* August 16, 2000.

12. Ibid.

Chapter 16: Banner Ad Sustenance in Cyberspace

1. Nielsen NetRatings, March 2000.

2. *eMarketer,* July 2000.

3. Ibid.

4. *eMarketer,* July 2000.

5. Jason Black, "Old Ads, New Metric," *Internet World,* August 1, 2000. Reprinted with permission.

6. "Case Study: iVillage & Hollywood.com," emarketingtoher.com, August 9, 2000.

7. Ibid.

8. Jim Meskauskas, "Online Media: Is the Price Right?" Clickz.com, May 9, 2000.

Chapter 17: Affiliate Marketing for the Future

1. Joel Gehman, "What Is Affiliate Marketing," Clickz.com, July 28, 2000.

2. Mana Tominaga, "Birds of a Feather," www.webtechniques.com, June 2000, detailing the basic considerations for affiliate merchants.

3. Ibid, detailing the basic considerations for affiliates.

4. Ibid.

5. *ICONOCAST,* March 2000, http://www.iconocast.com.

6. Shawn Collins, "Keeping Your Affiliates Loyal," Clickz.com, August 4, 2000.

7. Shawn Collins, "Communication 101 for Affiliate Managers," Clickz.com, July 21, 2000.

8. www.top10affiliates.com, February 2000.

9. www.cruelworld.com, Affiliate Program, September 2000.

10. www.vstore.com, Affiliate Comparison, September 2000.

11. www.lobsternet.com, Affiliate Program Benefits, September 2000.

Chapter 18: Driving Traffic on the Cyberhighway

1. Worldcom advertisement appearing in *Business Week,* September 11, 2000.

2. *PFS Marketwyse,* September 2000.

3. *ICONOCAST,* June 2000, http://www.iconocast.com.

4. Ibid.

5. Erdos & Morgan study, *ICONOCAST,* June 2000.

6. *eMarketer,* September 2000.

7. Susan Kuchinskas, "More for Less," *Business 2.0,* August 22, 2000.

8. Ibid.

9. "Case Study: AssociationCentral.com," emarketingtoher.com, September 11, 2000.

10. Stuart Elliott, "Campaign Stresses Customized Beauty Products Sold Online," *New York Times on the Web,* July 10, 2000.

Part V: Cyber Public Relations: The Credible Online Endorsement

Chapter 19: Is There Room for Tradition in Cyberspace?

1. Encyclopaedia Britannica, Micropedia, 15th Edition, Vol. 8. "Public Relations," p. 285.

2. E-mail correspondence between an undisclosed marketing company and a producer of ZDNet.com.

3. "Eyeball Wranglers: Are PR Firms Being Asked to Do Too Much?" Jill Hunter, *Silicon Alley Reporter,* Issue 36.

Chapter 20: PR Cybertools for Cyberspeed

1. www.cyberalert.com, CyberAlert, Inc., 2000.

2. www.cyberalert.com, copyright 1999-2000, CyberAlert, Inc.

3. Marcia Stepanek, "You Called Our Widget a What?" *Business Week,* The Best of Business Week Online, September 25, 2000.

4. Ibid.

5. www.prnewswire.com, October 2000.

Chapter 21: Relationship-Building Tactics with the Media

1. www.whackaflack.com, e-tractions, October 2000.

2. Ibid.

3. Matthew Drapeau, "This Ain't Your Mama's News Source," *WebPR,* October 2000.

4. Drapeau, "This Ain't Your Mama's News Source."

5. Jim Romensko's *MediaNews Extra!,* August 2000.

6. Jim Romensko's *MediaNews Extra!,* PR Beef Section.

7. Tom Gable, "Nine Easy Ways to Kill a Start-Up through PR," *The Standard,* June 2000.

8. Ibid.

9. Ibid.

10. www.grayrun.com, PR Toolbox, February 2000.

Chapter 22: Best PR Practices

1. "How to Hire and Get the Most from Outside PR Counsel," *O'Dwyer's PR Daily,* October 2000.

2. Ibid.

3. *Public Relations Tactics,* Bronze Anvil Winners, October 2000.

4. Ibid.

5. Ibid.

6. www.pharmaton.com, "Stand up for Leg Health Survey Results," May 2000.

7. "How the UK's DeskDemon.com Used Scantily Clad Males to Generate Press Internets," MarketingSherpa.co.uk, September 2000.

8. Vicki Hudson, "How Advertising Differs from Public Relations," *Small Business Administration,* January 1999.

INDEX

Flooz.com, 150
Focus groups, 171, 176–77
FogDog, 253
Ford Motor Company, 8, 144
Forrester Research, 171
Four "p's" theory, 47
Fraud, 210, 212–13
Fruitman, David, 216

G
Galloway, Michael A., 119
Gap, 11
Gartner Group, 171, 230
Gateway Computers, 233
Gear.com, 5
Gehman, Joel, 246
General Mills public relations
    campaign, 309
General Motors, 79, 225–26
GeoCities, 25
Giftcertificates.com, 150
Global brands, 11–13
  and cultural issues, 12–13
  ingredients for, 14–15
Global Online Telephone, Instant Call,
    158
Godfrey, Lawrence, 212
Goldberg, Whoopi, 150
GoTo.com, 72, 125
Graham, Jeffrey, 174
Grayrun Group, 299
Greenfield Online, 185–86
Gregory, James, 15
Gucci, 13
Guess jeans, 236
Gutenberg, Johann, 273

H
Half.com, 27
Hearon, David R. Jr., 119–20
Heinz brand, 7–8
Heinz, H. J., 8
Heller, Sabine, 277
Henderson, Florence, 150
Hewlett-Packard Web site, 91
Hindman, Leslie, 199
Historical brand promise, 6–8
Hits, 78
Holland, Anne, 67–69
Hollywood.com, 241
Home Depot Web site, 117

Homegrown research vs. online
    research, 181–82
Hotbot, 125
Hotmail.com, 126, 138
Hotwire.com, 224
HTML, 203, 205
HudsonValleyHelpWanted.com,
    35

I
IBM, 79, 144
  and cyberbranding, 162–65
IDcide, Inc., 201–2
  goal of, 201–2
  Privacy Companion, 201
Imported, use of term, 13
Inatome, Rick, 211
Incentive programs, 129–32
Industries, and the Internet, 28–31
Industry Standard, 126
Information, 47
  up-to-date information, provision
    of, 91–92, 95
Information overkill, 95
Instant Call, Global Online Telephone,
    158
Instinct, 47
Interactivity, 33, 47
Internal/external dimensions of brand,
    46, 48–49
International naming, 13
Internet, 15–16
  and advertising budgets, 26–27
  applets, 204
  ASP, 204
  branding, 23–24
  Cold Fusion, 204
  and company commitment, 23–24
  differentiating factors, 57–58
  e-commerce, 25
  and ethics, 208–9
  Flash files, 204–5
  HTML, 203, 205
  and industries, 28–31
  JavaScript, 203
  language behind, 202–5
  making transition to, 18–35
  most commonly purchased
    items/requests for information,
    25
  most frequently visited Web sites, 25

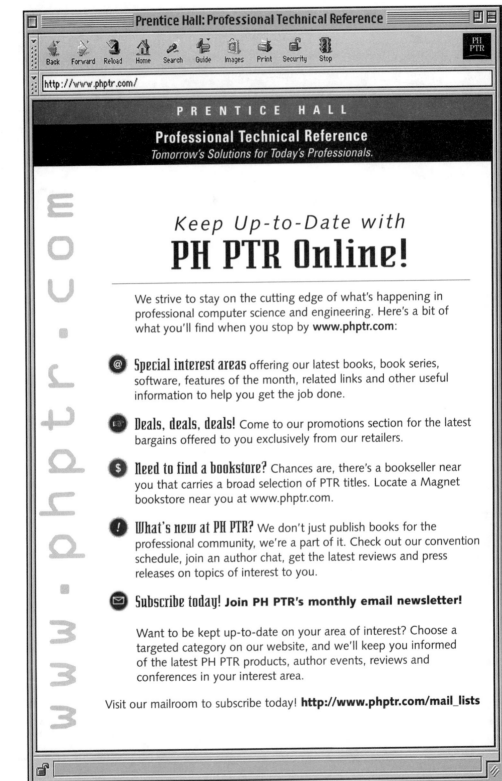